D0909069

The Indian Captivity Narrative, 1550–1900

Twayne's United States Authors Series

Pattie Cowell, Editor

Colorado State University

TUSAS 605

.F. Maij

.2.

"The French Sail to the River of May." Original picture (now lost) by Jacques Le Moyne de Morgues. Engraved and published by Theodor de Bry in *Brevis Narratio* [*A Brief Narrative*], Frankfurt-on-Main (Germany): T. de Bry, 1591. Part II of de Bry's series *Great Voyages*. The engraving shows French explorers arriving in Florida in 1562. *By permission of the British Library.*

The Indian Captivity Narrative, 1550–1900

Kathryn Zabelle Derounian-Stodola
James Arthur Levernier

Twayne Publishers • New York
Maxwell Macmillan Canada • Toronto
Maxwell Macmillan International • New York   Oxford   Singapore   Sydney

Twayne's United States Authors Series No. 622

The Indian Captivity Narrative, 1550–1900
Kathryn Zabelle Derounian-Stodola and James Arthur Levernier

Twayne Publishers   Maxwell Macmillan Canada, Inc.
Macmillan Publishing Company   1200 Eglinton Avenue East
866 Third Avenue   Suite 200
New York, New York 10022   Don Mills, Ontario M3C 3N1

Library of Congress Cataloging-in-Publication Data

Derounian-Stodola, Kathryn Zabelle, James Arthur Levernier.
    The Indian captivity narrative, 1550–1900 / Kathryn Zabelle
Derounian-Stodola, James Arthur Levernier.
        p.   cm. —(Twayne's United States author series ; **TUSAS 605**
    Includes bibliographical references and index.
    ISBN 0-8057-7533-1 (hc: alk. paper)
    1. Indians of North America—Captivities.   2.   American literature—
History and criticism.   3.   Indians of North America—Captivities—
    Literary collections. I. Levernier, James. II. Title.
    III. Series.
    E85.D47   1993
    813.009′3520397—dc20   92-42189
                                                            CIP

For our parents,
Kitty and Nubar Derounian
Florence and Arthur Levernier

Contents

Illustrations

Preface

Chance, rather than Divine Providence, we believe, brought us together as colleagues in the English Department at the University of Arkansas at Little Rock. Yet we both possess complementary strengths and backgrounds that coincidentally have helped us produce this analysis of the Indian captivity narrative. James Arthur Levernier's interest and expertise initially arose from his dissertation on the Indian captivity narrative, from his anthology (coauthored with Professor Hennig Cohen), *The Indians and Their Captives* (1977), and from articles on aspects of the captivity literature. Kathryn Zabelle Derounian-Stodola's interest and expertise focuses on early American women writers and specifically on the figure of Mary Rowlandson, which she first addressed in her dissertation and developed in subsequent publications.

In preparing this book, we tried to be sensitive to the political nature of many of the captivity narratives, produced as they often were with propagandistic and racist agendas. Such agendas especially involved negative stereotypes of Native Americans that regrettably remain in the popular imagination and culture even today.

One way to counter these stereotypes, we found, was to stress the vastness of the material and to refer to as many of the thousands of texts as we could. Too many commentators still focus on a relatively small core of familiar—canonized—narratives, so in this study we have tried to bring unfamiliar texts to light but still not neglect some of the better known accounts like those of Mary Rowlandson and John Williams.

Second, we also wanted to clarify that not all published captivities had European Americans as their main characters. For example, African Americans and Mexicans—among others—were taken hostage too, and we have tried to include references to their experiences and texts. Moreover, captivity narratives were so popular that they were published in Europe as well as America in languages other than English. We quote from some of these texts in translation.

A third strategy we considered important was to extend the accepted chronology of the Indian captivity narrative. Thus we look at accounts from the sixteenth century that are embedded within larger works and that predate the earliest separately published account—

Rowlandson's—by more than a century. We also extend our consideration to 1900, for even at that date manifestations and adaptations of the form appeared not only in fiction, but also in folklore, children's literature, and Southwestern humor.

Expanding the form's canon and chronology inevitably involved the corollary that the texts are far more complex than often recognized. Even apparently simple issues such as whether a particular narrative is factual or fictional and who wrote it can be surprisingly complicated. With this in mind, we have tried not to compromise the complexity of the material, but still make this study useful for both generalists and specialists.

In chapter 1, we provide an overview of the Indian captivity narrative by considering such issues as frequency of captivity, reasons for taking captives, definitions of the form, authorship, popularity, and historic phases and adaptations. Chapter 2 examines the mythology of the Indian captivity narrative as a way of explaining its continuing pull and popularity. We apply the various mythic approaches to a case study, the puzzling and provocative narrative known as the "Panther Captivity," first published in 1787 by the pseudonymous Abraham Panther. Chapter 3 assesses the different images of Native Americans in the captivity literature including negative, positive, and ambivalent images, sometimes all within the same text. By using a New Historicist approach, we reevaluate the contemporary context as well as the current significance of these images. In chapter 4, we look in detail at various aspects of the most anthologized and canonized narrative, Mary Rowlandson's *True History* (1682). Because most of the existing analyses of the form look at images of men or at images of both genders together, we felt it important to focus on images of women alone in chapter 5. By extending the usual range of material, we establish five dominant images of women in the captivity literature: as victims; as victors; as part of a female network of mothers, daughters, and sisters; as emotionally traumatized; and as transculturized. These areas gain added significance from the form's definition of these women as part of a family unit that has fragmented owing to the upheaval of captivity. In Chapter 6, we consider the Indian captivity narrative as usable past by looking at its later applications in history, folklore, and children's literature, as well as its more familiar fictional manifestations. For the convenience of readers, the back matter to this book includes an alphabetical checklist of title abbreviations.

In researching and writing this book, we are indebted to many people and institutions for their guidance and generosity. For grants that helped to defray expenses involved in research, we thank the Committee on

Faculty Research at the University of Arkansas at Little Rock and Samuel A. Covington, Director of Research and Sponsored Programs at the University of Arkansas at Little Rock, for his support.

For assisting us in publishing this book with the Twayne's United States Authors Series, we owe a special debt of gratitude to Pattie Cowell, of Colorado State University, whose professional expertise and enthusiasm for the project greatly facilitated its production from start to finish. We also wish to thank Elizabeth Fowler of G. K. Hall, Mark Zadrozny of Macmillan, and Therese Myers.

In addition, we express our appreciation to the many libraries and research institutions that opened their doors to us, especially the Newberry Library, the Haverhill Historical Society, the Boston Public Library, the Free Library of Philadelphia, the American Philosophical Society, the American Antiquarian Society, the Arizona Historical Society, the British Library, the Library Company of Philadelphia, the Northwestern University Library, and the Ottenheimer Library of the University of Arkansas at Little Rock. We especially wish to thank John Aubrey of the Newberry Library and Caroline Singer of the Haverhill Historical Society.

Finally, we also wish to acknowledge the use of materials that we previously published on the subject of Indian captivity. Portions of the chapter on Mary Rowlandson first appeared in *Early American Literature*. Sections of chapter 6 on the captivity narrative as children's literature and as history were published in the *Markham Review* and *Research Studies* respectively. Some of the information and ideas in chapters 1, 3, and 6 first appeared in *The Indians and Their Captives* (1977), edited by James Levernier and Hennig Cohen and published by Greenwood Press as an imprint of Greenwood Publishing Group, Inc., Westport, CT. We wish to thank both Hennig Cohen and the Greenwood Publishing Group for permission to use this material.

Chronology

1759   Beginning of Cherokee Indian War (1759–61).

1760   First African-American captivity account, Briton Hammon's *Narrative*, published.

1763   Treaty of Paris ends the French and Indian War. Pontiac's Rebellion (1763–64). More than 200 captives returned (some unwillingly) after a treaty with the Delawares and Shawnees is negotiated by Colonel Henry Bouquet.

1764   Henry Grace, *History*

1769   Dartmouth College, New Hampshire, founded for Native Americans. First of nine Spanish missions for Native Americans founded in California by Father Junipero Serra.

1774–1783   American Revolution rekindles publication of anti-British and anti-Indian propagandist captivities.

1777   Jane MacCrea abducted; the source for many stories, including Hilliard d'Auberteuil's novel, *Miss MacCrea*, published in 1784.

1778   U. S. Congress ratifies first treaty with an Indian tribe—the Delawares.

1779   John Dodge, *A Narrative*, the most famous of the anti-British accounts

1784   Congress adopts Land Ordinance. Iroquois cede all lands west of the Niagara River to the United States.
            John Filson, *The Discovery of Kentucke*, includes story of Daniel Boone

1787   Passage of Northwest Ordinance guarantees Native Americans' rights to their land and property (with some restrictions).
            Abraham Panther, *A Surprising Account*, better known as the "Panther Captivity," one of the most reprinted of early fictional accounts
            Shepard Kollock, *A True Narrative of the Sufferings of Mary Kinnan*

1790   Ann Eliza Bleecker, *The History of Maria Kittle*

1793   *The Affecting History of the Dreadful Distresses of Frederick Manheim's Family*

1794   Defeat of Native Americans at Battle of Fallen Timbers opens Ohio Territory to European–American settlement.

most widely read of the nineteenth-century anthologies

1842 John Todd, *The Lost Sister of Wyoming*, a famous account of a transculturated woman, Frances Slocum

1845 United States annexes Texas.

1846–1848 United States at war with Mexico.

1848 Bureau of Indian Affairs moved to U. S. Department of the Interior.

1848–1849 California Gold Rush leads to further westward expansion.

1849 Henry David Thoreau, *A Week on the Concord and Merrimack Rivers*

1857 Royal B. Stratton, *Life among the Indians,* the best-selling story of Olive and Mary Ann Oatman

1859 Gold discovered in Colorado and Nevada.

1861–1865 Civil War.

1862 Sioux Uprising (Minnesota).

1867 Francis Parkman, *The Jesuits in North America*

1871 U. S. government ends treaty-making era after negotiating approximately 600 treaties with some 350 Indian nations.
Fanny Kelly, *Narrative*

1876 Sioux Indians defeat General Custer at the Battle of Little Big Horn. Sioux Victory Day.

1877 Chief Joseph (Nez Perce) attempts to lead his tribe to Canada.

1879–80 Ute War in Colorado (murder of Agent Nathan Meeker becomes the source for a number of narratives).

1886 Chief Geronimo (Apache) surrenders in Arizona.
James T. DeShields, *Cynthia Ann Parker: The Story of Her Capture*

1890 Chief Sitting Bull (Sioux) assassinated. Massacre at Wounded Knee, South Dakota, of unarmed Sioux attempting to leave the reservation. Called the final battle of the "Indian Wars," the conflict was, in part, an attempt to stop the continued influence of the Ghost Dance religion, based on teachings of the Paiute medicine man Wovoka.

1893   Frederick Jackson Turner first advances his "frontier hypothesis." Cherokee Strip in Oklahoma open to European–American settlement.

1897   Charlotte Alice Baker, *True Stories of New England Captives*

Chapter One

The Captivity Tradition in Fact and Fiction

"This was *Indian Captivity!*"
—Cotton Mather, *Magnalia Christi Americana* (1702)

In *The Scarlet Letter* (1850), Nathaniel Hawthorne mentions that Roger Chillingworth had "been long held in bonds among the heathen-folk" and that his Indian captors, after a lengthy period of assimilating him into their culture, had accompanied him to Boston "to be redeemed out of [his] captivity." While this narrative detail can be easily overlooked today, its significance would not have been missed during Hawthorne's time. Like generations of American readers before them, Hawthorne's audiences would have been thoroughly familiar with stories of Indian captivity, and they would immediately have grasped the implications of Hawthorne's subsequent description of the "savage costume" Chillingworth wore and the fact that "during his Indian captivity" he was rumored to have "enlarged his medical attainments by joining in the incantations of savage priests" and to have willingly dabbled in "the black art" of their medicinal experiments with "native herbs and roots."[1] Indoctrinated to fear American Indian culture as the antithesis of everything civilized, they would have equated Chillingworth's captivity with the loss not just of civilization but possibly of salvation itself, for to them Chillingworth had forfeited his soul to the wilderness and ultimately to the devil.

Frequency of Indian Captivity

The Indian captivity that supposedly befell Chillingworth after his shipwreck along the New England coast was not simply an isolated incident that Hawthorne extracted from colonial history to inject verisimilitude into his novel. From the beginnings of European exploration and settlement in the sixteenth and seventeenth centuries through the end of the nineteenth century, Indian captivity was very much a historical reality for countless explorers and settlers living on the edge of the American frontier, and in one form or other it touched the imaginations and fears of virtually everyone for whom it was a possibility. In *Letters from an American Farmer* (1752), J. Hector St. John de Crèvecoeur lists Indian captivity among the worst "distresses of a frontier man," and he bemoans the fact that by the end of the eighteenth century literally "thousands of Europeans are Indians."[2] As Colin G. Calloway has aptly pointed out, "From seventeenth-century Massachusetts to twentieth-century Hollywood, Indian captivity has been regarded as a fate worse than death, and western frontiersmen advocated saving the last bullet for oneself to prevent it."[3]

Conservative estimates place the number of captives taken by Indians in the tens of thousands. In her study of the subject, Emma Coleman records the names of more than 750 New England captives taken to Canada during the French and Indian Wars alone, and she estimates that thousands more, whose names are lost, may either have died along the way or been adopted by the Indians.[4] A more recent survey compiled by Alden Vaughan and Daniel Richter documents that 1,641 New England settlers were known to have been captured by Indians between 1675 and 1763.[5] Although exact figures remain unavailable for later periods, a high frequency of Indian captivity continued until well into the latter part of the nineteenth century. According to Wilcomb E. Washburn of the Smithsonian Institute, "an estimated 900 to 1,000 Mexican captives, and a much smaller though not insignificant number of Anglo captives, were among the Comanches in 1850."[6] Presuming that many more captives must have been taken than retained by the Comanches, one can assume that the incidence of captivity among this single Western tribe must have been well into the thousands. As statistical research continues, other Western tribes such as the Apache and Sioux will no doubt be shown to have trafficked in similarly large numbers of captives. Hence, when Rip Van Winkle failed to return from an afternoon excursion into the Catskills, his friends and relatives could indeed logically assume that he had been "carried away by the Indians,"[7] for such had been the fate of many European settlers during Van Winkle's day.

Reasons for Taking Captives

Indians took captives for several reasons. One major reason was revenge. Angry at Europeans who stole their lands and massacred them in wars, Indians sometimes retaliated by subjecting enemy captives to ritualistic ceremonies of torture and death. A seventeenth-century Jesuit missionary captured by Mohawks in New France, Isaac Jogues mentions that male captives in their twenties were routinely tortured and killed, particularly if they were "full of life and courage." Such captives were "generally put to death," Jogues records, as a way "to sap as it were the life-blood of the hostile tribe" or to serve as a sacrificial offering to the *manes*, or spirit, of a slain warrior. Jogues was himself selected "to be offered" in this way but was spared when his captors brought in other prisoners who were sacrificed instead.[8]

One way in which Indians purportedly avenged themselves against their enemies involved burning a prisoner at the stake. This activity, usually presented in gruesome detail though almost certainly not as frequently or flagrantly practiced as many captivity authors would have their audiences believe, appears with such regularity in the captivity narratives that it becomes almost a stock feature. Other ritualistic forms of torture and death that Indians reportedly practiced on their captives included mutilation, dismemberment, decapitation, and cannibalism.[9] All of these activities are described by Rachel Plummer, who was taken captive in 1836 by the Comanches in Texas. According to Plummer, "These inhuman cannibals will eat the flesh of a human being, and talk of their bravery or abuse their cowardice with as much unconcern as if they were mere beasts." In fact, she states, "they appear to be very fond of human flesh. The hand or foot they say is the most delicious."[10]

Most of these tortures were reserved for adult male captives. Because captives were tortured primarily to avenge the death of Indian warriors, adult men were generally considered the appropriate object of Indian vengeance. There were, however, undoubtedly instances of female captives being tortured and killed, and one issue that remains beneath the surface of most narratives is whether such captives were sexually violated by the Indians. Except in the most egregious examples of narratives whose value as anti-Indian propaganda was being exploited by the press, most female captives either remained silent about any sexual abuse they may have experienced while in captivity or explicitly commented that their Indian captors respected their chastity. Writing in the seventeenth century, the Puritan captive Mary Rowlandson marvels, "I have been in the midst of those roaring Lyons, and Salvage Bears, that feared neither God, nor Man, nor the Devil, by night and day, alone and in company: sleeping all sorts together, and yet not one of them ever offered me the least abuse of unchastity to me, in word or action."[11] The eighteenth-century Quaker captive Elizabeth Hanson likewise maintains that the

Indians were "very civil toward their captive Women, not offering any incivility by any indecent Carriage (unless they be much overgone in Liquor), which is commendable in them so far."[12]

Such a view may not, in many instances, have been mere rhetoric to protect the captive's reputation once she had returned home. Evidence strongly suggests that Eastern tribes showed little sexual interest in their female captives. As Calloway explains, "Indians embarking on the warpath practised sexual abstinence lest their war medicine become 'contaminated'; additionally, they may have found white women unattractive." Calloway also indicates another powerful reason why Indian warriors usually respected the chastity of their female captives: "Should a captive be adopted into the tribe, she might become a member of the warrior's family, and he would not risk infringing incest taboos by forcing himself on a woman who soon might become his 'sister'" (Calloway, 203). While these practices seem later to have changed among Western tribes who came to emulate white society's less civilized war practices, they were evidently widely observed in the East, at least during the sixteenth and seventeenth centuries. For this reason, sexual abuse is less commonly mentioned or alluded to in Eastern narratives while it becomes a more frequent subject of discussion in Western ones.

Because distraught family and friends willingly paid whatever they could to regain their loved ones, ransom was a second major motive for Indians to take captives. In exchange for Mary Rowlandson, who was captured in 1675 during a raid on the Massachusetts town of Lancaster, the Indians demanded and received £20, an amount that equalled the annual income of a middle-class worker. Lonnie J. White notes that in 1867 "the military at Fort Arbuckle, Indian Territory, paid $210.00 in cash and $20.00 worth of uniforms for [Theodore Adolphus] Dot and $333.00 for Luella [Dot's sister]," who had been captured by Comanches the previous year.[13] General Samuel Houston is said to have paid $150.00 for the release of Elizabeth Kellog, who had been captured by Kiowas and Comanches during the 1830s in Texas.[14] Washburn points out that "ransoms as high as $2,000.00 were sometimes paid for captives who thus served as the economic equivalent of a large amount of guns, liquor, or other durable goods" (Washburn, "Introduction," xviii). To help captives' families raise funds, local governments sometimes established trusts specifically for ransoming captives. Such was the case, for example, during the French and Indian Wars in New England when the French in Canada furthered the war effort by offering the Indians money for English captives, thus creating a market between the French and English for captives and raising to exorbitant amounts the money needed for ransom. In fact, the high ransom captives could bring may have significantly reduced the number of captives who were ritualistically tortured and slain (Calloway, 195).

A third reason why American Indians took captives was to replace tribal numbers diminished by war and disease brought on by white colonization. As Calloway notes, "Among some of the Iroquois tribes to the west, adoption became such a vital means of replenishing the losses occasioned by constant warfare that adoptees came to outnumber pure-blooded Iroquois" (194). So common was this practice that adoption into the tribe, rather than torture and death, was the fate that most captives could reasonably expect. Taken captive in 1790 by Shawnees and Cherokees near the juncture of the Ohio and Scioto Rivers, Charles Johnston explains, "Among all the savage nations of America, the usage prevails, of adopting prisoners taken in war for the purpose of supplying any loss incurred by those, who have had their friends slain in battle, or otherwise."[15] Such captives were usually treated well. According to Jogues, once adopted, a captive "is subject thenceforward to no man's orders excepting those of the head of the family, who, to acquire this right, offers some presents" (*Jogues*, 20).

Many adopted captives grew to love their Indian families and opposed leaving them even when given the opportunity to do so. Writing in 1747 about captives who refused to leave the Indians, Cadwallader Colden records, "No Arguments, no Intreaties, nor Tears of their Friends and Relations, could persuade many of them to leave their own *Indian* Friends and Acquaintance[s]; several of them that were by the Caressings of their Relations persuaded to come Home, in a little Time grew tired of our Manner of living, and run away again to the *Indians*, and ended their Days with them."[16] Similarly, of some 200 captives redeemed through a 1764 treaty that Colonel Henry Bouquet negotiated with the Delawares and Shawnees at the close of the war with Pontiac, all but a few violently resisted leaving their Indian homes. "Unless they are closely watch'd," predicted Lieutenant Governor Francis Fauquier of Virginia, "they will certainly return to the Barbarians," and that is exactly what these captives did as soon as the first convenient opportunity arose (quoted by Axtell, "White Indians," 61).

For obvious reasons, children were the most likely candidates for adoption. In general less prejudiced and more culturally malleable than adults, children were more easily assimilated into the tribe. As James

Axtell explains, "The Indians obviously chose their captives carefully so as to maximize the chances of acculturating them to Indian life" (Axtell, "White Indians," 61). Girls in particular adjusted well to Indian life. Using Vaughan and Richter's study of New England captives, Washburn notes that "girls aged 7 through 15 were the most likely of all groups to be 'transculturated'" and that "almost 54 percent of this group refused to return to New England compared with less than 30 percent of the boys in the same age group" (Washburn, "Introduction," xvii). After an elaborate "educational process" designed to transform them into "affectionate Indian relatives," many of these captives chose to live their entire lives as Indians (Axtell, "White Indians," 66).

Such was the case, for example, with Mary Jemison (Dehgewanus), perhaps the most famous example of a white captive become Indian. Jemison was approximately 12 years old in 1755 when Shawnees attacked her home near Gettysburg, Pennsylvania, killing her parents and taking her captive. After an initial period of lament and regret, she embraced the culture of the Seneca family that adopted her. Remembered as the "white woman of the Genesee," she grew up in the Genesee River Valley of western New York, was twice married to Indian chiefs, and became a leader of her adopted tribe. She died in 1833 at age 90 and quickly became the subject of legend and folklore. An elegy written in her honor and published in 1844 records that Jemison "lov'd the Indian style of life."

Other examples of famous captives who also adjusted to Indian culture include Frances Slocum (We-let-a-wash), Eunice Williams, Cynthia Ann Parker, and John Tanner (Sha-shew-wabe-na-se). Remembered by her white family as the "lost sister of Wyoming," Frances Slocum was taken captive in 1778 by Delaware Indians who attacked her family's homestead in the Wyoming Valley of Pennsylvania, near the present site of Wilkes-Barre. Upon discovery by white society more than 50 years later, Slocum steadfastly refused to leave her Indian family. When urged by her white relations to "go back with us," Slocum replied:

"No I cannot. I have always lived with the Indians. They have always used me very kindly. I am used to them. The Great Spirit has always allowed me to live with them, and I wish to live and die with them. Your *Wah-puh-mone* (looking-glass) may be larger than mine, but this is my home. I do not wish to live any better, or any where else, and I think the Great Spirit has permitted me to live so long, because I have always lived with the Indians. I should have died sooner if I had left them. My husband and my boys are buried here, and I cannot leave them. On his dying day my husband charged me not to leave the Indians. I have a house, and large lands, two daughters, a son-in-law, three grandchildren, and everything to make me comfortable. Why should I go, and be like a fish out of the water?"[17]

Slocum chose to stay with the Indians for the remainder of her life. In the words of her biographer, the Reverend John Todd, "She had, to all intents and purposes, become an Indian" (*Sister*, 104).

Eunice Williams was taken captive during a raid on Deerfield, Massachusetts, on 29 February 1704. With her parents and two brothers, she was forced to march to Canada. Two younger sisters were killed during the attack, and her mother died shortly after the journey began. While her brothers and her father, who was the Puritan minister of Deerfield, were later ransomed, Eunice remained among the Indians, converted to Roman Catholicism, and married into the tribe. In later life, she and her Indian family returned to Massachusetts, but legend has it that she refused to enter her brother's house because their father had remarried.[18] In a final, unsuccessful effort to redeem her, the minister preached a sermon to her on the lawn. A memorial plaque in a Deerfield museum simply records that after being taken captive by Indians Eunice Williams "married a Savage and became one."

Even more dramatic were the captivities of Parker and Tanner. Captured in May 1836, Cynthia Ann Parker was 19 when a Comanche war party raided the Texas settlement where her family lived. Within a short time, however, she grew to appreciate Comanche culture. After marrying one of their chiefs, she bore three children, one of whom, Quanah Parker, himself became a legendary tribal hero. Although she repeatedly resisted the efforts of white negotiators to rescue her, Parker was eventually brought back to her white family by Texas rangers who came upon her while she was butchering buffalo meat. After several unsuccessful attempts to return to the Indians, she allegedly died of grief. At her funeral, her son is reported to have said that she loved the "Indian and wild life so well" that she had no desire whatsoever "to go back to white folks."[19] Captured in 1789 at age nine by Shawnees and later sold to Ojibwas, John Tanner so enjoyed his life as hunter and trapper among the Indians along the Minnesota and Canadian border that when white civilization began to assimilate the culture of his captors he grew sullen and violent. In 1846, Tanner is said to have destroyed his home near Sault Ste. Marie, murdered James Schoolcraft (brother of the Indian ethnologist Henry Rowe Schoolcraft), and fled into the wilderness, where he forever disappeared, despite pursuit by a posse and bloodhounds. His wife, a white woman from Detroit, had previously deserted him because of his brutality.[20]

Finally, Indians took captives for use as slaves. Those captives who were not immediately killed or adopted were often held as slaves. In such cases, the Indian who first seized the captive was usually considered the captive's owner. Remarking on the servile fate of two children taken captive with her in 1860 on the Oregon Trail near Fort Laramie, Emeline Fuller states, "The Indians were seen leading the two little girls with collars around their necks, and chains to them to lead them by. A thousand pities that they had not all been killed with their parents."[21] Commenting on the fate of a family taken captive by the French and Indians during the 1750s, Robert Eastburn, also a captive, wrote, "Here also, I saw one Mr. *Johnson*, who was taken in a Time of Peace, with his Wife, and three small Children (his wife was big with a *Fourth*, delivered on the road to *Canada*, which she called *Captive*) all which, had been prisoners between three and four Years, several young Men, and his Wife's Sister, were likewise taken *Captive* with them, and made *Slaves*!"[22] Becoming a slave did not, however, preclude the possibility of ransom or adoption at a later date. Such was the case, for example, with John Dunn Hunter, purportedly held by Kickapoos in the early part of the nineteenth century: "I was adopted into the family of one of the principal warriors, named Fongoh, who claimed me as his property, from having taken me prisoner; his wife, a squaw of an intermediate stature, and dark complexion, proved to me a kind and affectionate mother."[23]

Defining the Captivity Narrative

So extensive and so interwoven into the very fabric of early American culture was the experience of Indian captivity that a substantial body of literature was written about the subject. Known collectively as Indian captivity narratives, these works are so numerous that the full corpus of texts has yet to be identified. In *The Voice of the Old Frontier*, R. W. G. Vail compiled a descriptive bibliography of some 250 Indian captivity narratives.[24] Vail's study was limited primarily to works first published before 1800. Two additional bibliographies of captivity narratives contained in the Edward Ayer Collection of the Newberry Library, which houses the largest single repository of captivity texts, expand Vail's list by several hundred items.[25] Also compiled at the Newberry, a more recent unpublished checklist contains more than 2,000 items and is by no means exhaustive. In an attempt to standardize the canon, Alden T. Vaughan published a checklist of 281 titles.[26] The best known of these works, including various editions that involve substantial reworking of the same narrative, have been published in 111 volumes by Garland Press, thus making readily available the texts of the more standard narratives.[27]

Part of the problem bibliographers have experienced in identifying and cataloguing Indian captivity narratives stems from the difficult problem of defining exactly what the term *Indian captivity narrative* means. In attempting to catalogue the subject, Vaughan limits his list to works "that presumably record with some degree of verisimilitude the experiences of non-Indians who were captured by American Indians" and that were "printed separately in book or pamphlet form" (Vaughan, *Bibliography*, viii). As a basic guide for categorizing the most significant of the captivity narratives, this definition is appropriate. It aptly defines what we would consider the "classic" captivity narrative reduced to its most basic form: a single narrative whose primary focus is to record the experiences of individuals of European or African origin who had actually been captured by American Indians. Three narratives, for example, are known to have been written about the experiences of African Americans. They are *A Narrative of the Uncommon Sufferings, and Surprizing Deliverance of Briton Hammon, a Negro Man* (1760), *A Narrative of the Lord's Wonderful Dealings with John Marrant, a Black* (1785), and *The Life and Adventures of Nat Love* (1907). This definition also includes often overlooked narratives written and published in languages other than English. The narratives in the seventeenth-century *Jesuit Relations*, for instance, written in French, illuminate an important aspect of the captivity tradition, as do such works as *Die Erzehlungen von Maria Le Roy und Barbara Leininger, Welche Vierthalb Jahr unter den Indianem Gefangen Gewesen* (*The Narrative of Marie Le Roy and Barbara Leininger*, 1759), *Erzehlung Eines unter den Indianern Gewesener Gefangenen* (*The Captivity of Abraham Urssenbacher*, 1761), and *Merkwürdige und Interessante Lebensgeschichte der Frau von Wallwille, Welche Vier Jahre Lang en Einen Irokesen Verheyrathet War* (*The Remarkable and Interesting Life Story of Maria Wallwille, Who Was Married to an Iroquois Indian for Four Years*, 1809), originally dictated in German, about the captivities of German immigrants in Pennsylvania during the French and Indian Wars.

Inevitably, however, as the subject of Indian captivity is further probed, this definition must be expanded. A complete discussion of the captivity narrative must, for instance, include the hundreds of fictitious narratives on the subject. Many of these narratives were initially accepted as truthful and constitute a dimension of the literary tradition that often reveals more about the historical response of Americans to the captivity experience than do verifiable tales. So, too, should the captivity novels of James Fenimore Cooper, William Gilmore Simms, and Robert Montgomery Bird be considered part of the captivity tradition, as should oral tales about the captivities of such legendary American folk heroes as Tim Murphy and Tom Quick, whose exploits, most likely fictitious, were for generations circulated among the folk and only later recorded in writing.

And, finally, a definition of the captivity narrative must account for those narratives published as parts of other works, often written about other subjects. Some of the most widely discussed captivities—those of Captain John Smith, Hannah Dustan, and Daniel Boone, for example— were published not as narratives in themselves but as episodes in books primarily devoted to other subjects. The legendary story of his rescue by Pocahontas first appears in John Smith's *Generall Historie of Virginia* (1624), and the story of how Hannah Dustan slew and scalped her Indian captors while they slept was originally recorded by Cotton Mather to conclude his sermon, *Humiliations Follow'd with Deliverances* (1697). What is known about Boone's purported captivity among the Shawnees is recorded in John Filson's *Discovery, Settlement and Present State of Kentucke* (1784) and later embellished in Timothy Flint's *Biographical Memoir of Daniel Boone* (1833). Although only one of these narratives, Hannah Dustan's, can be verified in the historical record and although none of them were published individually as books or pamphlets devoted exclusively to the subject of Indian captivity, these narratives constitute an important part of the tradition and are included in most major discussions of the subject.

Authorship

Yet another vexing issue that must be addressed when discussing captivity narratives is the question of authorship. Assessing exactly who wrote what is far more complicated than it might appear. Considering later narratives alone, Roy Harvey Pearce observes, "the problem of authenticity in some of the narratives of the first half of the nineteenth century is hopelessly confused."[28] Indeed, distinguishing historically verifiable first-person accounts from edited or fictionalized ones is often impossible owing to multiple authorial contributions, unclear publishing conditions and copyright, and generic overlap within and between works. Some narratives are indeed first-person accounts told in a single clear voice and verifiable in the historical record. There is no reason, for instance, to doubt that John Williams, the Puritan minister of Deerfield, Massachusetts, when it was attacked by Indians in 1704, was not in fact the author of *The Redeemed Captive, Returning to Zion* (1707), the much publicized account of his subsequent captivity. But first-person writing by no means guarantees historical credibility. In fact, by the latter half of the eighteenth century, the historicity of any narrative written in the first person becomes suspect because, in imitation of the novel, wholly fictional narratives were customarily expected to use various strategies to appear factual. Thus, James Russell's fictionalized *Matilda: or, the Indian's Captive* (1833) has as its subtitle, "A Canadian Tale, Founded on Fact," and Russell states in its preface, "I am truly at a loss (Reader) what name to give this little work; to call it a Novel is an appellation which in some measure it does not deserve, as it is founded on fact."[29]

Even more baffling, however, are works where the line between fact and fiction is totally unclear. Written in the first person, John Dunn Hunter's *Manners and Customs of Several Indian Tribes Located West of the Mississippi* (1823) was long thought to be the account of an authentic captivity. A popular narrative, it was circulated throughout Europe and translated into German, Dutch, and Swedish. Recent research, however, calls into question the very existence of Hunter.[30] On the other hand, authorities long considered fictitious the first-person *Memoirs of Charles Dennis Rusoe d'Eres* (1800), about a Canadian captivity among the "Scanyawtauragahroote" Indians, because of the strange-sounding Indian tribe and because it mentions such unlikely details as a North American "monkey." Ethnological investigation, however, has uncovered the fact that *Scanyawtauragahroote* may simply be a white approximation of the Indian word *Skaniardaradihronnnon*, indicating "those who live across the river." Should that river be the Niagara, the word *Scanyawtauragahroote* may be a generic reference to "Canadian" Indians. Similarly, the "monkey" may have been nothing other than a flying squirrel or a bit of false information taken to expand the narrative from such sources as Jonathan Carver's *Travels through the Interior Parts of North-America* (1778).[31] Appropriations of this kind were common to many captivity accounts. Therefore, contrary to what was once thought, Rusoe d'Eres's *Memoirs* may indeed record an actual captivity.

More often than not the individual captivity narrative constitutes an amalgamation of voices and input, each with its own agenda and design. In such instances, identifying the author responsible for a given section of the narrative or, for that matter, sometimes the narrative as a whole, is extremely difficult, especially when editors become involved, who many times did not simply write the basic story but actually reoriented it as they saw it. One noteworthy example of authorial ambiguity involves complementary narratives by two women who journeyed West together on a wagon train bound for Idaho. In 1864, Fanny Kelly and Sarah L. Larimer were captured by Oglala Sioux in Wyoming, along with other members of their party. Kelly remained a captive for five months, but Larimer and her son escaped within days. Despite her brief captivity, Larimer published a 252-page volume, *The Capture and Escape; or, Life among the Sioux* (1870), padding her experiences with anthropological and historical information from other sources.[32] In her conclusion, she claims authenticity—"All that is not the result of personal observation has been gleaned from reliable sources" (*SL*, 251)—then promises as a sequel the story of her sister-in-suffering, Fanny Kelly, "For want of space in this volume, which is already larger than was originally intended, I am compelled to omit the particulars of her sufferings, privations and ransom, but give them, as related by herself in a book entitled 'Mrs. Kelly's Experience among the Indians'" (*SL*, 252).

Kelly's story appeared a year later, titled *Narrative of My Captivity among the Sioux Indians*, but it carried her own name—not Larimer's—and its preface included a startling expose of Larimer's attempts to appropriate Kelly's story: "Some explanation is due the public for the delay in publishing this my narrative. From memoranda, kept during the period of my captivity, I had completed the work for publication, when the manuscript was purloined and published; but the work was suppressed before it could be placed before the public. After surmounting many obstacles, I have at last succeeded in gathering the scattered fragments."[33] From the length of Kelly's work, from her prefatory remarks, and from verbatim passages in both narratives, it seems that Larimer did plagiarize Kelly's work and was about to mine her friend's manuscript still deeper when stopped by litigation.[34] Nonetheless, determining who wrote what in these two narratives is virtually impossible and certainly calls into question the authenticity of at least one, if not both, works.

A still more complex authorship scenario can be found in a series of narratives published from 1838 to 1851 about three Texas pioneers captured by Comanches: Caroline Harris, Clarissa Plummer, and Sarah Ann Horn. Harris's narrative appeared in 1838 told in the first person but intertwining Plummer's story with her own.[35] Embedded in the middle of her story is a particularly sensationalized summary of Plummer's "harsh and cruel treatment" that leads to the following sales pitch: "Mrs. Plummer (as the writer has been recently informed) is about preparing a Narrative of her Captivity, Sufferings, &c. for the press; to that we would refer our readers for a more particular account of her heavy trials and afflictions" (*CH*, 17). Did Harris really compose this advertisement on behalf of her "sister captive" (*CH*, 16), or did an editor or publisher insert it—and perhaps other material—in the story? The same year, Plummer's account duly appeared (before readers' memories could fade), carrying this reminder on its title page: "Mrs. Plummer was made prisoner and held in bondage at the same time with the unfortunate Mrs. Harris, with whose narrative the public have been recently presented."[36] Predictably, the same dual narrative strategy is evident here as in the Harris book because both women shared similar fates.

One year later, a man identified as "E. House" served as Sarah Ann Horn's "amanuensis"—as he says in her preface—because she "could not be induced to write it herself for publication."[37] The account is, however, presented in the first person and includes constant references to Harris, with whom Horn was supposedly captured. Yet if Plummer and Harris were taken together, as their narratives claim, and if Horn and Harris were also taken together, why do none of the narratives mention all three women together? Was one of them capitalizing on the name recognition of another? Harris is the only constant in these three narratives, as well as in a fourth, *An Authentic and Thrilling Narrative of the Captivity of Mrs. Horn . . . with Mrs. Harris* (1851), which is actually a revised, shortened, edition of the 1839 volume. This time, though, there is no reference to an "E. House," and the title page claims that the book is "Published by the Author."[38] A comparison of the 1839 and 1851 editions of the Horn story shows that background material and some of the more sensationalized incidents have been condensed or omitted from the latter book; in accordance with its title, it does *seem* more "authentic," but no one will probably ever know for certain.

To evaluate with certainty the historicity of any given text, then, requires the combined skills of historians, biographers, bibliographers, and textual critics. For this reason, the reader of captivity narratives must be extremely cautious when delving into these materials for historical or ethnological data. Ultimately, inferences should not be determined or differentiated by the vehicle of their presentation unless a thorough study has been completed concerning the background of the narrative. Any investigation of the captivity narratives must, therefore, be text- and culture-based, not author-based, because authorship is so problematical.

Popularity of Captivity Narratives

Despite difficulties of definition and authorship, narratives of Indian captivity share one thing: they were immensely, even phenomenally, popular. As Richard VanDerBeets explains, "First editions are rare today because they were quite literally read to pieces, and most narratives went through a remarkable number of editions" (VanDerBeets, *Held Captive*, xi). Washburn notes that "four captivity narratives—Rowlandson, John Williams, Jonathan Dickinson, and Mary Jemison—are listed by Frank Luther Mott," the noted historian of popular American literature, "as among the great best-sellers of American publishing" (Washburn, "Introduction," xi). Indeed, at the time of its publication in 1682, Rowlandson's *The Soveraignty & Goodness of God* was second in popularity among American readers only to the Bible, and it quickly established another audience in Europe, where it was published in the same year.[39] John Williams's *The Redeemed Captive, Returning to Zion* (1707) is estimated to have sold 1,000 copies during the first week after its publication (Calloway, 190).

Similarly, *The Remarkable Adventures of Jackson Johonnet*, first published around 1791, is known to have been printed in some 15 different editions before 1820 and to have been reprinted in newspapers and almanacs as well as in several popular anthologies of frontier literature. *An Account of the Captivity of Elizabeth Hanson* also illustrates the tremendous popularity that captivity narratives enjoyed both in the Americas and abroad. First published in 1728 by Samuel Keimer of Philadelphia with a simultaneous printing in New York, the story of the Kickapoo capture of Hanson, her four children, and a maid and their subsequent journey to Canada during the French and Indian Wars was printed in 13 editions before 1800. Within a few years after its publication in the Colonies, Hanson's narrative, like Mary Rowlandson's, was also printed and reprinted in London. During the nineteenth century, moreover, it was reprinted in 16 editions of Samuel Gardner Drake's *Indian Captivities* (1839–1872) and three editions of James Wimer's *Events in Indian History* (1841, 1842, 1843).[40] These narratives are by no means exceptions to the rule: the public simply could not read enough about Indian captivity. From the late seventeenth through to the end of the nineteenth centuries, captivity narratives about hundreds of captives among every major American Indian tribe were published, distributed, and read in virtually all sections of the country.

It is easy to understand why the captivity story had such popular appeal for early American audiences: "It combined dramatic form, thrilling adventure, exotic context, and personal relevance" (Washburn, "Introduction," xi). As long as Indians remained a viable threat to frontier settlement, white readers naturally wondered what "fearful things," in the words of Cotton Mather, happened to the "multitudes of families" unfortunate enough to be "dragg'd into the forlorn and howling wigwams of those wretched salvages."[41] Writing in the midnineteenth century about the captivity of Mary Jemison, James Everett Seaver summarized the omnipresent curiosity of early American audiences about Indian captivity:

These horrid tales required not the aid of fiction, or the persuasive powers of rhetoric, to heighten their colorings, or gain credence to their shocking truths. In those days, Indian barbarities were the constant topic of the domestic fireside, the parlor, the hall, and the forum. It is presumed that, at this time, there are but few native citizens that have passed the middle age who do not distinctly recollect the hearing of such frightful accounts of Indian barbarities, oft repeated, in the nursery and in the family circle, until it almost caused their hair to stand erect, and deprived them of the power of motion.[42]

During the seventeenth and eighteenth centuries, moreover, an additional factor contributed to the popularity of captivity narratives as a literary form. As Vail points out, "Our American ancestors did not believe in play-acting or the corrupting influence of the novel, so they limited themselves to true tales of horror in the form of deathbed confessions, stories of shipwreck, piracy, plague, and disaster, and of Indian captivity and torture" (Vail, 24). Captivity narratives were, simply put, "the escape literature of our ancestors" (Vail, 26).

Historical Phases and Cultural Adaptations

But captivity narratives did much more than merely entertain. As Roy Harvey Pearce first noted, the captivity narrative was a "vehicle for various historically and culturally individuated purposes" (Pearce, "Significances," 1947, 1). Throughout their long and complex history, they served Euro-American culture in a variety of ways. In theme, form, style, and purpose, Indian captivity narratives underwent a series of major and minor phases of development. These phases—beginning in the sixteenth century with European exploratory tracts that contained episodes about Indian captivity and extending through the nineteenth century, when

the captivity theme was appropriated by novelists such as James Fenimore Cooper and Mark Twain—evolved sequentially and were shaped by
the needs of the times. Although the phases within this progression often
intersected and distinctions between phases frequently become blurred,
they still provide the most generally accepted means for understanding
an extraordinarily complex literary and historical tradition.[43]

It must, however, always be remembered that while the narratives
may in general have been written and shaped by larger cultural concerns,
marketability was also a major motive behind the publication, and in
many instances, the writing of narratives from all periods. In addition,
authors themselves often had personal motives for writing that may or
may not have conformed to the cultural and economic forces that came to
bear on the telling of their stories. Sometimes these motives were
subconscious, as in the case of a captive who writes as a means of denying
the disunifying effect of a captivity by reunifying the experience in print,
thereby providing therapy for the narrator and perhaps even aesthetic
justification for the story. Other survivors of Indian captivity claim they
resorted to publication for a variety of more overt reasons. Such is the
case, for example, with Massy Harbison, who opened her *Narrative of the
Sufferings* by begging readers to "willingly patronize a poor widow, who
is left to provide for her family through her own industry."[44]

Still other reasons captives gave for writing included satisfying the
requests of friends and relatives (see Robert Eastburn, *Faithful Narrative*
[1758]); performing public duty by setting straight the record (see
Theresa Gowanlock, *Two Months in the Camp of Big Bear* [1885] and Clara
Blynn, *General Sheridan's Squaw Spy and Mrs. Clara Blynn's Captivity*
[1869]); warning against naive missionary zeal (see Mary Barber, *The
True Narrative of the Five Years' Suffering & Perilous Adventures* [1872]);
earning ransom money for the rescue of other captives (see Nelson Lee,
Three Years among the Comanches [1859]); and providing genuine educa-
tional value in the form of ethnological and historical data (see Grace E.
Meredith, *Girl Captives of the Cheyennes* [1927]). Sometimes captives
provide truly outrageous reasons for authorship. Among these are mar-
keting an Indian blood tonic (see Edwin Eastman, *Seven and Nine Years
among the Comanches and Apaches* [1873]) and promoting a touring "Wild
West" gun show that included a franchise for shooting lessons (see
William F. Carver, *Life of Dr. Wm. F. Carver of California: Champion
Rifle-Shot of the World* [1875]).

Written during the sixteenth and seventeenth centuries, the first
captivity narratives were essentially the result of New World coloniza-

tion by European nations. Despite extensive contact with American Indians that long predated the first captivity narratives, Europeans remained basically ignorant about Indians. Moreover, what they purported to know was often based less on fact than on speculation. Narratives of exploration such as the anonymous *True Relation of the Gentleman of Elvas* (Evora, 1557), Richard Hakluyt's *Virginia Richly Valued* (London, 1609), Captain John Smith's *Generall Historie of Virginia* (1624), and Captain John Underhill's *News from America* (1638), among many other such works, often contained captivity narratives that offered European readers firsthand, though distorted, information about Indian culture.

In general, the narratives in these works projected stereotypes that conveniently supported the political aims of the European country that published them. Spanish narratives thus portrayed Indians as brutish beasts so that the native populations of the New World could, without serious objections from Europe, be more easily exploited, along with whatever wealth they possessed. French captivities, on the other hand, reflected a different design for Indians. Because the French agenda for the New World involved a network of outposts throughout the Canadian wilderness, the French wanted their colonists to remain on friendly terms with the Indians, who were therefore depicted as souls needing education and spiritual redemption. In Virginia, where the colonists initially sought a peaceful mercantile relationship with the Indians, British captivities viewed American Indians as innocent exotics, while in New England, where Pilgrims and Puritans saw Indians as a grave threat to the religious utopia they sought to establish, captivity narratives presented Indians in collusion with satanic forces bent on the annihilation of English colonial enterprises and all things godly.

As time passed, and New World settlement by European colonial powers became permanent, Indian captivity narratives entered an essentially religious phase of expression. For Puritans, Quakers, and Roman Catholics who sought to bring God's kingdom to the newly discovered lands across the Atlantic, Indian captivity assumed an increasingly pronounced theological dimension. Seeking scriptural justification for their existence, the New England Puritans structured their society upon that of ancient Israel. Following this concept, they viewed Indians as neo-Canaanite infidels who must and would be subdued in the name of the Puritan Jehovah. Eventually they elaborated on this concept until Indians were seen as devils in human guise. An avid collector of captivity narratives, the Puritan divine Cotton Mather perhaps best summarized the Puritan view of Indians and their role within the cosmos: "These

Parts were then covered with nations of barbarous *Indians* and infidels, in which the *prince of the power of the air* did *work as a spirit*; nor could it be expected that nations of wretches, whose *religion* was the most explicit sort of *devil-worship*, should not be acted by the devil to engage in some early and bloody action, for the extinction of a plantation so contrary to his interest as that of *New England* was" (*Magnalia*, II, 479–80). For the Puritan, then, becoming a captive involved direct domination by diabolic spirits. Indian captivity was thus a religious experience with profound spiritual and social ramifications.

Accordingly, to the Puritan, Indian captivity was considered a religious trial by God for purposes known only to Him. "I cannot express to man the afflictions that lay upon my Spirit," wrote Mary Rowlandson, the most famous of all Puritan captives. In her words, "The portion of some is to have their Affliction by drops, now one drop and then another; but the dregs of the Cup, the Wine of astonishment, like a sweeping rain that leaveth no food, did the Lord prepare to be my portion" (*MR*, 36). Rowlandson's view was also felt by Quakers to the south and Roman Catholics to the north. Although both Quaker and Roman Catholic attitudes toward Indians were more tolerant than Puritan ones, captives nonetheless interpreted their captivities providentially. When in 1699 the Quaker merchant Jonathan Dickinson was captured by Indians off the coast of Florida, he viewed his experience as an "afflicting tryal" from God sent for the betterment of his soul. Similarly, a captive missionary priest like Father Francis Joseph Bressani, while hesitant to condemn Indians as diabolic agents, saw redemptive spiritual possibilities in his captivity experience: "What consoled me much was, to see that God granted me the grace of suffering some little pain in this world, instead of the incomparably far greater torments, which I should have had to suffer for my sins in the next world."[45]

Like Father Bressani, the Puritans also considered Indian captivity a divine chastisement for wrongdoing. In the narrative of his captivity, John Williams records that "It would be unaccountable Stupidity in me, not to maintain the most Lively and Awful sense of Divine Rebukes, which the Holy GOD has seen meet in Spotless Sovereignty to dispense to me, my Family and People, in delivering us into the hands of those that Hated us."[46] Another Puritan captive, Hannah Swarton, felt certain that she merited her captivity as a punishment for her transgressions against God. In recounting her captivity, she remembered that she and her husband "had Left the Publick Worship and Ordinances of God . . . to Remove to the North part of *Casco-Bay*, where there was no Church, or Minister of the Gospel . . . thereby Exposing our Children, to be bred Ignorantly like Indians."[47] For Swarton and for other Puritan captives, Indian captivity became "the symbolic equivalent of a journey into hell" (Levernier and Cohen, xviii). Mary Rowlandson, for instance, dramatizes this concept in her description of an Indian celebration shortly after the destruction of her home in Lancaster, Massachusetts: "Oh the roaring, and singing, and dancing, and yelling of those black creatures in the night, which made the place a lively resemblance of hell" (*MR*, 3). Puritans customarily described Indians as "copper-colored," and they called Satan "the Prince of Darkness."[48]

During its religious phase, Indian captivity was often translated into spiritual allegory. Living through the experience and returning home was considered a sign of divine favor. This concept was frequently emphasized in the titles of the Puritan captivity narratives. It can be seen, for example, in the title of the first American edition of the Rowlandson narrative: *The Soveraignty & Goodness of God, together, with the Faithfulness of His Promises Displayed* (1682), and in the title Williams chose for his narrative: *The Redeemed Captive, Returning to Zion* (1707). For both Rowlandson and Williams, escaping from the Indians to the freedom of Boston typologically suggested their future redemption in heaven (Levernier and Cohen, xviii). Accordingly, captivity narratives written during the religious phase often contain mention of any "special providences" which befell captives along the way. An unexpected cup of broth, an act of kindness or courtesy, crossing a river without getting overly wet, giving birth to a child—in short, anything unusual that benefited the captive—were seen as signs of divine intervention and worth notice. Among the many *"Memorable Providences"* that Mather notes about Puritan captives were the "Astonishing Deliverances" that were "sent from Heaven, to many of our Captives." In recording the experiences of these captives, Mather notes the "numberless" stories of divine interventions on their behalf:

Astonishing Deliverances have been sent from Heaven, to many of our Captives. They have been many a time upon the Point of Destruction; but, *These poor ones have Cryed unto the Lord*, and He has Remarkably delivered them.

'Tis a Wonderful Restraint from God upon the Brutish Salvages, that no *English Woman* was ever known to have any Violence offered unto her *Chastity*, by any of them.

'Tis wonderful, that no more of the Captives have been murdered by them, neither when they were Drunk, nor when the Caprichio's, and the Cruelties of their Diabolical Natures were to be Gratified.

'Tis Wonderful, that when many of the Captives have been just going to be Sacrificed, some strange Interposition of the Divine Providence has put a stop to the Execution, and prevented their being made a Sacrifice. The Stories are numberless.[49]

This view of Indian captivity as an allegorical interpretation of God's working on behalf of the captive also is reflected in the titles of Quaker narratives—Elizabeth Hanson's *God's Mercy Surmounting Man's Cruelty, Exemplified in the Captivity and Redemption of Elizabeth Hanson* (1728) and Jonathan Dickinson's *God's Protecting Providence Man's Surest Help and Defence in Times of the Greatest and Most Imminent Danger* (1699). And it surfaces as well in the narratives of Roman Catholic captives who, like Father Bressani and his colleagues, believed that God used their captivities as a means for improving their souls and as an instrument for converting the Indians through prayer and exemplary Christian behavior.

Often the religious messages inherent in the captivity experience were seen as having meaning not just for the captive but for the community at large. As a result, Puritans, Catholics, and Quakers alike took interest in passing these lessons on to others. In *Reports of Divine Kindness* (1707), for example, Williams explains that "The Infinitely Wise disposer of all things, who aims at His own Glory, doth sometimes bring Persons into the depths of distress, and then magnify his Power & Grace in raising them up out of their afflictions: and in many respects by such things, He has a design of advancing His own Honour & Glory in the World.[50] It is, continues Williams, therefore "very acceptable to God for Christians to entertain the report of the experiences of others, to excite their own hearts to glorify God. For if God make it a duty in the receiver to report, it layes the hearer under an obligation, to set such remarks upon the passages of Divine Providence in others, as may be useful to engage their hearts to Glorify God, for the favours and blessings He has bestowed upon others" (*Reports*, 8–9). In a "Pastoral Letter" published by Mather in *Good Fetch'd Out of Evil* (1706) and subtitled *A Collection of Memorables Relating to Our Captives*, Williams specifically instructs his fellow captives "that it well becomes them who have had Eminent Mercies, to be shewing to others *what great things God has done for them*," for in so doing they will "stir up others to Glorify God" and "may be instrumental in putting others upon trusting God, and making Him their Refuge in an Evil Day."[51] Recognizing this obligation to the community, Swarton makes explicit the reason why she gave Mather an account of her captivity: "I knew not, but one Reason of Gods bringing all these Afflictions and Miseries upon me, and then Enabling me to bear them, was, *That the Works of God Might be made manifest"* (*Humiliations*, 70). Indeed, the lessons to be drawn from the captivity experience shaped the very form in which many early captivities were told. The narratives of such captives as Rowlandson, Williams, Swarton, and Dickinson, for instance, assume the form of spiritual autobiography. By writing the events of their captivities in the way that Providence had allowed them to occur, captives could scrutinize their experiences for any spiritual patterns that might emerge and then pass those lessons to the entire community.

Well aware of the instructional value of the captivity narratives, clerical authorities of all denominations encouraged their publication, sometimes even assisting in the writing process itself. For nearly 50 years, the Jesuits published yearly installments of *The Jesuit Relations* (1632–73) in the hopes that the lessons gained from the captivities and hardships of their missionaries among the Indian peoples of North America would not be lost to the faithful worldwide. Likewise, the Quakers of Pennsylvania financed the publication of the Dickinson captivity, *God's Protecting Providence*. Like the Jesuit editors who compiled and printed *The Jesuit Relations*, the anonymous Quaker editor of the Dickinson narrative felt a public obligation to reveal to others the many "Signal favors" of this captivity experience. Concerning people like Dickinson who had undergone "remarkable outward deliverances from God," the editor voices a communal imperative for them to instruct others about the spiritual import of their experiences:

Remarkable outward deliverances, ought in a more than commonly remarkable manner, to be the objects of their gratitude, to their great *Deliverer*. I must confess, thanks giving (which is what we poor *Mortals* can return, for the manifold favours we daily receive from him) that it's rise in the heart; and as *out of the abundance of the heart the mouth speaketh*, how can those who are truly thankful in heart; but *render the calves of their lips;* in telling to their Friends and acquaintance, *how great things GOD hath done for them*: Nay, they are so affected, with such eminent appearance of the Protecting hand of Providence, for their help, preservation and deliverance; that they are not willing to confine in them only, but to publish it to the World; that the Fame of their God may be spread *from Sea to Sea*, and from one end of the Earth to the other.[52]

Not to be outdone by their Catholic and Quaker counterparts, Puritan religious leaders not only assisted in the publication of captivity narratives, they also used them in their homilies and historical writings. As Vaughan and Clark explain, "of the best New England narratives before 1750, only a few can be considered purely lay products. Several were written by clerics or their immediate kin; others were transcribed and embellished by clergymen."[53] Increase Mather is thought to have been involved in the publication of Mary Rowlandson's narrative and to have written the preface of the first edition.[54] Among the many accounts of "memorable events" that he included in his *Essay for the Recording of Illustrious Providences* (1684) was the account of Quentin Stockwell's captivity among the Wachusett Indians during King Philip's War.

Ever aware of his filial responsibilities, Increase Mather's son Cotton continued to promulgate the public interest in Indian captivity narratives begun by his father. In *Good Fetch'd Out of Evil,* the younger Mather includes accounts of the captivities of John Williams and another Puritan captive named Mary French, and in *A Memorial of the Present Deplorable State of New-England* (1707), he prints an account of the captivity of Hannah Bradley, a Puritan woman unfortunate enough to have been captured by Indians in 1697 and again in 1703. In addition, variants of the Swarton and Dustan captivities, transcribed and edited by Mather himself, appear in *Humiliations Follow'd with Deliverances,* a fast-day sermon delivered by Mather in Boston on 6 March 1697, and later published. As part of the sermon, these captivities were designed to alert Puritans throughout New England to the possibility and even likelihood of God using His power to punish them, through acts of Indian hostility, for their spiritual transgressions and apostasies. Just two years later, Mather again used his account of the Dustan captivity, this time in *Decennium Luctuosum* (1699), as an illustration of "*A Notable Exploit*" performed for God during wartime by "poor Women," who "had nothing but fervent *Prayers*"[55] to assist them. Along with several other narratives, both the Swarton and Dustan materials were resurrected still one more time for publication in Mather's *Magnalia Christi Americana* (1702) as instances of "memorable providences" and "wonderful deliverances." So powerful a precedent was the early tendency to view Indian captivity within a religious context that even as late as the mid-nineteenth century, when cultural pressures toward an exclusively theological exegesis of the captivity experience had subsided, the clergy still continued to take an active interest in collecting, preserving, popularizing, and publishing captivity accounts, and some captives still attributed religious concerns as a primary motivation behind the writing of their narratives.

By the mid-eighteenth century, captivity narratives entered another phase of development. A general decline in religious authority and a corresponding increase in secular concerns, especially on the frontier, markedly changed the character of the captivity narratives. Once primarily an occasion for religious expression, captivity narratives became instead a means for spreading propaganda against those nations and powers that blocked Anglo-American westerly settlement. Accordingly, this propaganda was directed against the French, the English, and the American Indian, all of whom at different times and in different degrees were seen as enemies. Even the very form of the captivity narrative was altered to suit the changing cultural purposes to which it was put.

Frequently reprinted, these narratives sometimes appeared as broadsides or as filler material in almanacs sold by travelling booksellers like Mason Locke Weems (1759–1825). As Moses Coit Tyler states in his *History of American Literature* (1878), until after the Civil War, when newspapers replaced them, almanacs were "the supreme and only literary necessity" in nearly every American household.[56] Sold and read throughout the United States, almanacs provided an excellent medium for advertising the potential of the frontier territories for private and commercial development and the need to remove and protect those lands from the Indians. Serving this purpose, "A True and Faithful Narrative of the Captivity and Travels of Capt. Isaac Stewart" was published in *Bickerstaff's Genuine Boston Almanack for 1787,* where it was used to bolster American claims to lands southwest of the Mississippi River by encouraging Americans to settle there. With the signing of the Peace of 1783, all lands from Florida to the Mississippi had been ceded by the United States to Spain, which in turn attempted to keep Americans from the region by allying itself with the Indians. In order to ensure an American presence in the area, settlement of the region by American citizens was urgent. Obviously fictitious (the narrative alludes to Welsh-speaking Indians and another tribe "whose arrows were pointed with gold"), the Stewart narrative simultaneously describes the "horrid barbarity" of the Indians, who it implies are an impediment to progress and must therefore be removed, and the wealth of the land, with "gold dust in the brooks and rivulets," there for the taking. According to Stewart, "I was not acquainted with the nature of the ore, but I lifted up what he [a guide] called gold-dust from the bottom of the little rivulets issuing from the cavities of the rocks: It had a yellowish cast and was remarkably heavy."[57] Throughout the eighteenth and nineteenth centuries, almanacs such as *Bickerstaff's* played a major role in disseminating propagandistic narratives like the Stewart one. Indeed, the first of the Bickerstaff almanacs (that for 1768) includes a selection with the title, "Adventures of a Young British Officer among the Abenakee Savages."

Like almanacs, broadsides offered a convenient medium for the publication of captivity narratives whose primary purpose was propagandistic and immediate. Easily produced and marketed, broadsides were printed on one side of a sheet of paper and then distributed by travelling vendors who brought them to distant places where they were purchased by individuals and publicly displayed. Distributed during the Second Seminole War (1835–41), the broadside "Captivity and Sufferings of Mrs. Mason," for example, was designed to enlist support for the war by publicizing propaganda about alleged Indian war crimes. According to the Treaty of Payne's Landing (1832), Seminoles of Florida had agreed to move west of the Mississippi River. As compensation for their ancestral lands, the Seminoles would receive $15,400 in cash, and each member of the tribe would get a new shirt and a blanket for the journey (Levernier and Cohen, 85). Incensed at the treachery of white officials who had tricked their leaders into signing this agreement, large numbers of the Seminoles resisted deportation. The result was a protracted war that cost thousands of casualties and millions of dollars and that deeply humiliated government leaders in Washington who were beset by protests from an outraged constituency that largely sided with the Seminoles. Framed by two woodcuts—one depicting an Indian with upraised tomahawk in the act of murdering Mrs. Mason and her child and the other "a battle with the Indians"—the central feature of the broadside is a short recital of the "sufferings of Mrs. Mason, with an account of the Massacre of her youngest Child."

Preceding the narrative is a short prefatory remark that clearly reveals the blatantly inflammatory intent of the author:

At the Great Council of the principal Chiefs and Warriors of the different Indian tribes bordering on the Southern frontiers and Florida, assembled in the spring of 1836, the solemn vows then entered into have been kept. The Indians then agreed that so long as the Sun should continue to rise or the grass to grow, they would never leave the land of their fathers. And so inveterate and deadly was their hatred towards the white people that many of them pledged themselves neither to eat or sleep until they had taken the scalp of a pale face.

Under these feelings commenced the *Florida Indian War*. The distress and cruelty which has been inflicted and the hardships endured are beyond description, and although an incessant war has been waged to an enormous expense and the lives of many a brave soldier, the Indians still remain unsubdued, and almost every mail brings the news of some horrid massacre. The following account given by Mrs. Mason of her captivity and suffering, are from her own pen.[58]

Both Mrs. Mason and the events described in her narrative are probably fictitious, but broadsides like this one helped justify the Indian wars and unify public opinion. Other broadsides about Indian captivity include the "Narrative of the Tragical Death of Mrs. Darius Barber" (c. 1816) and "War! War!! War!!! Women and Children Butchered" (c. 1832). The similarity between these broadsides illustrates much about their purpose and medium. The central illustration on the Mason broadside, an Indian threatening to tomahawk a woman and a child, appears on all three broadsides. So common were such publications that printers apparently shared a manufactured engraving that they used to embellish them (Levernier and Cohen, 86).

In the vast majority of instances, however, captivity narratives intended as propaganda were published as inexpensive pamphlets, ranging from 20 to 100 pages and printed on cheap paper. In that class of literature sometimes referred to as pulp thrillers, shilling shockers, and penny dreadfuls, they "constitute the stereotypical Indian captivity narrative" (Levernier and Cohen, xxii) as it has been historically envisioned by the white popular culture. Typical of this type of narrative are *The Horrid Cruelty of the Indians Exemplified in the Life of Charles Saunders, Late of Charles-town, in South Carolina* (1763) and the *Narrative of the Massacre, by the Savages of the Wife and Children of Thomas Baldwin* (1836). Sixteen pages in length and surviving only by chance, the Saunders narrative reflects the propagandistic concerns of the times of its publication shortly after the conclusion of the French and Indian Wars. It begins by mentioning "several instances of the Indians being prejudiced against the English" because they had been "stirr'd up by the perfidious French," but most of the narrative focuses on the more immediate problem reflected in the title, namely "the Horrid Cruelty of the Indians," who, in the tradition of the earlier Puritan captivities, are condemned throughout the narrative as "inhuman monsters," "diabolical Fiends," "infernal ministers of Vengeance," and "brutal barbarous Villains."[59]

Published more than 50 years later, the Baldwin narrative is similarly brief, and its main focus, as its title states, is the presentation of anti-Indian propaganda, which it amply accomplishes by recounting the story, probably fictitious but presented as absolute fact, of an old man, then supposedly living as a hermit on the frontier, whose entire family was purportedly massacred by Indians. Retreating into the religiosity of the earlier captivity narratives, the surviving Baldwin has spent his life in prayer. But unlike that in earlier Puritan captivities, the piety in this narrative is merely sentimental, reflecting instead "the softer religiosity into which Puritan severity had declined" by the mid-nineteenth century (Levernier and Cohen, 179). More indicative of its intent is an elaborate engraving that illustrates the "Massacre of the Baldwin Family by the Savages" and is accompanied by the following caption:

The scenes which the above Plate is designed to represent (as described by Baldwin) are—Fig.1 his House in Flames—2 a Savage in the act of Tomahawking Mrs. B. (his wife)—3 his youngest child (a daughter) eleven years of age on her knees intreating a Savage to spare her life—4 two Savages, one in the act of tomahawking and the other in that of scalping his oldest son—5 Baldwin (the elder) intercepted and taken captive in his attempt to escape by flight—6 the Savages burning his second son at a stake, around which they are dancing to and fro in savage triumph—7 the Savages returning (with the unfortunate Baldwin and his Only surviving child, captives) to the settlement.

The degeneration of the captivity narratives into pulp fiction presented, for purposes of propaganda and sensation, as fact is revealed by the popularity of this type of narrative during the nineteenth century. A garbled reworking of the Baldwin narrative, titled *A Narrative of the Horrid Massacre by the Indians, of the Wife and Children of the Christian Hermit* (1840), contains added examples of Indian cruelties against white settlers and argues "the folly of attempting to civilize the savage." Yet another version of this captivity, *A Narrative of the Extraordinary Life of John Conrad Shafford, the Dutch Hermit* (1840), takes place in Canada rather than in the United States and draws special attention to "the most shameful treatment" of Shafford's daughter at the hands of "a lusty and most powerful looking savage" who forces her to "become his adopted squaw!"[60]

The evolution of the captivity narrative from primarily a document of religious statement to one of propaganda and outright bigotry began in 1692 with the intercontinental wars between the English and the French which concluded in the French and Indian War (1754–63), known in Europe as the Seven Years' War. Often appearing to be religious in nature, many of the captivity narratives from this period actually had very little to do with spiritual instruction. Instead, they were designed to evoke anti-French sentiment by claiming that the French hired Native American mercenaries to massacre British colonists from Maine to Pennsylvania. Purportedly written "to glorify God, for his Goodness and Faithfulness to the Meanest of his Servants, and to encourage others to trust in him," *A Faithful Narrative of the Many Dangers and Sufferings as Well as Wonderful Deliverances of Robert Eastburn* (1758), for example, contains numerous instances of French-inspired Indian atrocities (*RE*, 42). "Even in Time of *Peace*," states Eastburn, the French governor of Canada "gives the *Indians* great Encouragement to *Murder* and *Captivate* the poor Inhabitants of our Frontiers" (*RE*, 38). According to Eastburn, the French are so "*barbarous*" that "contrary to the *Laws* of *War*, among all *civilized Nations*," they trained the young men their Indian allies captured from the English as recruits for the French military who are then "employed in *Murdering* their *Countrymen*; yea, perhaps their *Fathers* and *Brethren*" (*RE*, 33–34).

Similar accusations likewise appear in *A Narrative of the Sufferings and Surprizing Deliverance of William and Elizabeth Fleming* (1756) and *French and Indian Cruelty Exemplified in the Life and Various Vicissitudes of Fortune of Peter Williamson* (1759). According to the Flemings, the French gave the Indians "*a certain Sum per Scalp and for Prisoners, if they were young, and fit for Business*," but "*the Old People and Children*" were to be "*kill'd and scalped, as well as such as were refractory and not willing to go with them.*"[61] In this way, they charge, the French encouraged the Indians to kill the helpless and infirm rather than to take them captive. A preface to the Williamson narrative clearly pronounces its author's anti-French biases.[62] It states that "Herein is exhibited, in a concise manner, a scene of many barbarities, and unheard of cruelties, exercised by the savage *Indians* instigated by the treacherous French, in *America*, upon many innocent families, sparing neither the aged, nor the most tender of infants." In the opinion of Williamson, the Indians, whose "numberless and unheard of Barbarities" (*Williamson*, 21) he details at great length, were "well supplied by the *French* with Arms and Ammunitions, and greatly encouraged by them in their continual Excursions and Barbarities, not only in having extraordinary Premiums for such Scalps as they should take and carry home with them at their Return, but great Presents of all Kinds, beside, Rum, Powder, Ball, &c. before they sallied forth" (*Williamson*, 37). Had the French not "tempted" the Indians "with the alluring Bait of all-powerful Gold," states Williamson, "myself as well as hundreds of others might still have lived most happily in our Stations" (*Williamson*, 16).

In keeping with the earlier religious mission of the captivity tradition, anti-French captivity narratives often contain anti-Catholic propaganda as well. "O! may not the *Zeal* of *Papists*, in propagating *Superstition* and *Idolatry*," laments Eastburn about the efforts of the French clergy to convert New England captives to Roman Catholicism, "make *Protestants* ashamed of their *Lukewarmness*, in promoting the Religion of the *Bible*!" (*RE*, 21). When Elizabeth Fleming's Indian captors told her about the many "*old People and Children they kill'd and scalped*," she "asked them if they did not think it was a Sin to shed so much innocent Blood." The Indians promptly replied "*That the French were much better off than the English, for they had a great many old Men among them that could forgive all their Sins, and these Men had often assured the Indians it was no Sin to destroy Hereticks, and all the English were such*" (*Fleming*, 16).

In his *Travels and Surprizing Adventures* (1761), another captive, John Thompson, also blames the Roman Catholic church for inciting Indians against the British, pointing to a collusion between the Catholic clergy and French government officials to destroy all British outposts in the Americas:

The reason for which they [the Indians] killed our British people then, was first, because the French King hired them; he having Governors in his Plantations in America, who gave the savage Indians 15 l. sterling for every one of our British people they killed; thinking thereby to destroy all our British settlements. The second reason for their killing the British people, was because the French Priests told the savages, that when the Son of GOD came into the world, the British people killed the Son of GOD, or the good man as they call him . . . for which cause, they intend to destroy all the English or British people.[63]

Similarly, *A Journal of the Captivity of Jean Lowry* (1760) concludes with a spirited discussion between her Catholic inquisitors and Lowry, who claims that Jesuit priests "attacked" her "about Religion" and the infallibility of Rome. When Lowry attempts to argue with a Jesuit, he accuses her of being "in a damnable Condition."[64]

Predictably, at the time of the American Revolution, captivity writers turn their attention away from the French and toward the British, who are accused of doing the same acts of barbarism formerly associated with France. The first paragraph of *A Narrative of the Capture of Certain Americans at Westmorland by the Savages* (c. 1780), for example, points responsibility toward the British for having used their Indian allies to perpetrate the horrors that it records: "The savages who occasioned the following scenes, were sent from the British garrison at Niagara, some time in the fore part of March A.D. 1780, through a deep snow, on a wretched skulking Indian expedition, against a few scattered people which they hoped to find about Susquehannah; especially those who were making sugar in the woods at that time of the year."[65] The various "scenes" that the narrative occasions include the torture, killing, and mutilation of several captives by Indians who receive encouragement from the British for whatever harm they can inflict on American settlers and soldiers. By offering the Indians a reward for scalps but not for prisoners, the British are said to encourage the Indians to keep their captives alive "for the purpose of carrying the baggage" until they reach the British garrison at Niagara, where the captives were then toma-hawked "and their scalps, not themselves," redeemed (*Westmorland*, 7).

Like the Westmorland narrative, *A Narrative of the Capture and Treat-ment of John Dodge* (1779) is vituperatively Anglophobic in the senti-ments it expresses. According to Dodge, who had worked in Sandusky, Ohio, as an Indian trader before he was taken captive by Indians and turned over to the British at Detroit, the Indians were "no ways inter-ested in . . . the unhappy dispute between Great-Britain and Amer-ica" before the British had "roused [them] to war" by offering them a twenty-dollar reward for every American scalp and telling them that the Americans intended "to murder them and take their lands."[66] Through-out the narrative, Dodge singles out for special criticism the inhumane behavior of the British leaders whom he encounters. Angry at their lack of humanity, Dodge calls these men "barbarians" (*JD*, 13) and is particularly angry with Governor Henry Hamilton, who he claims ordered Indian war parties "not to spare man, woman, or child" because "the children would make soldiers, and the women would keep up the flock" (*JD*, 13). Even "some of the Savages," states Dodge, "made an objection, respecting the butchering of women and children," but, he continues, because "those sons of Britain offered no reward for Prisoners" and a generous bounty for scalps (an accusation frequently leveled by captivity writers against both the French and the Indians), the Indians would murder and scalp their captives in the sight of the British, who "shewed them every mark of joy and approbation" by running "to meet and hug them to their breasts reeking with the blood of innocence" (*JD*, 13–14). Frequently reprinted and widely distributed, captivity narra-tives such as that by Dodge greatly helped further American indepen-dence by uniting public opinion against the British, even in Great Britain itself, where Dodge's narrative was published in a popular periodical, *The Remembrancer*. After the war, Dodge's narrative drew the notice of George Washington and the United States Congress, who interviewed Dodge about his experiences and used them as evidence against the British for "their former inhuman treatment of prisoners, who fell into their hands."[67]

Significantly, while the impulse toward anti-British sensationalism subsided with the conclusion of the American Revolution, narratives like Dodge's reappear during times of political rivalry between Great Britain and its former colonies.[68] During the 1790s, for example, when Great Britain angered the United States by insisting on the retention of its military outposts in the Northwest and arguing for the existence of a separate Indian nation under British protection, anti-British propaganda reasserts itself as a dominant impulse in the captivity narratives that were written and reprinted at the time, and it again surfaces with the approach of the War of 1812. *A True Narrative of the Sufferings of Mary Kinnan* (1795) is a case in point. One of the more popular captivity narratives, it recounts the captivity of a Virginia settler who, as the subtitle of her narrative indicates, "was Taken Prisoner by the Shawnee Nation of Indians on the Thirteenth Day of May, 1791, and Remained with them till the Sixteenth of August, 1794," and offers the following statement, Shakespearean quotation included, about the "perfidy" of "British agents" to the west who encourage the Indians "to persevere in their warfare" against "the people of the United States":

O Britain! how heavy will be the weight of thy crimes at the last great day! Instigated by thee, the Indian murderer plunges his knife into the bosom of innocence, of piety, and of virtue, and drags thousands into a captivity, worse than death. The cries of widows, and the groans of orphans daily ascend, like a thick cloud, before the judgment-seat of heaven, and

> "Plead like angels, trumpet-tongued,
> "For your damnation:
> "And pity, like a naked, new-born babe,
> "Striding the blast, or heav'n's cherubin, hors'd
> "Upon the sightless couriers of the air,
> "Shall blow your horrid deeds in every eye,
> "That tears shall drown the wind."[69]

Writing at the time of the War of 1812, Elias Darnall is similarly incensed at the British, whom he accuses of "employing the savages to murder the defenceless inhabitants of the frontiers."[70] Among other things, he claims that the British "paid the Indians for infants' scalps that were taken out of their mothers' wombs" and that "when the Indians *sent home to them scalps, from the unborn infant, to the grey hairs, in bales, like goods; they* [the British] *had days of feasting, rejoicing and thanks giving to the Lord for the victory they had gained*" (*Kentucky*, 53). Although the British may "call themselves Christians," continues Darnall, "*the D***l would be ashamed to acknowledge such a people as any part of his offspring*" (*Kentucky*, 53).

With the conclusion of the American Revolution and the withdrawal of British military forces from North America, anti-Indian propaganda becomes a major motivation for writing and publishing captivities. As Washburn indicates, "It was easier to express outrage at the cruelty of the Indian in capturing white women and children than to defend the policy of separating the Indian from his land" (Washburn, "Introduction," 1983, xi). While an occasional narrative drew favorable attention to Native American culture, most were shaped by publishers exploiting a mass market that thrived on sensationalism, in a natural alliance with land speculators who wanted to implement a policy of Indian extermination in the interest of real estate development. Accounts like *The Remarkable Adventures of Jackson Johonnet* (1793), the *Narrative of the Tragical Death of Mr. Darius Barber . . . Inhumanely Butchered by the Indians* (1818), *A Narrative of the Sufferings of Massy Harbison from Indian Barbarity . . . with an Infant at Her Breast* (1825), the *Narrative of the Captivity and Providential Escape of Mrs. Jane Lewis* (1833), and *In Captivity: The Experience, Privations and Dangers of Sam'l J. Brown, and Others While Prisoners of the Hostile Sioux* (1862), among dozens of others, were in large measure designed to horrify audiences into hating what the novelist Hugh Henry Brackenridge (1748–1816), himself an editor of captivity narratives, referred to as "the animals, vulgarly called Indians."[71] In these narratives, American Indians are depicted as so "fierce and cruel" that "an extirpation of them would be useful to the world, and honorable to those who can effect it" (*Expedition*, 31).

The locale for these narratives accompanies the westerly movement of the frontier. Initially, they are set primarily in the western parts of Massachusetts, Pennsylvania, New York, Maryland, and Virginia. As these areas were settled by whites and the Indians either contained on reservations or pushed further westward, the setting for captivity narratives shifts to the Midwest, specifically Ohio, Indiana, Illinois, Minnesota, Iowa, and the territories surrounding the Ohio, Mississippi, and

Missouri Rivers, which provided the major avenues of access for white pioneers in search of inexpensive lands. During the late nineteenth century, the primary setting for captivity narratives becomes Texas, Arizona, Colorado, Oregon, Utah, and the Dakotas, where the last of the wars between Indians and whites took place. As late as 1874, the impulse toward propaganda was still markedly evident in the narratives being written and circulated. Published in Lawrence, Massachusetts, the 7 February issue of the *Essex Eagle* contains a captivity story titled "One more Chapter of Indian Barbarities: Fiendish Treatment of a Lawrence Man by the Rocky Mountain Snake Indians." Eventually, the setting for the captivity narrative extends westward across the Pacific Ocean to the islands of Polynesia, where, in a work such as the *Narrative of the Capture, Sufferings, and Miraculous Escape of Mrs. Eliza Fraser* (1837), New Guinea islanders are referred to as "Indians" and "squaws." They live in "wigwams," brandish "tomahawks," travel in "canoes," and have children called "papooses" and leaders referred to as "chiefs."[72]

Each of the various wars that took place between whites and Indians also produced its share of propaganda narratives. *A Journal of the Adventures of Matthew Bunn* (1796) tells about its author's captivity in 1791 by Kickapoos, who were then under assault by a military unit sent to bring the Indians of the Old Northwest into the jurisdiction of the newly confederated United States. *An Affecting Account of the Tragical Death of Major Swan and the Captivity of Mrs. Swan and Infant Child by the Savages* (1815) occurs near St. Louis during the border disputes that followed the War of 1812. *A Narrative of the Life and Sufferings of Mrs. Jane Johns, Who Was Barbarously Wounded and Scalped by Seminole Indians in East Florida* (1837) involves a Florida captivity and, like the broadside "Captivity and Sufferings of Mrs. Mason," was published during the Second Seminole War. *The Narrative of the Capture and Providential Escape of Misses Frances and Almira Hall* (1832) concerns a captivity purported to have taken place in the Midwest at the time of Black Hawk's War. Royal B. Stratton's *Captivity of the Oatman Girls* (1857), *General Sheridan's Squaw Spy, and Mrs. Clara Blynn's Captivity among the Wild Indians of the Prairies* (1869), Fanny Kelly's *Narrative of My Captivity among the Sioux Indians* (1871), and Josephine Meeker's *The Ute Massacre* (1879) are set in the West during the late nineteenth century.

In an obvious attempt to engender as much anti-Indian hostility as possible, these narratives contain highly evocative descriptions of Indian brutalities. Accounts of murder and torture, usually described in lurid detail, predominate and are often accompanied by graphic woodcuts and illustrations. Babies are thrown into cauldrons of boiling water, fried in skillets, eaten by dogs, or dashed against trees or rocks (see Fig. 2). The aged are dispatched with tomahawks and scalped. Women are sexually violated, and captives of all ages and both sexes are burnt at the stake, dismembered, and sometimes even devoured in orgiastic rituals said to be of almost, but not quite, "too shocking a nature to be presented to the public."[73] In these narratives the line between fact and fiction becomes blurred. Plagiarisms abound, and the most egregious fictions are frequently presented as absolute fact and are sometimes even accompanied by bogus testimonials and affidavits.

Such is the case, for instance, in *A Narrative of the Life and Sufferings of Mrs. Jane Johns* (1837). According to its anonymous author, who begins by placing the narrative within the context of others of its kind, "Many have been the victims who have fallen beneath the tomahawk, or before the Indian arrow or rifle; of these some have been scalped after, and some undoubtedly before, life became extinct; but few have survived the combined effects of the rifle, the scalping knife and fire, as occurred in the case of this young lady, whose sufferings we are now about to detail."[74] After being scalped, set aflame, and left for dead, Mrs. Johns recovers, and, states the author, "Finding all quiet, her first thought was to extinguish the fire of her clothes, to accomplish which, she scraped the blood from her denuded head in her hands, and cautiously (for she still feared some Indians were near,) applied it to the fire, which was actually consuming her" (*Johns*, 12).

To authenticate the tale, the author includes testimonials from two military officials, a judge, an aunt ("much respected in Florida"), and Mrs. Johns's personal physician, who provides the following account of what he witnessed when Mrs. Johns was first brought to him for medical treatment:

"Here I beheld a sight, at the bare recollection of which my very heart sickens. I until then thought I had viewed, in the course of my professional career, wounds of the most revolting character. I have witnessed many horrors in the practice of surgery, I might almost venture to acknowledge without wincing— but when I looked upon this young widow, prostrate, in calm resignation, with one arm deeply lacerated, so much so that the muscles absolutely gaped open nearly to the bones. The same rifle ball which had effected this wound passed through the neck; these, in themselves, were painful to behold in one so peculiarly wretched, but who can depict in colors sufficiently powerful to convey to the imagination the appalling spectacle of her head, divested of the scalp to

This lurid engraving from *Miss Coleson's Narrative of Her Captivity* (1864) typifies the visual sensationalism that often accompanied anti-Indian propagandist narratives during the eighteenth and nineteenth centuries. *Courtesy of the Edward E. Ayer Collection, the Newberry Library.*

the bare bone, in two places, of which it was not only denuded and scraped, but portions absolutely cut out by the knife of the demon who had inflicted such unheard of torture!!! I measured the extent of skull divested of its natural integuments, which was from the upper part of the forehead (leaving at its commencement only a few hairs) to the occiput, nine inches—on the right side of the head it appeared to me that the knife had slipped, a cut had been made obliquely, otherwise the circumcision of the scalp was tolerably regular. Her legs were considerably burned, but not to the extent I apprehended, from the appearance of her dress when shewn to me." (*Johns*, 8–9)

Despite extensive efforts to verify the personages and events described in this narrative, there is no reason to think that Mrs. Johns ever experienced these torments or, for that matter, that she even existed.

Perhaps the most notorious example, however, of the mass proliferation of anti-Indian propaganda was the publication and frequent reprinting during the late eighteenth and nineteenth centuries of anthologies of captivity narratives whose avowed purpose was the total extermination of the American Indian. To facilitate this ignoble end, the editors of these volumes strung together highly evocative tales "of the dreadful cruelties exercised by the Indians on persons so unfortunate as to fall into their hands," as the anonymous editor of *The Affecting History of the Dreadful Distresses of Frederick Manheim's Family* (1793), the earliest and most famous of these collections, explains.[75] The titles of the anti-Indian anthologies openly display their militaristic and racist intents: *Horrid Indian Cruelties* (1799); *A Selection of Some of the Most Interesting Narratives of Outrages Committed by the Indians in Their Wars with the White People* (1808–11); *Indian Anecdotes and Barbarities: Being a Description of Their Customs and Deeds of Cruelty, with an Account of the Captivity, Sufferings and Heroic Conduct of the Many Who Have Fallen into Their Hands, or Who Have Defended Themselves from Savage Vengeance; All Illustrating the General Traits of Indian Character* (1837); and *Indian Atrocities! Affecting and Thrilling Anecdotes Respecting the Hardships and Sufferings of Our Brave and Venerable Forefathers, in Their Bloody and Heartrending Skirmishes and Contests with the Ferocious Savages* (1846).

Ironically, although anti-Indian captivity narratives continued to be produced about Western captivities until the twentieth century, a different impulse began to dominate the publication of narratives in the East. By the 1830s, when the Indian wars of the West were just beginning, in the East the Indian was already becoming a historic relic. Perhaps the most striking example of the contrast at this time between how the East and the West responded to the American Indian was the treatment that the Sauk leader Black Hawk received after his defeat in 1832. In Washington, D.C., and throughout the East, he was received as a hero. In response to public pressure, President Andrew Jackson, normally not an admirer of Indians, entertained him at the White House, and former President John Quincy Adams awarded him a medallion for his valor. On his return to the Midwest, however, a military escort was needed to protect Black Hawk from angry crowds who called for his execution. Still absent in the Midwest, there had, by the 1830s, emerged in the East a sentimental and antiquarian interest in the past and an appreciation for primitive culture inherited from the Enlightenment *philosophes* and reinforced by their Romantic successors, Rousseau, Chateaubriand, and Keats.

This changing attitude toward Indians is, in turn, reflected in the captivity narratives written and published in the East. In contrast to the propaganda narratives, the Indian ceased to be an object of white hatred and was transformed instead into a symbol of America's national heritage, whose legacy was to be preserved not just in literature but also in sculpture and on porcelain, canvas, postcards, and advertisements. At the very least, the American Indian was seen as a pathetic anachronism carelessly discarded as white society, with its increasingly more obvious apparent flaws and problems, moved relentlessly forward into the future. Affected by this shift in attitudes, historians, tellers of folktales, ballad singers, playwrights, and novelists turned toward the Indian and Indian captivity as a theme for their nationalistic and imaginative literary endeavors, and as a result the captivity narrative assumes a character far different from any that it previously exhibited.

During the nineteenth century, for example, numerous captivity narratives were published in local and regional histories of several Eastern towns and states, where they reminded white Americans of their past, which could in turn be used to inspire patriotism and national pride.[76] Captivity accounts also appear in American Indian and military histories. In these contexts, they became a means, respectively, for preserving historical and ethnological information about the Indian and for illustrating frontier heroism. In addition, captivity materials appear in large-scale historical works such as George Bancroft's *History of the United States* (1834–82), Washington Irving's *Astoria* (1836), Henry David Thoreau's *A Week on the Concord and Merrimack Rivers* (1849), and Francis Parkman's *The Jesuits in North America* (1867), where they were used to explore—not always positively—nationalistic assumptions about progress, race, and Manifest Destiny.

As part of a growing body of information that Eastern writers of the nineteenth century were assimilating into a collective definition of America's past, captivity narratives were written as children's literature, and they were incorporated into a rapidly growing body of folklore that similarly attempted to provide Americans with a national heritage and cultural identity.[77] Stories of Indian captivity appear, for example, in McGuffey's Readers, where they were read by countless thousands of young people, who found in them lessons in history, ethics, and adventure. Ballad singers in turn romanticized their nation's frontier heritage by composing folksongs about Indian captivity, and tellers of folktales utilized the subject as well. On the basis of their exploits as Indian captives, folk celebrities even developed around the subject. Included in this last category are Davy Crockett and Jim Bridger, as well as Daniel Boone, Tim Murphy, and Tom Quick.

Finally, Indian captivity enters the mainstream of nineteenth-century American belletristic literature in the form of poems, plays, short stories, and novels. Like their counterparts in history, children's literature, and folklore, nineteenth-century American poets, dramatists, and novelists turned to Indian captivity as a theme for their works. Striving to develop a uniquely American literary tradition that would reflect, in a noticeable way, what Philip Freneau and others called "the rising glory of America,"[78] they attempted to write in established forms about distinctively New World themes. Dramatic, exotic, and in every respect thoroughly American, the Indian captivity narrative served this function well. It was decidedly American, and its theme and setting could readily be transferred to Old World forms of writing.

Dramatists, for example, were quick to realize the adaptability of Indian captivity to the stage. Searching for decidedly nationalistic themes for their dramatic productions, they found history, romance, and high adventure in stories of Indian captivity. For novelty and dramatic splendor, nothing in Europe could match Indian chiefs and maidens who, when arrayed in brightly colored feathers and wilderness costumes, provided a distinctively New World alternative to the more urban dramas then in vogue. While only a few of these plays survive, playbills and mention of them in other sources attest to the popularity of such productions. James Nelson Barker's *The Indian Princess; or, La Belle Sauvage* (1808), about the rescue of Captain John Smith by the Indian princess Pocahontas, was so popular that it became the first in a series on the subject that later included a satiric rendition by John Brougham titled *Po-ca-hon-tas, or the Gentle Savage, an Original Aboriginal Erratic Operatic Semi-Civilized and Demi-Savage Extravaganza, Being a Per-Version of Ye Trewe and Wonderrefulle Hystorie of Ye Renowned Princess* (1855).

Eventually, through the novel, the captivity narrative became legitimized as the subject for serious literary endeavors. Captivity materials could easily be molded to conform to the conventions of sentimental, gothic, and historical fiction. Ann Eliza Bleecker's *The History of Maria Kittle* (1790) is basically a novel of sensibility, and Charles Brockden Brown's *Edgar Huntly; or, Memoirs of a Sleepwalker* (1799), a gothic novel. Both of these works are structured around the subject of Indian captivity. Drawn to the tradition through his interest in the frontier and his reading on the subject, James Fenimore Cooper also incorporated captivity materials into many of his most successful novels, including each of his much publicized Leatherstocking Tales (1826–41), where they are used as the basis for historical romance and adventure.

Even painters and sculptors recognized the aesthetic and dramatic potential in Indian captivity for the development of a national artistic legacy. The celebrated artist Thomas Cole based two of his paintings on captivity episodes in Cooper's *The Last of the Mohicans*. Also influenced by Cooper, the New York sculptor Erastus Dow Palmer (1817–1904) used Indian captivity as the subject of one of his most famous works, a marble statue called *White Captive* (1856). On display at New York's Metropolitan Museum of Art, this work, like the paintings of Cole, uses captivity as a means for infusing a classical art form with American subject matter. It depicts a nude young woman, in the tradition of Greek and Roman statuary, rudely tied to the stump of a tree, suggestive of the American frontier, awaiting her fate, whatever it might be.[79]

Known as the *Rescue Group* (1851), a sculpture by Horatio Greenough (1805–52) uses the subject of Indian captivity for similar purposes. Portraying a white frontier mother and infant standing between an Indian warrior, who apparently is intent on abducting them, and a white woodsman, who attempts to secure their release, the *Rescue Group* uses a classical medium to illustrate the nature of the American past as a heroic blending of white European civilization and the New World wilderness. As Washburn explains, "The size of the figures represents the significance of each. The woman is tiny and frail, the Indian powerful in comparison with her, but diminutive in comparison with the Bunyanesque rescuer" (Washburn, "Introduction," xxi). For more than a century this work was displayed in front of the U.S. Capitol in Washington, D.C. (Washburn, "Introduction," xxi).

Chapter Two
The Mythology of the Captivity Narrative

A mythology is a complex of narratives that dramatizes the world vision and historical sense of a people or culture, reducing centuries of experience into a constellation of compelling metaphors.
>   —Richard Slotkin, *Regeneration through Violence* (1973)

Like Iceland, the United States is fortunate in having a body of narratives that cover the periods of her settlement in new lands and the violence that attended that settlement. . . . It is my contention that these captivities deserve better treatment as literature.
>   —Phillips D. Carleton, "The Indian Captivity," *American Literature* (1943)

The discrete historical and cultural significances of the Indian captivity narrative, however illuminating they may be in their religious, propagandistic, and visceral applications, are subordinate to the fundamental informing and unifying principle in the narratives collectively: the core of ritual acts and patterns from which the narratives derive their essential integrity.
>   —Richard VanDerBeets, "The Indian Captivity Narrative as Ritual," *American Literature* (1972)

The male imagination, for better or for worse, tends to transform the tale of captivity into one of adoption, to substitute the male dream of joining the Indians for the female fantasy of being dragged off by them.
>   —Leslie A. Fiedler, *The Return of the Vanishing American* (1968)

For what the captivity story provided was a mode of symbolic action crucial to defining the otherwise dangerous or unacknowledged meaning of women's experience of the dark and enclosing forests around them.
>   —Annette Kolodny, *The Land before Her* (1984)

Immensely and immediately popular in their day, captivity narratives were not merely flashes in the publishing pan: they also maintained their appeal through the centuries. In a regular rhythm, while new captivity accounts were published, the more durable old ones were revamped and republished alongside them.[1] The reading public seemed to crave both the new and the novel as well as the old and the classic.[2] While the popularity of captivity narratives is well-established, the central issue behind their popularity is *why* they appealed—and continue to appeal—to so many people. Why, for example, do we as modern readers still relate to a seventeenth-century text like Mary Rowlandson's when many other popular texts of the time have lost their appeal for all but a few scholars and antiquarians? What underlying universalities exist in a work such as Rowlandson's that touch profound emotional and intellectual chords in us, just as they did in generations of readers before us?

Archetypal patterns and literary substructures form one means of explaining the continuing attraction of captivity narratives beyond the cultural contexts in which they were originally published. As Richard VanDerBeets indicates, their "cultural significances" are secondary to their primary, unifying principle, namely, "the core of ritual acts and patterns from which the narratives derive their essential integrity."[3] Different ways of identifying the rituals that provide a mythological backdrop to the captivity corpus furnish different answers to why this group of texts remains so perennially captivating that it forms "a constellation of compelling metaphors."[4]

Myth-Ritual Archetypes

The most basic approach to understanding the captivity narrative's power is the theory that behind it lies an archetypal pattern—common in American literature generally—of separation, initiation, and return. As Phillips D. Carleton first noted, not only did the content of captivity narratives provide unity, but their standard formal elements of attack, capture, and escape or return also gave them coherence and definition as a group.[5] In addition, this pattern stresses the archetypal significance of the newcomers' struggle for identity as Americans and of their interactions with Native Americans, who taught them wilderness survival but who lost the land to them (Carleton, 180). The captivity literature thus provides a means to explore the subconscious ramifications of westerly American settlement.

Included in this experience are "ritual acts and patterns"—markers for decoding the social issues underlying the archetypal pattern of capture, initiation, and return. These are defined as human acts that seem to possess common meanings and functions despite their documentation in records that are not otherwise related. Two such ritual acts stressed in many myths, including the captivity accounts, are cannibalism and scalping. Further information on these rites comes from Sir James Frazer's classic work on myth, magic, religion, and ritual, *The Golden Bough*, first published in 1890.[6] Because these rituals define the initiate in terms of the capturing culture, they constitute boundaries that, once crossed, also define the initiate in terms of "the other." Additionally, the captivity archetype itself can be linked to the monomyth established by Joseph Campbell in *The Hero with a Thousand Faces* (1949), for the narratives' primary pattern is that of the hero's initiation journey, or quest, which "is a variation of the fundamental death-rebirth archetype and traditionally involves the separation of the Hero from his culture, his undertaking a long journey, and his undergoing a series of excruciating ordeals in passing from ignorance to knowledge. In the monomyth, this consists of three stages or phases: separation, transformation, and enlightened return" (VanDerBeets, 553).

The general nature of the myth-ritual archetype explains the captivities' popularity and even cross-cultural appeal, defines their collective power as narrative acts, and draws them together into what has been called "an American genre."[7] It applies to texts ranging from the factual—such as Rowlandson's *A True History* (1682), James Everett Seaver's *A Narrative of the Life of Mrs. Mary Jemison* (1824), and James Smith's *Account* (1799)—to the largely or totally fictional—such as Ann Eliza Bleecker's *The History of Maria Kittle* (1790), Andrew Coffinberry's epic poem *The Forest Rangers* (1794), and James Fenimore Cooper's *The Last of the Mohicans* (1826)—as well as stories about captivity in the folklore, dime novels, and even humor of the nineteenth and twentieth centuries. In other words, it unifies the narratives despite all other differences such as date of composition, overall length, authorship, literary genre, and gender of captive.

The Hunter-Predator Myth

In addition to the universal myth-ritual archetypes, more particular interpretations of the captivity literature have been advanced, including the hunter-predator myth. As Richard Slotkin explains, "The first colonists saw in America an opportunity to regenerate their fortunes, their spirits, and the power of their church and nation; but the means to that regeneration ultimately became the means of violence, and the myth of regeneration through violence became the structuring metaphor of the American experience" (Slotkin, 5). Captivity by Indians not only constituted a uniquely American phenomenon but also an archetypal clash of cultures (Slotkin, 21). Thus captivity accounts encapsulated the very essence of the frontier myth, and as they evolved as literature, they continued to incorporate cultural preoccupations and symbols.

The hunter-predator myth is perhaps most clearly illustrated by two narratives: Mary Rowlandson's *A True History* (1682) and John Filson's *The Discovery, Settlement and Present State of Kentucke and the Adventures of Daniel Boon* (1784). The earliest separate full-length captivity narrative, Rowlandson's dramatic account of her three months' capture by Narragansetts and Nipmucks functions as a generic archetype, that is, it creates "a paradigm of personal and collective history that can be discerned as an informing structure throughout Puritan and (with modifications) in later American narrative literature" (Slotkin, 102). This text is the first and also "perhaps the best of the captivity narratives" (Slotkin, 102) owing to its skillful dramatization of the settlers' desire for emigration and adventure versus their accompanying guilt and anxiety, in other words, of their ambivalent psychic accommodation to the New World (Slotkin, 107).

As European culture became established, and as colonists began defining themselves not just in terms of their difference from, and hostility to, Indians, but also in terms of their identity as Americans, the captivity myth emphasized the captive as mediator between savagery and civilization. In this capacity, Daniel Boone, "the solitary, Indian-like hunter of the deep woods" (Slotkin, 21), became the prototypical myth-hero. Equally at home in the wilderness and the drawing room, Boone represented the archetypal balance Americans sought between nature and tradition. His story first appeared in an appendix to jack-of-all-trades John Filson's promotion document on the geography and settlement of Kentucky. Although the section on Boone is written in the first person, it is actually Filson's literary creation from various sources. Boone's adventures, which include temporary capture and adoption by the Shawnees, constitute a set of wilderness initiations that deepen his identity, moral sense, and insight into primitive nature. Each adventure is succeeded by a return to family and civilization, where Boone can reflect on his experiences and then apply his conclusions to further his own community's success: "As a result of these rhythmic cycles of immersion and emergence, he grows to become the commanding genius of his people, their hero-chief, and the man fit to realize Kentucky's destiny" (Slotkin, 278–79). That destiny is not to preserve the integrity of the land and its original people, the Native Americans (Slotkin, 293), but to wrest control of the whole environment through settlement and cultivation, through exploitation, through what we ironically call *progress*.

This paradigm makes it possible to trace the influence of the captivity mythology and tradition on the works of Cooper, Melville, Thoreau, and other nineteenth-century American Romantics. Although this myth of "regeneration through violence" can be illustrated with captivities by and about both genders, it seems most applicable to the male narratives, which are more likely to emphasize aggression and independence.

Freudian Interpretations

Freudian perspectives, when applied to the captivity narrative, also explain its popularity—at least in part—as an essentially male form of fantasy literature reflecting the white Anglo-Saxon Protestant (WASP) American male's subconscious ambivalence when confronted by the wilderness.[8] Two such gender-based impulses can be discerned within the captivity literature.

First, in trying to shed the constraints of civilization and merge with nature, the male imagination transforms captivity into adoption. The *male* captive thus identifies with the American Indians and the wilderness and reveals through his captivity initiation "the wild man that lives next to the mild husband at the heart of all American males" (Fiedler, 104). Two ways to illustrate this myth include analysis of what Leslie A. Fiedler calls "The Myth of Love in the Woods," the archetypal story of Pocahontas and John Smith, and "The Myth of the Good Companions in the Wilderness," the story of a European and a Native American "who find solace and sustenance in each other's love," exemplified by the fur-trapper Alexander Henry's *Travels and Adventures in Canada and the Indian Territories* (1809) (Fiedler, 51). Henry's text recounts the experiences of a trader captured and later adopted by American Indians in the late eighteenth century. During his captivity, he forms a strong bond of friendship and respect with his Indian family, especially with his adopted brother. Such close ties between Indian and white hunters, freed from repressive contact with white "civilization"—particularly marriage with a white woman—form the powerful prototype of such Western American narratives as Cooper's *The Last of the Mohicans*, in which

Leatherstocking, a variant of Daniel Boone, befriends Uncas, the "last of the Mohicans," according to the same rituals evident in the Henry narrative. This provides one explanation for the lasting hold of the Leatherstocking Tales and those like them on the white (male) imagination.

Second, narratives about the *female* captive also conform to Freudian archetypes, but of course from a different perspective. Women such as Mary Rowlandson and Hannah Dustan, who survived Indian captivity without their husbands, are said to awaken subconscious male fears of impotence and castration through their ability to live through the experience without male intervention. The story of Hannah Dustan, "a New England lady who, snatched out of childbed by an Indian raiding party, fought her bloody way to freedom," initiated this approach, which can be termed "The Myth of the White Woman with a Tomahawk" (Fiedler, 51). This woman, an inversion of the Pocahontas figure, is "our other—alas, realer—mother, the Great WASP Mother of Us All, who, far from achieving a reconciliation between White men and Red, turns the weapon of the Indian against him in a final act of bloodshed and vengeance" (Fiedler, 95).

According to the Freudian archetype, whether the captivity account has a male or a female protagonist, it ultimately entails a patriarchal vision and fulfills male fantasies. For through this literature, American men can recapture the primordial dream of "a natural Eden," lost when civilization—symbolized by matriarchy—interfered.

Feminist Perspectives

Feminist revisionists sense other mythic impulses beneath the captivity narratives' popular appeal. Annette Kolodny, for example, condemns the male mythology's aggression and violence. Instead, she discerns in the women's materials symbols of their domestic aim to create and cultivate individual gardens in the wilderness as havens from the surrounding wild: "Massive exploitation and alteration of the continent do not seem to have been part of women's fantasies. They dreamed, more modestly, of locating a home and a familial human community within a cultivated garden."[9]

To illustrate the radically different female psychology, Filson's *Adventures* of Daniel Boone can be contrasted with *A Narrative of the Captivity, and Extraordinary Escape of Mrs. Francis Scott*. Scott's story initially received considerable exposure in newspaper articles published in 1785.

Her homestead on the Virginia/Kentucky border was attacked by Delawares who killed her family and took her captive. Although she managed to escape, as a woman unused to the wild she had difficulty finding food and help, and even after returning to "civilization," she remembered the wilderness experience with horror. In 1786, these two accounts by Filson and Scott appeared as complementary texts in a book published by John Trumbull, the well-known printer in Norwich, Connecticut (Kolodny, *Land*, 29). In Boone's fascination with the fertile Kentucky landscape, "the white male imagination continued to project, ever westward, its endless dream of rediscovering Paradise. As represented by the captivity narrative of Francis Scott, the white female continued to encounter only the implacable and hostile American wilderness" (Kolodny, *Land*, 31).

Daniel Boone showed the American male as victor over the American Indian, and Scott's story showed the American female as victim. But was there another kind of white woman who could accommodate herself to the wild? The answer is yes if we consider the experiences of women who were originally captured by American Indians but who remained with them—who became transculturated or transculturized, in other words.[10] For example, *A Narrative of the Life of Mrs. Mary Jemison*, dictated to James Everett Seaver by Jemison herself and first published in 1824, tells the story of a woman captured by French and Shawnees in 1758 at age 13 or 14 who was adopted into Seneca tribal culture and who adapted to it willingly. While Jemison's story is clearly mediated by Seaver, it still forms one of the few instances in which a transculturated captive's own voice penetrates the narrative.[11] In 1823, when Seaver and Jemison met, Jemison had lived among the Senecas for 65 years, had long ago taken the name Dehgewanus, had married two Indian men—first Sheninjee then, some years after she was widowed, Hiokatoo—and had a large family network of eight children (though she outlived all but three daughters) and 39 grandchildren. As Kolodny states, "Jemison's *Life* was 'revolutionary' . . . because it represented the first text in American literature to move a real-world white woman beyond the traditional captivity pattern to something approaching the *willing* wilderness accommodations of a Daniel Boone" (Kolodny, *Land*, 80). The hunter-predator and Freudian mythologies can be further differentiated from this feminist approach by considering that "In sharp contrast to the Adamic paradisal longings of the men . . . Mary Jemison brought home and family into the cleared spaces of the wild—an act of survival, if not of romance" (Kolodny, *Land*, 80).

Kolodny acknowledges her debt to another feminist theory advanced by Dawn Lander Gherman, whose study, "From Parlour to Tepee: The White Squaw on the American Frontier," reaches a still different conclusion regarding the mythology of the captivity literature.[12] This response begins with "the traditional image of the white woman as Civilizer: alien to the landscape, racially prejudiced and sexually inhibited" (Gherman, vii), but it suggests that this figure of woman as victim is based not so much on historical fact as on social sanction. The counterimage presented is that of "the White Squaw" (Gherman, viii), that is, the woman who breaks through the "wilderness taboo" by rebelling against white patriarchal society and finding new roles. Many of the examples used concern women who were captured by American Indians but who became acculturated or transculturated, for example, Eunice Williams, daughter of the Puritan minister John Williams, taken captive in 1704, and Mary Jemison and Frances Slocum, both taken in 1758. All three had the opportunity to return to white society; all three declined to do so. Thus, the implicit focus of this approach is what might be termed "feminine wildness", defined as "a propensity to break social taboos which restrict self-expression and exploration" (Gherman, vi).

To appreciate the range of the four approaches described above, we can apply each in turn to a single case study, the popular but puzzling narrative known as the "Panther Captivity."

A Case Study

The fictional captivity titled *A Surprising Account of the Discovery of a Lady who was taken by the Indians in the year 1777, and after making her escape, she retired to a lonely Cave, where she lived nine years* was first published in 1787 as a six-page letter by the pseudonymous Abraham Panther to a male friend and is now generally referred to as the "Panther Captivity."[13] It proved to be so popular it was reprinted, sometimes in pirated form, several dozen times in New England and New York between 1787 and 1814.[14] Subsequently, while its popularity declined among general readers, its significance increased among critics.

The account begins with the letter-writer describing to a male reader how he and a companion, Isaac Camber, travelled westward for 13 days on a hunting expedition. On the fourteenth day, they are surprised to hear a young woman singing in the wilderness at the mouth of a cave. A guard dog barks, and when the beautiful woman sees the men, she faints. She recovers when they assure her they intend her no harm, and she invites them into her cave and hospitably offers them ground nuts, apples, Indian cake, and fresh water—the produce of the earth—before she tells her story in her own voice. Born to a good family in Albany, New York, she and her lover eloped because her father disapproved of the match. They were attacked by Indians who killed her lover, but she was able to escape into the wilderness and feed on "the spontaneous produce of the earth" (*Panther*, n. p.). After two weeks, she encountered a giant who spoke to her in an unknown language and indicated that she must sleep with him. He bound her with ropes, but she was able to bite through them and free herself. She then took the hatchet he had threatened her with, killed him with three blows, decapitated and quartered him, took the pieces into the forest, and buried them. With only a faithful dog as companion, she lived alone for nine years and sustained herself by planting corn she fortuitously found in the cave. Here the woman's narrative breaks off and Panther resumes. He tells how after some resistance she agrees to accompany them home and how she returns to her father's house. Her ailing father, much affected by her story and apparently guilt-stricken at having precipitated her elopement, faints and dies, leaving his daughter a large fortune.

The "Panther Captivity" is woven from various generic sources, including the adventure narrative (the story of the two male explorers), the captivity narrative (the Indian attack on the woman and her lover), the sentimental novel (the woman as heroine and the standard plot resolution in which her father forgives her, dies, and leaves her well provided for), and the fertility myth (the giant whom the woman kills) (Kolodny, *Land*, 60). All these elements conform to the basic archetypal pattern of capture, initiation, and return, which applies to the main characters: the woman and the two hunters. Only the unnamed woman is captured by Indians, but that action affects everything—and everyone—else, so that there is both a female and a male quest.

The woman, actually the "Lady" as the title identifies her, willingly separates herself from a patriarchal society that denies her freedom. She is initiated into a wilderness experience that in fact forces her to be independent and self-sufficient from the time her lover is "barbarously murdered" (*Panther*, n. p.) and she switches from the dependent heroine typical of sentimental fiction to the resourceful frontier woman (albeit temporarily). When the Earth offers her food, she takes it; when the giant accosts her, she strategically and ritually kills him; when she discovers corn, she plants and harvests it. Only when the two hunters find her does she revert to the sentimental heroine (for example, by fainting and then being persuaded to leave her cave) and return with them to "civilization," where her newfound independence is validated by her changed status from penniless daughter to wealthy heiress.

The giant himself is a mythic fertility figure with ties to Indian legends about "the ritual slaying of a vegetation god" (Slotkin, 257) and to the figure of the Green Giant in the fourteenth-century alliterative poem *Sir Gawain and the Green Knight*. However, it is not a question of ascertaining whether the "Panther Captivity"'s unknown author was influenced either by Indian legends or by the medieval text, but rather of acknowledging that "any writer who involves his imagination in the literary exploitation of such mythy material as the captivity narratives seems bound to uncover the archetypal patterns concealed deep beneath the conventionalized surface form of the narratives" (Slotkin, 258).

The two hunters also embark on their own quest, which takes the form of capture, initiation, and return. The men are not so much captured as captivated by the landscape and by the emblem of civilization, the Lady of the Cave. They are initiated into the surprising discovery that the land is not necessarily there for hunters to exploit, but perhaps more importantly for settlers to cultivate (Kolodny, *Land*, 64). Indeed, the woman cultivator has beat them to it. As Panther observes after tracing the source of the singing he hears, which is the only woman-made sound in the wild (as opposed to the man-made sound of gunshot): "We desired her to be under no uneasiness, told her we were travellers, that we came only to view the country but that in all our travels we had not met with any thing that had surprised us so much as her extraordinary appearance, in a place which we imagined totally unfrequented" (*Panther*, n. p.). Panther and Camber return eastward with the lady and with newfound knowledge about themselves and their role in the wilderness.

Exploring the myth-ritual archetypes of the "Panther Captivity" inevitably involved some aspects of the hunter-predator myth, which can now be examined separately. Several commentators point out the significance of the story-within-the-story of the "Panther Captivity," that is, the lady's tale, beginning in 1776, the year she and her lover escape from her father into the woods. Although the text was not published for another decade, it is easy to see it as an allegory of the new nation's birth. The work thus dramatizes Americans' dilemma at the point of independence between maintaining ties to Europe (symbolized by the "Panther Captivity"'s affinities to the traditional—Puritan—captivity form) and acculturating themselves to the native wilderness (symbolized by the fertility myth associations). Both choices involved violence and change.

Perhaps the "Panther Captivity"'s contemporary popularity lay in its ability to simultaneously articulate *both* alternatives and suggest "many levels of human and colonial anxiety in a single, emotionally evocative, symbolic drama" (Slotkin, 259). Thus, in this interpretation, the narrative deals with issues of independence, identity, and power as applied to the national and to the individual consciousness. One of the "Panther Captivity"'s analogues, Filson's *Discovery*, "quieted fears of white male degeneracy in the woods by substituting for those fears the heroic myth of white male conquest of the wilderness" (Kolodny, *Land*, 56) in the figure of Daniel Boone. To understand how the "Panther Captivity" itself addressed corresponding fears "for the fate of white women in the wilderness" (Kolodny, *Land*, 57), we must next turn to a Freudian interpretation.

Secure in their male companionship, Panther and Camber determine "to penetrate the Western wilderness as far as prudence and safety would permit" to hunt the startled game, which, "as we had our muskets contributed not a little to our amusement and support" (*Panther*, n. p.). But despite the phallic subtext, the "rich and fertile land" is not dominated by these men or by any of the male characters: not the lady's father, nor her lover, nor the Indians, nor the "gigantic figure" of the cave. It is the newly independent lady who controls the land and to whom the Earth gives up its "spontaneous produce" (*Panther*, n. p.). Here indeed is "The Myth of the White Woman with a Tomahawk," the story of a woman who delivers herself from a fate worse than death and from death itself by axing, decapitating, and quartering the giant—by symbolically castrating then killing him. All the male characters are displaced by this woman: she survives her father, whose abusive authoritarianism had initially caused her rebellion; she survives her lover, who is unable to defend himself against the Indians, let alone her; she outwits the Indians by quietly withdrawing while they are celebrating; she survives the giant by pitting her mental strength against his physical strength; and finally, she denies Panther and Camber their fantasy of a masculine wilderness adventure untouched by a woman's (corrupting) influence. The male perspective of such a Freudian interpretation would see this female figure as distorted and defeminized, except that by the end of her story the lady obligingly slips back into the passive role of sentimental heroine. However, the figure undergoes a metamorphosis within a feminist mythology.

The "Panther Captivity" is unusual because "it adhered to the essential male fantasy of woodland intimacy while, at the same time, it offered a positive image of the white woman's capacity to survive and plant gardens in that same wilderness" (Kolodny, *Land*, 66–67). In its dual interest, it symbolically fulfilled opposite fantasies. For as women really did arrive on the frontier, agriculture began to displace hunting for subsistence (Kolodny, *Land*, 67). Yet even though cultivation— symbolized by women's gardens—historically marked the overturn of the frontier, ultimately "the nation took to its heart the heroic mythology of the wilderness hunter, eschewing the hybridized romance of the wilderness cultivator suggested by the Panther Captivity" (Kolodny, *Land*, 67). The independence and identity of the woman cultivator were too threatening to the male hunter, so the stronger male stereotypes prevailed. In the "Panther Captivity," America simply was not ready for the figure of the White Squaw. A final issue of feminist significance concerns the true identity of the pseudonymous author, Abraham Panther. The author has still not been identified, though all previous commentators have assumed he is male. Yet given the feminist subtext, it is tantalizing to speculate that the author could well have been a woman wishing to present a female viewpoint under the guise of the outrageously fake pen name Abraham Panther. Certainly, it is well-known that women who published in the eighteenth century often did so under a pseudonym.

The "Panther Captivity" is almost certainly derived from Filson's *Adventures* (originally published three years earlier) and, in turn, it almost certainly influenced later American literary texts, including Charles Brockden Brown's *Edgar Huntly* (1799). Applying all four structural approaches to the "Panther Captivity" works particularly well because its disparate elements invite deeper examination. But other captivity narratives do not necessarily respond to such a multi-layered approach.

This chapter has presented the dominant mythologies of the captivity narrative. The diversity of both the texts and the analyses suggests that the material offers literary critics and cultural theoreticians a particularly rich resource for continued interpretation. However, because each approach tends to use a restricted number of narratives to illustrate its thesis, we do not believe that any single one applies consistently to the entire corpus. As we suggest throughout this book, valid mythologies to account for the appeal of these narratives are probably as varied and complex as the texts themselves.

Chapter Three
Images of Indians

They are so guileless and so generous . . . that no one would believe it
who has not seen it.
> —Christopher Columbus, *The Letter by Christopher
> Columbus Describing the Result of His First Voyage*
> (1493)

. . . for Mercy who'd expect / From *Cannibals* that gorge on Human
Flesh, / And Swill like *Polypheme*, the reeking Gore?
> —John Maylem, *Gallic Perfidy: A Poem* (1758)

Such monsters of barbarity ought certainly to be excluded from all the
privileges of human nature, and hunted down as wild beasts, without
pity or cessation.
> —Mary Smith, *An Affecting Narrative of the Captivity
> and Sufferings of Mrs. Mary Smith* (1815)

Notwithstanding all that has been said against the Indians, in
consequence of their cruelties to their enemies—cruelties that I have
witnessed, and had abundant proof of—it is a fact that they are naturally
kind, tender and peaceable towards their friends, and strictly honest; and
that those cruelties have been practised, only upon their enemies,
according to their idea of justice.
> —James Everett Seaver, *A Narrative of the Life of Mrs.
> Mary Jemison* (1824)

The Character of the savage mind, naturally fierce, revengeful and cruel,
will not receive and cherish the introduction of the arts and sciences: but
on the contrary renders it more debased and inveterate—therefore, the
policy of a great nation ought to be, and is, to overawe and intimidate,
and not to extirpate them.
> —Jane Lewis, *Narrative of the Captivity and Providential
> Escape of Mrs. Jane Lewis* (1833)

For more than four centuries, Indian captivity narratives provided white
audiences, both European and American, with a major source of infor-

mation about American Indians. Because Indians lived on the frontier segregated from white settlements, Indian contact with European settlers generally consisted of limited, carefully defined exchanges. Genuine cultural interaction that might significantly meld white and Indian communities was the exception rather than the rule.[1] What early readers knew about Native Americans was, for the most part, filtered through the perspective of explorers, missionaries, traders, trappers, and captives who wrote about their experiences with Indians.[2] Predictably, these accounts were, in most instances, culturally biased. Such was particularly the case with captivity narratives, whose authors, despite a multiplicity of purpose, rarely considered the welfare of the Indian, often harboring ingrained prejudices, not to mention outright personal vendettas, against Native Americans.

Recent anthropological and historical studies have noted that two distinct images of Indians predominate in white American culture from colonial times through the present: one negative and one positive. On the negative side exists the stereotypically "bad" Indian often associated in the white popular culture with stories of Western adventure. Portrayed as culturally and often mentally deficient and incapable of what white society considered civilization and progress, this Indian lived a rude, nomadic existence generally characterized by the basest of emotions and motives. Simply put, the "bad" Indian was a barbarian. Alongside this Indian, there also exists the image of the "good" Indian, who opposes what the "bad" Indian represents, often siding, like Tonto with the Lone Ranger and Chingachgook with James Fenimore Cooper's Leatherstocking, with the values of white society.[3]

These bipolar images possess roots that reach back to the first extended intercultural contacts between Europeans and American Indians during the fifteenth century. Beginning with Columbus, the native inhabitants of the Americas were classified as either "bad," meaning foreign, dangerous, and expendable, or "good," meaning simple and inferior but tractable and useful. At the same time that Columbus described a "guileless" and "generous" people who lived in a prelapsarian harmony with nature, for example, he also described other "very fierce" and "ferocious" natives who "eat human flesh."[4] This same view was later reinforced by the sixteenth-century navigator and cartographer Amerigo Vespucci, who simultaneously described Indians as either "gentle and amenable" and "amicable and hospitable" or "unwonted and monstrous" and "very libidinous." Indeed, Vespucci records the behavior of one Indian "who was reputed to have eaten more than three hundred human bodies," and he notes that "human flesh" is such "a common article of diet" that some fathers have been known "to eat children and wife."[5]

Significantly, both negative and positive stereotypes of Native Americans were in no way an accurate portrayal of Indian culture, which, at the time when Columbus sailed, included some 2,000 tribes, each representing a unique civilization (Berkhofer, 3). Ironically, from the start, Europeans seemed less capable of fathoming the complexity of Native American cultures than Indians, who were labelled incapable of progress, were of understanding European values. The very term *Indian* illustrates the unilateral perception that early explorers and colonists imposed on the Indians of the Americas. From the Eskimos of the Canadian tundra to the Incas of Peru, all Native American peoples were, in the eyes of the European usurpers, essentially identical, and all were referred to simply as *Indians* (Berkhofer, 4–5).

There was, in fact, a utilitarian reason why white American culture refused to develop an accurate image of American Indian cultures. Whether negative or positive, stereotyping Indians ultimately served the same pragmatic racist purpose regarding the so-called Indian problem encountered by an essentially expansionistic, white, agrarian society that needed new territories as it grew in both size and military strength. Depicted as inferior to Europeans but tractable, the "good" Indian could assist the white settler in exploiting the continent and its resources, most notably by helping to eradicate the "bad" Indian, whose unwillingness to adapt to European cultural norms necessitated a policy of extermination. Predictably, for whites, "bad" Indians usually outnumbered "good" Indians, who are often, like Chingachgook in Cooper's *The Last of the Mohicans*, the "last" of their tribes. Once their negative counterparts were eliminated, the "good" Indians, having served their purpose, also became expendable, and that fewer "good" Indians seemed to exist than "bad" Indians in turn provided a convenient justification for why Indian culture, in the eyes of white culture, would vanish along with the frontier. In the end, after more than four centuries of genocide, simply too few Indians were left to matter.

Within this context, Indian captivity narratives played a major, though often insidious, role. Viewed collectively, the captivity narratives reveal four major images of the American Indian, all of which to one degree or another reflect the biases and racist preoccupations of white America. First, early Colonial narratives provided what appeared to be an

experiential, empirical foundation for stereotypes of the American Indian that later solidified in the white culture generally. Second, the
propaganda narratives that emerged during the eighteenth and nineteenth centuries encouraged negative images of Indians that both directly and indirectly fueled white hostilities toward Indians as European
colonists advanced across the continent. Third, those few narratives that
intentionally presented sympathetic images of Indians also contributed
to the Indians' demise as the dominant culture in the New World. That
such narratives were few, especially when compared to the hundreds of
narratives that openly vilified Indians, only served, ironically, to further
validate the negative image of the Indian as barbarian and brute, for they
conveyed the impression that only a few Indians were worth salvaging
while the threat of countless more dangerous Indians necessitated the
genocide of the entire race. Finally, a fourth, more realistic but usually
disguised, image of the Indian emerges in retrospect from captivity
narratives by writers who, despite their ethnocentric prejudices, sometimes revealed realities about the American Indian that they themselves
failed at a conscious level to recognize or acknowledge.

Colonial Images

The first captivity narratives, those written and published during the
period of European colonization of the New World, confirmed stereotypes of Indians that, for purposes of convenience, Old World powers
wished to promulgate. These stereotypes varied with the aims of the
colonizing nations but were generally based on principles of convenience, greed, exploitation, and deliberate misrepresentation. In seeking
to understand Indians, Europeans first turned to philosophers, theolo-
gians, and historians, whose theories, often drawn from folklore, established images of Indians that provided a framework that Europeans could
use in their dealings with the native populations of the New World.
These initial images were remarkably varied, ranging from the "wild
men" of medieval legend, to the prelapsarian innocents of Montaigne's
Essays, to subhuman degenerates like Caliban in Shakespeare's *The
Tempest* (1611), whose ancestry had diabolic origins.[6]

As European colonization of the New World began in earnest, theoretical images of Indians were adapted to the needs of the colonizing
nations, and fixed stereotypes began to emerge. How each colonizing
power wanted Indians to behave determined what image that nation
developed as the basis for its treatment of the people it encountered in the

New World. Supposedly based on fact, captivity narratives provided experiential evidence to support whatever stereotypes about Indians that individual European nations found it convenient to confirm. Spain, for instance, wanted to exploit the New World for its wealth. To the Spanish, Indians were thus part of the plunder. Indeed, it required a papal bull from Paul III, *Sublimus Deus* (1537), to determine that Indians were "truly men—capable of understanding the Catholic faith," and not "dumb brutes created for our service."[7] While missionaries like Bartolomé de Las Casas insisted that Indians were "a simple people without evil and without guile" (quoted in Berkhofer, 11), such a view clearly reflected a minority opinion. More useful for the Spanish colonial agenda was the attitude of Juan Ginés de Sepúlveda, who saw little of value in Indians except their usefulness as slaves. According to Sepúlveda, Indians "scarcely" exhibited "traces of humanity" and "were involved in every kind of intemperance and wicked lust," including the stereotypically "monstrous hunger" for "human flesh" (quoted in Berkhofer, 11–12).

Predictably, early Spanish captivities confirmed Sepúlveda's view that Indians were meant for exploitation, and they served to counter the objections of individuals like Las Casas, whose benevolent view of Indians impeded Spanish objectives to exploit the New World. While captivity narratives that projected favorable images of Indians were suppressed by the Spanish authorities, narratives that supported Sepúlveda's views were published and encouraged. Such was the case, for instance, with *Cautiverio Felix* (*The Happy Captivity*), about the experiences of Alvaro Francisco Núñez de Pineda y Bascuñán, a Spanish conquistador who largely enjoyed his captivity among the Indians of the New World. This narrative, with its essentially favorable depiction of Indian culture, remained in manuscript until 1863, when it finally saw publication, more as a historical curiosity than a document with potential political import.[8]

By contrast, the captivity story of Juan Ortiz, with its less than flattering portrayal of Indians, was quickly published and widely circulated, both in Spain and throughout Europe. A member of a relief party sent from Cuba to assist the conquistador Panfilo de Narváez whose expedition into the interior of North American had fallen into trouble, Ortiz was captured in 1529 by natives near Tampa Bay. After some 10 years among the Indians, Ortiz was rescued by Hernando De Soto, who utilized Ortiz's skills as a translator of Indian languages. The story of Ortiz's captivity was first told in the anonymous *True Relation of the Gentleman of Elvas* (1557). The Indians whom Ortiz encountered are described as bloodthirsty, barbaric, superstitious, and cruel. They delight in torturing their prisoners, and they participate in human sacrifices, whose remains Ortiz is forced to guard from the depredations of wolves, which are seen as less violent, less dangerous, and more predictable than the Indians. Among the bodies that Ortiz protects is that of the chief's son, who was brutally sacrificed to gain the favor of monstrous Indian deities. First published in Spain in 1557, the Ortiz narrative was later reprinted in Portugal, and eventually in England, where it was included, among other places, in Richard Hakluyt's *Virginia Richly Valued* (1609) as a warning from Spain to British colonists about the hazards of the Indian character.[9]

Unlike their Spanish counterparts, the French *coureurs de bois* who colonized Canada maintained objectives that depended on preserving Indian culture and developing a mutually profitable mercantile interchange between France and the New World over furs and woodland goods. Indians could assist French colonists in extracting these products from the interior of the continent. Rather than force the Indian into slavery, the French encouraged peaceful interaction between their colonists and the Indians. The French thus developed friendships with Indians, freely intermarried, and, as Samuel de Champlain explains, brought missionaries "to teach the [Indian] people the knowledge of God, and inform them" about French culture, "so that together with the French language, they may acquire a French heart and spirit" (quoted by Levernier and Cohen, xvi). For de Champlain and other French explorers and commentators, Indians differed from Europeans only in cultural particulars, not in their potential for material and spiritual development. If, as Jacques Cartier stated, "These men [Indians] may truly be called wilde because there is no poorer people in the world," they were, in the minds of the French, nonetheless "men" and therefore fully human. Their "wilde" existence was more the result of poverty and ignorance than of any innate mental deficiencies. According to André Thevet, all that the "marvelous, strange, wild, and brutish people" of the New World lacked to transform them into Europeans was simply "faith" and "laws." With "religion," explained Thevet, would come "civility," and with civility would come agreement between cultures (quoted in Berkhofer, 13–14).[10]

Captivity narratives written by captive French missionaries reflected these images of the Indian and reinforced them among readers in France, thus indirectly encouraging continued European investment in French colonial expansion. Because French Jesuit captives see tremendous spiritual and social value in their Indian captors, they willingly undergo any torture, privation, and hardship in order to redeem Indians, whom they consider as worthy of God's love and salvation as any European, from their pagan ways. Isaac Jogues, for instance, actually views his captivity and torture by the Iroquois as a blessing from God that he is unworthy to receive: "Surely it is pleasing to suffer at the hands of those for whom you would die, and for whom you chose to suffer the greatest torment rather than leave them exposed to the cruelty of visible and invisible enemies" (*Jogues*, 15). Not only does Indian captivity afford Jogues the opportunity to grow in personal holiness, but it allows him the chance to instruct and baptize many souls that would otherwise have been lost: "I was resolved to suffer all that could befall me, rather than forsake, in death, Frenchmen and Christian Hurons, depriving them of the consolation which a priest can afford" (*Jogues*, 13). According to Jogues, one unexpected benefit of his captivity was that it enabled him "to make greater progress" in learning Indian languages, so that through "God's grace" but "chiefly by the kindness of one [Indian] who knew both languages," he was able "to instruct and baptize" many Indians from among his enemies (*Jogues*, 36).

In the French captivity narratives, the contrast between the Iroquois, whom the Jesuit missionaries labor to convert, and the Hurons, who have already experienced conversion, illustrates the potential that the French saw in Indians for embracing European values. Jogues quite genuinely laments the torments that his Huron converts, with whom he clearly identifies, experience at the hands of the unconverted Iroquois, and he extols their courage and piety as superior to his own. About the torture of Christian Hurons by the Iroquois, Jogues writes, "While each of them suffered but his own pain, I suffered that of all; I was afflicted with as intense grief as you can imagine a father's heart to feel at the sight of his children's misery; for, with the exception of a few old Christians, I had begotten them all recently in Christ by baptism" (*Jogues*, 16). He refers to these converts as "companions" (*Jogues*, 18). In addition, he praises "the Christian spirit" of one Indian who "implored his countrymen" not to hold his death as an obstacle for "the concluding of a peace with the Iroquois" (*Jogues*, 19–20), and he notes the "heroic charity" of another "generous man," also a convert, who "had repeatedly" offered himself as a sacrificial offering in place of "those who had begotten him in Christ" (*Jogues*, 20). Moreover, if the Iroquois act cruelly, they do so out of ignorance and fear, errors that Christianity will correct. Without doubt or hesitation, Jogues looks forward to the day when the French and

Indians will form one culture and in the "lapse of time" the powers of ignorance and darkness that then held the Indians "in bondage" will "be overthrown" (*Jogues*, 33).

In contrast to the Spanish and French, considerable diversity exists in the images of Indians projected in narratives about British captives. Each British colony had its own preconceived expectations, and this diversity is reflected in the captivity narratives. Like the French, the Virginia colonists wanted to trade with the Indians, and they brought with them a view of Indians that was designed to encourage peaceful interchanges between British and Indian cultures. Drawing on classical theories about native peoples, they saw the New World and its inhabitants in Arcadian terms—"Earth's onely Paradise," where "the golden Age / Still Natures lawes doth give,"—as it was described by the poet Michael Drayton in his ode "To the Virginian Voyage" (1606).[11] Within this context, they considered Indians to be innocent and naive "naturals." To Sir Francis Drake, for example, the natives of Roanoke appeared a "people of a tractable, free and loving nature, without guilt or treachery."[12] This is exactly the image that John White, the painter who took part in the first expedition to Roanoke, captured in his watercolors (see Fig. 3).

The explorer Arthur Barlowe described Indians in similar terms. After his visit to the New World, he reported that the Indians, whom he likened to "such as lived after the Golden Age," received him "with all love and kindness, and with as much bountie, after their manner, as they could possibly devise" (quoted in Berkhofer, 17). With training and instruction, wrote Thomas Hariot, Indians would make excellent British subjects: "Although they have no such tooles, nor any such craftes, sciences and artes as wee, yet, in those things they doe, they show excellencie of wit."[13] Hoping to encourage British colonization to the New World, the Hakluyts shared this view and promulgated it in England. "Though simple and rude in manners," reported the Hakluyts, the Indian "people" were "yet of nature gentle and tractable, and most apt to receive the Christian Religion, and to subject themselves to some good government."[14] Not until the Jamestown Massacre of 1622 did this image of the Indian change. Only after it became evident that using Indian lands to grow tobacco and cotton held more economic promise than trade did a more negative stereotype of the Indian begin to emerge in the literature about Virginia.

The view of the Indian presented in Captain John Smith's *Generall Historie of Virginia* (1624) aptly illustrates the growing ambivalence that Virginia colonists eventually came to see in the Indian. One of the most

This sixteenth-century watercolor by John White originally appeared as an engraving by Theodor de Bry in his edition of Thomas Hariot's *A Briefe and True Report* (1590). It reflects the early views of the American Indians as benign. Here, the Carolina Algonquians are shown dancing around a circle of posts probably as part of a harvest festival or fertility ritual. In later illustrations, this image is deliberately distorted to emphasize the Indians' supposed malice: the circular dance becomes a war dance, and instead of holding leafy branches in their hands as they do in the original, they hold bows, arrows, and hatchets. The most famous propagandist adaptation of this watercolor appears as the frontispiece to the *Manheim* anthology (1793) of captivity accounts and is, according to Edwin Wolf II, the first American illustration of Indian torture. *Reproduced by Courtesy of the Trustees of the British Museum.*

famous of captivities, the story of Smith's capture by Powhatan Indians
and his romantic rescue from execution through the intercession of the
chief's daughter, Pocahontas, forms a significant dramatic episode in the
book:

At last they brought him to *Weronomoco*, where was *Powhatan* their Emperor.
Here more then two hundred of those grim Courtiers stood wondering at him,
as he had beene a monster; till *Powhatan* and his trayne had put themselves in
their greatest braveries. Before a fire upon a seat like a bedsted, he sat covered
with a great robe, made of *Rarowcun* skinnes, and all the tayles hanging by. On
either hand did sit a young wench of 16 or 18 yeares, and along on each side the
house, two rowes of men, and behind them as many women, with all their heads
and shoulders painted red; many of their heads bedecked with the white downe
of Birds; but every one with something; and a great chayne of beads about their
necks. At his entrance before the King, all the people gave a great shout. The
Queene of *Appamatuk* was appointed to bring him water to wash his hands, and
another brought him a bunch of feathers, in stead of a Towell to dry them:
having feasted him after their best barbarous manner they could, a long
consultation was held, but the conclusion was, two great stones were brought
before *Powhatan*: then as many as could layd hands on him, dragged him to
them, and thereon laid his head, and being ready with their clubs, to beate out
his braines, *Pocahontas* the Kings dearest daughter, when no intreaty could
prevaile, got his head in her armes, and laid her owne upon his to save him from
death: whereat the Emperour was contented he should live.[15]

That the Indians intended to bludgeon Smith to death anticipates later
Virginia views about the potential for Indian treachery, but the generosity of Pocahontas, who shields Smith with her own body, simultaneously illustrates earlier reports about the inherent nobility of the
Indian. Powhatan himself is described as an "emperor" and Pocahontas
as "the Kings dearest daughter," and while the Indians who surround the
royal family are depicted as "grim" and "barbarous," they are nonetheless
presented as "courtiers" and nobles. Whether this incident actually
occurred is a matter of historical debate.[16] At the time when Smith wrote
his *Generall Historie of Virginia*, he was out of favor with the crown.
Pocahontas was then visiting England, where she was entertained at
court and the subject of much publicity, especially after her untimely
death shortly before she was to return to Virginia. Evidence suggests that
Smith fabricated the episode to draw public attention to himself and his
New World exploits. What is important to note about the episode,
however, is the image of the Indian it conveys. Political changes in

England and Virginia were necessitating a gradual reassessment of earlier views about the "gentle" character of the Virginia natives.

In New England, where Puritans and Pilgrims hoped to establish a theocracy where the forces of good would combat the powers of evil, an image of the Indian prevailed that associated Indian culture with the devil. Although in their charter the Massachusetts Puritans stated that their primary mission in colonizing New England was converting the natives to a "knowledge and obedience of the onlie true God and Saviour of mankinde,"[17] missionary efforts were generally considered useless, if not outright dangerous, to the entire Christian community. Despite occasional protests from missionaries such as John Eliot, Roger Williams, and Thomas Mayhew, Indians were viewed, in the words of the Puritan poet Benjamin Tompson, as "monsters shap'd and fac'd like men" (quoted by Slotkin, 89).

Many Puritans developed this concept even further. For them, Indians were direct instruments of Satan's bidding, if not actual devils themselves. "As for their religion," recorded William Hubbard in his *General History of New England*, the Indians "never were observed by any of the first comers or others, to have any other but what was diabolicall, and so uncouth, as if it were framed by the devil himselfe."[18] For most Puritans, Indians could never be trusted, and eradicating them through genocide was seen as the best way for devout Christians to deal with the problem. About King Philip's War, for instance, Increase Mather states that the Indians "were so *Devil driven* as to begin an unjust and bloody war upon the English, which issued in their speedy and utter extirpation from the face of Gods earth."[19]

Captivity narratives provided Puritans an opportunity for confirming and then publicizing their suspicions about the character of the Indian, who was generally depicted as hopelessly beyond the pale of civilization and therefore deserving of annihilation. In the captivity narratives that he included in his *Decennium Luctuosum*, Cotton Mather refers to Indians as "Barbarous Opressors," "hideous *Loup garou{s}*," "merciless *Tyrant{s}*," "Diabolical Master[s]," "Cowardly Miscreants," "Blood-Hounds," "furious Tawnies," and "Raging Dragons" (*DL*, 50, 52, 54, 56, 84, 139, 140). Mather characterizes the typical Indian as having "*Fire* in his *Eyes*, the *Devil* in his *Heart*, and his *Hatchet* in his *Hand*." Clearly, Mather considers the Indians to be subhuman, monstrous, and irredeemably cruel. "Truly, the *Dark places* of *New England*," states Mather, "where the *Indians* had their Unapproachable *Kennels*, were *Habitations of Cruelty*: and no words can Sufficiently describe the *Cruelty* undergone by our *Captives* in those *Habitations*," where, among other things, "they must ever now and then have their Friends made a *Sacrifice of Devils* before their Eyes" (*DL*, 50). According to Mather, not even babies remained safe from Indian cruelty. After detailing the slaughter by Indians of several infant captives, he concludes, "In fine; when the *Children* of the *English Captives* Cryed at any Time, so that they were not presently quieted, the manner of the *Indians* was, to dash out their Brains against a *Tree*" (*DL*, 57).

In keeping with Mather's image of the Indian, the captive Puritan minister, John Williams, refuses to acknowledge his Indian captors capable of even the most rudimentary acts of human kindness. Typically Puritan, Williams credits God, not the Indians, whom he terms "Heathen," for assisting the English children from his town who had difficulty marching through the snow to Canada: "God made the Heathen, so to Pity our Children, that though they had several Wounded Persons, of their own to carry, upon their Shoulders, for Thirty Miles, before they came to the River, yet they carried our Children, uncapable of Travelling, upon their Shoulders, and in their Arms" (*Zion*, 6–7). God is also credited with having saved Williams's son from death: "My youngest Son, aged *Four* years, was Wonderfully preserved from Death; for though they that carried him, or draw'd him on *Sleyes*, were tired with their Journeys, yet their Salvage cruel Tempers, were so over-ruled by God, that they did not kill him, but in their pity, he was spared, and others would take care of him" (*Zion*, 15).

Mary Rowlandson also expresses this attitude toward Indians. In her narrative, she describes them as "hell-hounds," "merciless Heathen," "ravenous Beasts," and "Barbarous Creatures" who "triumphed and rejoyced in their inhuman, and many times devilish cruelty to the English" and who decorated themselves with necklaces "strung with *Christian* fingers " (*MR*, 2, 3, 23). For Rowlandson, salvageable Indians were rare. She reserved special disdain for those Indians known as "praying Indians" who seemed to have adopted English manners and beliefs. "Little do many think what is the savageness and bruitishness of this barbarous Enemy," writes Rowlandson, "even those that seem to profess more than others among them, when the English have fallen into their hands." It was one of "*Marlborough's* Praying *Indians*," discovers Rowlandson during her captivity, who was responsible for having "slain and mangled in a barbarous manner" seven Christian men from a neighboring Massachusetts town (*MR*, 3).

Just as England eventually dominated the other European powers struggling for control of North America, so too did the Puritan image of Indians gain ascendancy over other colonial views of Indians, including the more benevolent opinions put forth in the British colonies of the Middle Atlantic and the South. Shared by early New England leaders such as William Bradford and John Winthrop, it began as a religious view that quickly became secularized. Political in its implications, it anticipated the nineteenth-century doctrine of Manifest Destiny that held as a corollary that because Indians were incapable of progress they deserved to be deprived of the lands they inhabited. As a general Western stance toward primitive cultures, the Puritan view of Indians had its roots in the attitudes of the ancient Greeks and Romans toward the barbarians and was essentially the same view of foreigners that the British held toward the native Irish, whose lands were also colonized by England during the sixteenth century (Levernier and Cohen, 17). Racist and chauvinistic, this view would ultimately establish a fixed stereotype of Indians that would determine the future course of Anglo-American Indian policy and thereby seal the fate of hundreds of thousands of Native Americans.

Propaganda, Racism, and the Image of the Indian

While ambivalence often characterized the image of Indians presented in the Colonial narratives of exploration, later captivities tended to present a predominantly negative view of Indians. Eager for white society to acquire Indian territories, captivity writers of the late eighteenth and nineteenth centuries rarely attempted, at least consciously, to depict Indians favorably or even, for that matter, ambivalently. In these narratives, the Indian is seen as devoid of nearly every characteristic valued by *white* civilization, epitomizing instead every degradation of the human personality that the *white* imagination could devise. Rankly chauvinistic, this image of Indians embodies archetypal racist stereotypes traditionally used as propaganda against enemies of Western cultures during periods of war, conquest, and domination. Such propaganda typically begins as misunderstanding, quickly evolves into deliberate distortion of truth, and eventually degenerates into slanderous fiction masquerading as fact.[20] As Berkhofer has explained, European Americans used "counterimages of themselves to describe Indians and the counterimages of Indians to describe themselves." "Such a negative reference group," continues Berkhofer, was "used to define White identity or to prove White superiority over the worst fears of their own depravity" (Berkhofer, 27). In the Americas, the foundation for this image of Indians was established in the captivity narratives of earlier periods, but not until the mideighteenth century, when the Indian clearly became the major obstacle to easy westward migration, did it predominate in the captivity narratives as a whole and come to be a stock feature.

In constructing a negative stereotype for American Indians, captivity writers generally describe them as barbarous and animalistic in their living habits. They are said, for example, to eat food that no civilized person would consume, and their behavior is depicted as based largely, if not totally, on instinct rather than reason. Captured by Indians near Fort Stanwix, New York, in July 1779 and later taken to Canada for ransom, William Scudder typifies this point of view. "Being in the midst of their whoopings screaming and yellings," Scudder states, "I could scarce think myself among human beings," for "I could not have supposed so uncommon a contrast in the display of mortals, ever possible."[21] In Scudder's opinion, "no kind of an idea, amongst the basest of white people, could bear any affinity to the hideousness of their noise" (*WS*, 47). Scudder was by no means alone in voicing this view. In fact, it becomes a major feature of the anti-Indian captivity narrative.

In keeping with this propagandistic stereotype, Hannah Lewis focused on another aspect of Indian culture that she, like many of the anti-Indian captivity writers, wished to emphasize: the image that Indian males were lazy. By describing Indians as lazy, captivity writers reinforced the white racist notion that Indians were unworthy of the lands they inhabited because they lacked the industry needed to develop them. According to Lewis, "The men are remarkable for their indolence, in which they even seem to value themselves, saying that labor would degrade them, and belongs solely to the women, while they are formed only for war, hunting and fishing."[22] Captured during the nineteenth century by Crees, Theresa Gowanlock had similar things to say about Indian males: "The squaws perform all manual labor, while the big lazy, good-for-nothing Indian lolls about in idleness."[23] Criticizing the favorable view of the American Indian portrayed in Eastern romances, Sarah Larimer states that her respect for Indians was "fearfully diminished" by contact with them. "Instead of the Indian being a noble lord, holding a patent of nobility from heaven," she found her captors "repulsive, lazy, unprincipled, cunning, and ruthless" (*SL*, 128). Larimer's friend in captivity, Fanny Kelly, perhaps best summarizes the general characteristics that many captivity writers associated with Indian men. She reports that "instinct, more than reason, is the guide of the red man. He repudiates improvement, and despises manual effort. For ages his heart has been imbedded in moral pollution" (*FK*, 187).

Such "moral pollution," as Larimer terms it, predictably includes a total disregard for family. Because their instinct for self-preservation was seen to dominate over other behaviors, Indians are depicted as having little regard for children or the aged. To underscore this opinion, Charles Saunders describes the "cruel" Indian "practice" of murdering the elderly:

This cruel practice has been of long standing among the Indians, as I am well authorized to affirm, even long before the first discovery of *America* by us; they account it more humane and tender to put such as labour under old Age or any acute disorder to death than to allow them to languish in the extremity of affliction, by which means they free them from pain and save them from becoming troublesome to Society: This old Man, whom I saw put to death, had signalized himself in his Youth by having performed several Feats of Arms against their common Enemies. He was placed in a Pit dug in the ground about four Foot deep, and his Companions furnished him with a Tomahawk, scalping Knife, &c. &c. which was a declaration that he merited to be rank'd among the Heroes of his Country in the other World; and so great stress do they lay upon this Ceremony that they imagine without a due performance of it, the Person has no title to those Rewards prepared above for good Men, and Heroes, but lies for ever buried in oblivion; so romantick are their notions of Futurity! After having thus armed him, they next kneel'd and in a solemn manner poured out Ejaculations to their Gods: This done they next laid their hands upon his head and spoke to the Victim, who did not appear concern'd at his approaching Fate, being fully persuaded he was going to be infinitely more happy: After this they appointed three of their number who, encompassing him in the form of a semi-circle, two of them instantly stabb'd him in each side, while the other plung'd a dagger in his Breast; he lay some time exulting in the midst of his Torments, and then expired without a Groan. This Custom tho' barbarous, is the means of making most part of their enterprizes successful; because when (as 'tis often the Case) a quick march is requisite, and a most precipitate retreat, the great fatigues of which occasion the weakest to fall sick, it lops off all those who could give no aid to the Enterprize, but tend to encumber it. (*CS*, 15–17)

Within the context of Saunders's narrative, the "barbarous" treatment that the Indians afford their elderly is made to seem especially cruel because it immediately follows an account of how the daughter of a white male captive, "labouring under the infirmities of old Age" and thus "incapable of sustaining the load" given him to carry by his captors, "besought the Indians earnestly to allow her to carry her Father's burden" (*CS*, 15). Even though suffering from "a wound in her Leg," this "virtuous Lady," unlike the Indians, who are said to care nothing for their elderly, demonstrated such "great Care about her aged Father," that she would not tend to her own sufferings until her father was first treated (*CS*, 19).

Indian males are also stereotyped as prone to drunkenness and passion, thus making them appear dangerously unpredictable. Claiming to have been captured while serving in the military during the early 1750s, Henry Grace records that Indians "were fondest of spirituous Liquors," which, when obtained through plunder or trade, they "drank to such a Degree," that they would become "stark staring mad." At such times, notes Grace, they became especially dangerous, seeking out "poor unfortunate Prisoners, in Order to kill them for their diversion."[24] Captured by Shawnees and Cherokees near the juncture of the Scioto and Ohio Rivers, Charles Johnston wrote in his *Narrative* (1827) that Indians "indulged to the utmost excess in drinking whiskey." According to Johnston, "Their invariable habit is, not to quit the bottle or cask while a drop of strong drink remains" (*CJ*, 26, 60).

In keeping with their intention to dehumanize Indians, captivity writers frequently accuse them of sexual atrocities. Caroline Harris, for instance, reports that she was forced to satisfy the appetites of the sachem who claimed her as his property: "I was doomed to spend eleven months in a state of bondage and misery that beggars description! being not only compelled to cohabit, but to yield to the beastly will of a Savage brute!" (*CH*, 13). Generally more hesitant than Harris to admit having been themselves sexually violated, white female captives are nonetheless quite forthright in suggesting that such activities commonly occurred. Allegedly captured in 1814 by Kickapoos and Chickasaws, Mary Smith reports in her *Affecting Narrative* that the Indians "ravished, rifled, murdered and mutilated the inhabitants without distinction of age or sex, without any other provocation or incitement than brutal lust and wantonness of barbarity!"[25] Similarly inflammatory language is used by Eunice Barber, captured in Georgia at about the same time as Smith: "The particulars of many of the instances of barbarity exercised upon the prisoners of different ages, and sexes, and to which I was an eye witness, are of too shocking a nature to be presented to the public—It is sufficient here to observe that the scalping knife and tomahawk, were the mildest instruments of death—that in many cases torture by fire, and other execrable means were used."[26]

Equally suggestive are Charles Johnston's comments about what Peggy Fleming, a woman taken captive along with himself, experienced while among the Indians. When Johnston first meets Fleming, he states, "She enjoyed a high flow of spirits; and, indeed, I had never seen any one who appeared to be more contented and happy" (*CJ*, 33). When he encounters her several weeks later, however, Johnston notes that "she was no longer that cheerful, lively creature, such as when separated from us." Rather, "her spirits were sunk, her gayety had fled: and instead of that vivacity and sprightliness which formerly danced upon her countenance, she now wore the undissembled aspect of melancholy and wretchedness." In response to this change in Fleming's demeanor, Johnston writes, "I endeavoured to ascertain the cause of this extraordinary change, but she answered my inquiries only with her tears; leaving my mind to its own inferences" (*CJ*, 65).

In addition to the sexual excesses and atrocities Indians were said to have committed, captives also accuse their captors of cannibalism. In his poem, *Gallic Perfidy*, for example, John Maylem, a soldier captured by Indians at the battle of Fort William Henry in August 1757, accuses his Indian captors of disemboweling their prisoners, eating their hearts, and then "swilling" their blood:

> Nor must omit, how on *Montreal* Plains,
> The inhuman Banditti (in drunken Mood)
> Ript up the Bowels of a Prisoner;
> Then, with extended Jaw, the beating Heart
> (Yet warm with parting Life) varacious swallow'd;
> And swill'd the Blood, and revell'd on the Carcase![27]

Similar accusations are made by Henry Grace, who writes about the "fine diversion" Indians supposedly had when they mutilated and then devoured the body of an English captive:

I heard them relating their Treatment of an Englishman in an Island opposite Fort *Duquesne*, which they called fine diversion. They stripped him quite naked, and tying him to a Tree, made two large Fires on each Side of him and perfectly roasted him alive, while they danced around him, paying no Regard to his moving Lamentations; when they had danced till they were almost tired, one of the young Indians ran in between the two Fires and cut off his private Parts, and put them into his Mouth to stop his crying; they then danced round him again, and another Indian ripped his Belly open, and then they had another Dance, after which another Indian cut out his Heart, broiled and eat it, and sucked his

Blood, while the other two Prisoners were tied to Trees, and Spectators of this
dismal Tragedy. (*HG*, 47–48)

Whether Indians actually practiced cannibalism[28] made little difference.
Anxious to foster the image that Indians were truly beyond the limits of
all things civilized, captivity writers were quick to accuse Indians of this
practice.

In the anti-Indian captivity narratives, virtually every vice associated
with Indian men is also assigned to Indian women. "One of the principal
objects of my attention, whilst I lived among the Indians," wrote Mary
Kinnan, "was the humiliating condition of their women": "Here the
female sex, instead of polishing and improving the rough manners of the
men, are equally ferocious, cruel, and obdurate. Instead of that benevolent disposition and warm sensibility to the sufferings of others, which
marks their characters in more civilized climes, they quaff with extatic
pleasure the blood of the innocent prisoner, writhing with agony under
the inhuman torments inflicted upon him—whilst his convulsive groans
speak music to their souls" (*MK*, 8–9).

Such is also the attitude of Henry Grace, whose sensationalized
depiction of Indian women expresses the biased viewpoint common in
captivity narratives written as anti-Indian propaganda:

The old Squaws drink as bad as the Men, but the young ones do not care for it,
so that they get out of their Way when they are drinking, but the Squaws that
have their Companions, which they call their Husbands, will dance and drink
quite naked along with the Men. They have all blood-thirsty Minds, and are a
very jealous sort of People; insatiable in their Revenge, so to gratify which they
will refuse no Difficulty or Danger. Otherwise they are lazy and sluggish, and
hate all Employment except hunting and fighting; in their Lodging, Diet, and
Dress, they are filthy and nasty to the last Degree, Strangers to all the Rules of
Decency and Modesty, and seem almost void of natural Affection, being more
careless of their Offspring than Brutes. As soon as their Children come into the
World, they will carry them to the Water, and duck and wash them all over,
after which they will wrap them in a Bit of Cloth, and put them upon a Board
which is made on Purpose, with a large Hoop bent round at Top, and comes
down even on both Sides, and they lace the Child with a List of Cloth to the
Board, and carry them upon their Backs through the Woods, or wherever they
go, and in all Weathers.
    The way that they marry is as they sit round the Fire at Night, the Indian Man
takes something he has some Value for, and flings it into the Squaw's Lap that
he has a Liking to; the Squaw flings it back again to the Indian, he returns it

three Times, and the third Time, if the Squaw keeps it they are married. This is all the Ceremony of their Marriage, as far as I know. (*HG*, 22–23)

Like their male counterparts, Indian women are here portrayed as sexually promiscuous, prone to drunkenness, "blood-thirsty," "lazy," "filthy and nasty" in matters of "Lodging, Diet, and Dress," and "void of natural Affection, being more careless of their Offspring than Brutes."

It is, however, in the cruelty Indians are said to exhibit in torturing their captives that captivity writers most graphically attempt to promulgate their racist agenda. Eliza Swan, taken captive with her husband in April 1815 near her home in St. Louis, Missouri, records the following account, typical in the anti-Indian captivity narratives, of the "diabolical cruelty" of Indian tortures:

Things being thus concluded upon, the whole village set up the death-cry; when they began to make preparation for rioting in the most diabolical cruelty. They first stripped the prisoners, and fixing two posts in the ground, fastened to them two pieces from one to the other: one about a foot from the ground, the other six or seven feet higher; they then obliged the unhappy victims to mount upon the lower cross piece, they tied their legs to it a little asunder, and then in a similar way secured their hands to the upper piece; they next daubed their bodies with pitch. The whole village, men, women, and children, now assembled round them, when their torments began, every one torturing them in whatever manner they pleased, each apparently striving to exceed the other in cruelty—they first tore off their scalps, and then cut off their fingers and toes, joint by joint; they next dug out their eyes and filled their sockets with hot embers; and next drew out their tongues by the roots! until they were thus deprived of their speech. . . . Brands of fire were not occasionally applied to the naked bodies of the prisoners, until life becoming nearly extinct, they beat out their brains with their tomahawks! In this situation they left them hanging in the frames, while the whole tribe joined in one general powwow, which was attended with capering and singing and dancing to and fro around the wretched victims of their torture.[29]

In ending this account, Swan states that the Indians had the audacity to "invite" her "to take a part with them in this barbarous revel," an invitation that she says she indignantly "declined." "Such," concludes Swan, "is the disposition of a savage!" (*Swan*, 20–21).

Accounts of Indian cruelty like that given by Swan, as outrageous and biased as they were, are by no means rare and generally function as the propagandistic climax of the anti-Indian captivity narrative. Almost always fictitious and often repeated verbatim from captivity to captivity, they constitute what became in the white popular culture of the late-eighteenth and nineteenth centuries the characteristic *topos* associated with the theme. But whether they were truth or fiction ultimately mattered little. What finally mattered was both their audience appeal as visceral thriller and the inflammatory racist stereotype of the American Indian that they deliberately evoked. Charles Johnston, for instance, graphically relates the "horrible" death of Dr. William Flinn, who was taken captive with Johnston:

The miserable Flinn . . . had been conducted to one of those Miami towns which were, at that period, fatal to white captives, . . . where every preparation was immediately made for his sacrifice. Incisions were made through the muscular parts of his arm, between the elbows and shoulders, and, by thongs of buffalo hide passed through them, he was secured to a strong stake. A fire was kindled around him. . . . All the ingenuity of the savages was exerted in aggravating his torments, by all those means which they know so well how to employ. . . . At length the fire around him began to subside. An old squaw advanced to rekindle it. When she came within his reach, he kicked her so violently, that she fell apparently lifeless. His tormentors were then exasperated to the highest point, and made incisions between the sinews and bones at the back of his ankles, passed thongs through them, and closely fastened his legs to the stake. [An] old squaw . . . lighted pine torches, and applied their blaze to him; while the men bored his flesh with burning splinters of the same inflammable wood. His agonies were protracted until he sunk into a state of insensibility, when they were terminated by the tomahawk. (*CJ*, 75–77)

Aware that his readers expected sensational tales of torture from captivity writers, Johnston states that such "acts of barbarism and unrelenting cruelty" as this one about Flinn have so frequently "been related by others" that his "narrative would be imperfect without it." Despite their frequency of publication, Johnston nonetheless asserts that a "horror" story such as his will still "interest the hearts of those that may read it," "shock every feeling of humanity," and thereby "exhibit the savage character in a strong light" (*CJ*, 75).

Especially effective in this regard were lurid accounts of captive women being tortured by Indians. To further incite hatred of Indians, these tales were even more horrific and more visceral than those about men. One such example is the outrageously sensationalized, and almost certainly fictitious, account of the torture by Indians of the 16-year-old twin "virgin" daughters of Frederick Manheim, "an industrious German" who was supposedly living on a farm near the Mohawk River in upstate New York, when "hostile *Canasadaga* Indians" attacked and captured the two girls:

At length, with countenances distorted by infernal fury, and with hideous yells, the two savages who had captured the hapless *Maria* and *Christina*, leaped into the midst of their circle, and dragged those ill-fated maidens, shrieking, from the embraces of their companions.

These warriors had disagreed about whose property the girls should be, as they had jointly seized them; and, to terminate the dispute, agreeably to the abominable usage of the savages, it was determined by the chiefs of the party, that the prisoners, who gave rise to the contention, should be destroyed; and that their captors should be the principal agents in the execrable business. These furies, assisted by their comrades, stripped the forlorn girls, already convulsed with apprehensions, and tied each to a sapling, with their hands as high extended above their heads as possible; and then pitched them from their knees to their shoulders, with upwards of six hundred of the sharpened splinters above described, which, at every puncture, were attended with screams of distress, that echoed and re-echoed through the wilderness. And then to complete the infernal tragedy, the splinters, all standing erect on the bleeding victims, were every one set on fire, and exhibited a scene of monstrous misery, beyond the power of speech to describe, or even the imagination to conceive. It was not until near three hours had elapsed from the commencement of their torments, and that they had lost almost every resemblance of the human form, that these helpless virgins sunk down into the arms of their deliverer, Death. (*Manheim*, 5–7)

Selected by the nineteenth-century editor and Indian-hater Archibald Loudon as decidedly one "of the most interesting narratives of outrages committed by the Indians in their Wars with the white people,"[30] this account of Indian cruelty, first published in 1793 as *The Affecting History of the Dreadful Distresses of Frederick Manheim's Family*, was frequently reprinted under other titles about the experiences of several different captives. During the nineteenth century, for example, the same story was told about the "virgin daughters" of many other captives, most notably Mary Smith, whose daughters seem to have coincidentally befallen the same fate as the Manheim sisters and in almost exactly the same words.

Even pregnant women, children, and infants were, according to the anti-Indian propaganda writers, subject to acts of barbarism. During her captivity among the Indians, Jane Wilson claimed to have "endured repeated acts of inhumanity." Among other things, Indians supposedly placed her "on an unbroken mule without a bridle." The mule "would frequently top [her] over its head." As Wilson explains, "You may understand one object the Indians had in view of putting me on this wild animal and causing me to be thrown so often when I tell you I expected to become a mother in a few weeks."[31] When Sarah Horn asked an Indian for some flour so that her starving child could have something to eat, the Indian took the child, "swung it by its arms, and threw it up as high as he could, and let it fall upon the ground at his feet" (*Horn and Harris*, 12). Fanny Kelly saw her Indian captors take an "infant child . . . from its little bed" and "thrust it into [a] heated oven, its screams torturing the wretched mother, who was immediately after stabbed and cut in many pieces." "Taking the suffering little creature from the oven," the Indians "then dashed out its brains against the walls of the house" (*FK*, 117). Usually fictitious, incidents such as these were used to reinforce the racist claim that Indians lacked all feelings of humanity and were therefore deserving of whatever fate befell them at the hands of the United States militia.

In fact, the killing of infants by knocking their heads against trees was a stock propaganda device that appears in captivity narratives from the seventeenth through the twentieth centuries. The wanton killing of infants is seen as the ultimate badge of barbarism, so it comes as little surprise that such accusations are repeatedly hurled against Indians. In his seventeenth-century account of Hannah Dustan's captivity, for example, Cotton Mather records that "e're they had gone many Steps," the Indians "dash'd out the Brains of the [Dustan's] *Infant* against a Tree" (*Humiliations*, 43). Repeated dozens of times down the centuries, this extraordinary image became, through captivity narratives like Dustan's, so ingrained in the white popular imagination that it was still being told anew as late as 1912. According to the *Old Record of the Captivity of Margaret Erskine*, who had been taken captive in 1779 but whose story waited nearly 125 years for publication, when Erskine refused to surrender her baby to her captor, the Indian "caught it by the heels and dashing out its brains against a tree flung it on the ground at her feet."[32]

Eventually, the relentless way in which captivity writers fostered a blatantly anti-Indian stereotype took its final toll. Mary Smith, mother of the ubiquitous twin girls tortured at the stake, summarizes why white audiences accepted and encouraged the promulgation of captivity stories that featured these outrageously racist portrayals of the American Indian. According to Smith, "Such monsters of barbarity ought certainly to be excluded from all the privileges of human nature, and hunted down as wild beasts, without pity or cessation" (*MS*, 20). This same view is expressed in the Lewis narrative: "The character of the savage mind, naturally fierce, revengeful and cruel, will not receive and cherish the introduction of the arts and sciences; but on the contrary renders it more debased and inveterate—therefore, the policy of a great nation ought to be, and is, to overawe and intimidate, and not to extirpate them."[33] Elias Darnall elaborates on this theme by commenting that "this country was designed for a more noble purpose than to be a harbor for those rapacious savages, whose manners and deportment are not more elevated than the ravenous beasts of the forest." He confidently anticipates "the time not far distant, when this country will be interspersed with elegant farms and flourishing towns, and be inhabited by a free and independent people under an auspicious republic" (*Kentucky*, 23). By 1867 and the publication of such captivities as *General Sheridan's Squaw Spy and Mrs. Clara Blynn's Captivity*, the "time" predicted by Darnall seemed to have arrived. In the words of its author, "any parleying with the Savages under existing circumstances is worse than folly . . . for the Indians are bloodthirsty, and cannot be tamed." "Thus," concludes the author, "in the war of races extermination must certainly be the fate of the Indians."[34]

Transculturation and the Image of the Indian

Not all captivity narratives conveyed a negative image of the American Indian. Just as in the early Colonial narratives positive images of Indians coexisted with negative ones, so too did some captivity stories project an essentially positive view of Indian culture. Such accounts were, however, relatively rare, especially considering the large number of captives who chose to stay among the Indians when given the opportunity to leave. Precisely because many of these captives chose to disassociate themselves from white culture, most of their captivities went unrecorded. Due to illiteracy or a lack of interest or opportunity, the vast majority of transculturated captives chose to remain silent (Axtell, "White Indians," 63–64).[35] Having embraced Indian culture as their own, many of these captives probably had little, if any, desire to communicate with white audiences.

Not only was there little for transculturated captives to gain from writing, but in some instances there was undoubtedly fear that speaking freely with white society about themselves could jeopardize their security. Such was certainly the case with Frances Slocum (We-let-a-wash). When after more than 50 years her white family succeeded in locating and visiting her, her biographer John Todd mentions that "on being told who they were, she received them with great reserve, coolness, and indifference. While they were walking the room in tears, not a feature of her countenance moved. She shed not a tear, she evinced no emotion" (*Sister*, 124–25). According to Todd, "She was coy, reserved, and seemed to fear they were contriving some way to cheat her out of her property" (*Sister*, 126). "It was not," continues Todd, "till the family had with great efforts, obtained the confidence of the lost sister, that she could be prevailed upon to relate, through the Interpreter, so much of her history as she could remember. She was especially cautious when she saw them produce writing materials in order to note it down" (*Sister*, 131). Clearly Slocum feared the recording of her life experiences, for she suspected that her audience might later use what she said against her, perhaps, as Todd suggests, to swindle her property from her.

In addition, white audiences of the eighteenth and nineteenth centuries appear to have had little desire to read accounts of Indian culture that went counter to the negative image of Indians that an expansionistic white society created to dispossess them of their Western properties. One indication of this phenomenon is the obvious editorializing of such narratives by white editors seeking to market them. In the subtitle to *A Narrative of the Life of Mrs. Mary Jemison* (1824), James Everett Seaver, who purports to have "carefully taken" the account of Jemison's life "from her own words," deliberately misrepresents the content of the book. Rather than emphasize the positive nature of Jemison's life among the Indians, he describes her captivity as "An Account of the Murder of Her Father and His Family; her sufferings; her marriage to two Indians: her troubles with her Children; [and] barbarities of the Indians in the French and Revolutionary Wars." Indeed, Seaver seems almost bored with what Jemison (whose Indian name was Dehgewanus) told him about herself and certainly somewhat disappointed about not having found more to legitimately sensationalize about her life, for in the introduction to the narrative, he writes, "The vices of the Indians, she appeared disposed not to aggravate, and seemed to take pride in extolling their virtues. A kind of family pride inclined her to withhold whatever would blot the character of her descendants, and perhaps induced her to keep back many things that would have been interesting."[36]

Captives who spoke favorably about their experiences faced stiff editorial and public resistance. James Smith (Scoonwa), who lived from 1755 to 1759 as an adopted son of the Delawares, delayed the publication of his *Account* (1799) for almost half a century because he felt the public simply would not believe what he had to say: "At that time the Americans were so little acquainted with Indians affairs, I apprehended a great part of it would be viewed as fable or romance."[37] Indeed, as Smith recognized, narratives about purported Indian atrocities were vastly more profitable to the publishing industry than were accounts such as his. Ironically, they also seemed more credible because they conformed to the distorted preconceptions of white audiences who wanted to view Indians negatively and whose negative assumptions had been amply reinforced by a multitude of propaganda narratives. Edwin James, the editor of *A Narrative of the Captivity and Adventures of John Tanner* (1830), anticipates, for example, that his audience is unlikely to accept the essentially positive account of Tanner's (Sha-shew-wabe-na-se) transculturized experiences among the Ojibwas and Chippewas of the Northwoods: "Some particulars in Mr. Tanner's narrative will doubtless excite a degree of incredulity, among such as have never attended particularly to the history and conditions of the Indian tribes. . . . He will appear to some weakly credulous—to others, stupidly dishonest."[38]

Moreover, when publishing the narrative of a captive who favored Indian society, editors almost universally attempt to distance themselves and their audiences from the experience, usually by presenting it as an example of the social dangers of prolonged contact with Indians rather than as a positive counterimage of the negative Indian stereotypes present in the white popular imagination and fueled by the anti-Indian propaganda narratives. Thus, although she was content among the Indians and defended their kind treatment of her, Slocum's captivity transformed her from a "fair-haired, pale-faced little girl" to an "old, jealous, ignorant, suspicious savage" (*Sister*, 126). As her biographer takes pains to reiterate, "She was rich, and much respected and beloved;—but she was a poor, darkened savage!" (*Sister*, 129). Her preference for Indians is explained away as a "perversion from civilization,"[39] and her narrative is considered of "interest" primarily "because of the peculiar developments which followed her association with the Indians, the loss of her mother tongue, and the tenacity with which she clung to the strange people with whom she cast her lot" (*Frances*, iii). Similarly, the "Publisher's Note" to the 1856 edition of *The Life of Mary Jemison* describes her "transformation" from white captive to "the wife of an Indian, and the mother of Indian children" as "the reverse of the order of nature," adding that "as if in punishment of this unnatural alliance, two of her sons meet with a violent death at the hands of their brother, and afterward, to complete the tragedy, the fratricide himself dies by the hands of violence."[40] Ending in much the same way the Jemison narrative began, *The Life and Adventures of William Filley* (1867), about a captive abducted as a boy in Michigan who spent 29 years living among the Indians, concludes with an editorial disclaimer for the many positive things this captive says about his life as an Indian: "Notwithstanding the many years that this boy was a captive among the Indians, and in the face of many hardships through which he was compelled by them to pass, his friendship for them is of that enduring kind which time, even, cannot change or efface. The slightest insinuation against their honesty or friendship, is resented by him as a personal insult. In fact, his long residence among them, HAS MADE HIM AN INDIAN."[41]

Nonetheless, when the accounts of transculturated captives are disentangled from their editorial overlay, an image of Indians emerges that is highly positive. Above all, transculturized captives express an enthusiastic, often passionately eloquent, preference for Indian culture over that of their birth. When Slocum was asked if she "'ever tired of living with the Indians,'" her response was unequivocal: "'No. I had always enough to live on, and to live well. They always used me very kindly . . . I do not wish to live any better, or any where else. . . . The Indians are my people. I do no work. I sit in the house with these my two daughters, who do the work, and I sit with them'" (*Sister*, 139–42). John Dunn Hunter was even more "enthusiastic" than Slocum about his "attachment" to the Indians: "I have no hope of seeing happier days than I experienced at this early period of my life, while sojourning with the Kansas nation, on the Kansas river, some hundred miles above its confluence with the Missouri" (*Manners*, 35). "My attachment for the Indians and Indian mode of life was," states Hunter, "ardent and enthusiastic" (*Manners*, 114). When Cynthia Ann Parker was asked if she wished to return to white society, she said, "'I am happily wedded,'" and then added, "'I love my husband, who is good and kind, and my little ones, who, too, are his, and I cannot forsake them!'" (*Parker*, 32).

The reason why these captives expressed such an enthusiasm for Indians is easy to discern in their narratives. Like Slocum, they appreciate the kindness the Indians are said to have shown them, and they do not feel they could necessarily expect the same treatment elsewhere. As Hunter explains, "It is a remarkable fact, that white people generally when brought up among the Indians, become unalterably attached to their customs, and seldom afterwards abandon them" (*Manners*, 21). About his own experiences with transculturation, Hunter wrote,

This, to those who have been bred in refinement and ease, under the fond and watchful guardianship of parents, may appear gross and incongruous. If, however, the imagination be allowed scope, and a lad ten or twelve years of age, without kindred or name, or any knowledge by which he could arrive at an acquaintance with any of the circumstances connected with his being, be supposed in the central wilds of North America, nearly a thousand miles from any white settlement, a prisoner or sojourner among a people, on whom he had not the slightest claim, and with whose language, habits and character, he was wholly unacquainted; but, who nevertheless treated him kindly; and it will appear not only natural but rational, that he should return such kindness with gratitude and affection. Such nearly was my situation, and such in fact were my feelings at that time. (*Manners*, 35)

When given the opportunity to leave his Indian captors, John Tanner (see Fig. 4) thus concluded that he was better off among the Indians, whom he felt sure would care for his needs, than among the people of his birth, who he suspected would neglect and perhaps even abuse him:

At this time, I was suffered to go entirely at large, being subject to no manner of restraint, and might, at almost any time, have made my escape from the Indians; but I believed my father and all my friends had been murdered, and I remembered the laborious and confined manner in which I must live, if I returned among the whites; where, having no friends, and being destitute of money or property, I must, of necessity, be exposed to all the ills of extreme poverty. Among the Indians, I saw that those who were too young, or too weak to hunt for themselves, were sure to find some one to provide for them. I was also rising in the estimation of the Indians, and becoming as one of them. I therefore chose, for the present, to remain with them. (*JT*, 46)

Captives also seem to enjoy the freedom they found among the Indians. As Jemison points out, "Our labor was not severe; and that of one year was exactly similar, in almost every respect, to that of the others, without that endless variety that is to be observed in the common labor of the white people. Notwithstanding the Indian women have all the fuel and bread to procure, and the cooking to perform, their task is probably not harder than that of white women, who have those articles provided for them; and their cares certainly are not half as numerous, nor as great. In the summer season, we planted, tended and harvested our corn, and generally had all our children with us; but had no master to oversee or drive us; so we could work as leisurely as we pleased" (*MJ*, 46–47). Tanner also found Indian society to be less confining and restrictive than

Portrait of John Tanner used as frontispiece to his *Narrative* (1830). Tanner, whose Indian name was Shaw-Wabe-Na-Se (The Falcon), was one of the most famous of the transculturated Indian captives. He lived much of his adult life among the Chippewas and Ojibways. *Courtesy of the Everett D. Graff Collection, the Newberry Library.*

that of his birth. At one point in his *Narrative*, Tanner is almost induced to leave the Indians by a trader, but after considering the prospect he quickly concludes that life among the whites would be "intolerable" after having experienced so much freedom: "He said so much to induce me to leave the Indians, that I felt sometimes inclined to follow his advice; but whenever I thought of remaining long at the trading house, I found an intolerable irksomeness attending it. I felt an inclination to spend all my time in hunting, and a strong dislike to the less exciting employments of the men about a trading house" (*JT*, 96).

Consistent with the reasons captives give for why they stayed with the Indians, Indians are seen, throughout this group of narratives, as kind, generous, and just in their dealings with one another. According to Jemison, "Indians love their friends and their kindred, and treat them with kindness" (*MJ*, 73). Tanner was particularly impressed by the generosity and justice he observed among the Indians. Even when food was scarce, states Tanner, "They are commonly ready to divide what provisions they have, with any who come to them in need" (*JT*, 66). About Indian justice, Tanner maintains, "The customs of the tribe are as a law to the Indians, and anyone who ventures to depart from them, can expect neither support nor countenance. It is rare that oppression or injustice in affairs of private right, between man and man, take place among the Indians" (*JT*, 92). Concerning the honesty of Indians, William Filley asserts, "I am not going to hold the Indian up to the last point of honesty, for I know there are some who are not honest. But there are more honest Indians, according to their numbers, than there are whites." "If this is not so," continues Filley, "your State prisons would not be so full" (*WF*, 80). According to John Dunn Hunter, "Bravery, generosity, and magnanimity form most important traits in the character of the warrior; and the practice of these qualities is much more strictly inculcated in early life, and observed in maturer years by them, than are the commands of the Decalogue by the respective sects, which profess to believe in and obey them" (*Manners*, 56). James Smith was equally impressed by the moral character of his captors: "They appeared to be fulfilling the scriptures beyond those who profess to believe them, in that of taking no thought of to-morrow and also in living in love, peace and friendship together, without disputes. In this respect they shame those who profess Christianity" (*JS*, 29).

In addition, Indian living habits are seen as wholesome and Indians as kind and generous toward the more vulnerable members of their society, particularly the aged. Filley, for example, notes that Indians were extremely conscientious about matters of personal hygiene: "As a regular thing they wash their hands, face, and neck every morning, noon, and night; and at other times, especially when they have been handling flesh or anything else of an unclean nature they will wash themselves in several waters, in order to be sure that their hands are perfectly free from any bad smell" (WF, 95). Indians were also deeply attached to their children. According to Charles Dennis Rusoe d'Eres, whose *Memoirs* (1800) describe his lengthy experiences as a transculturated captive in Canada, "The parents are remarkably fond of their children, especially while in their infantile state. Nothing can exceed the mother's attachment to her infant; she takes unwearied pains to nurse it, never omitting any means or pains to prevent its being unuseful when coming into an active life."[42] Regarding the treatment of the elderly, Hunter writes, "Each warrior makes provision for the aged, infirm, and needy, which are nearly related to him; and, where it is not wholly beyond his power, for those also more remotely connected. . . . They are very assiduous and attentive to the wants and comforts particularly of the aged, and kind to all who require their assistance. And an Indian who failed in these respects, though he otherwise merited esteem, would be neglected and despised. To the credit of their morals few such are to be found, except where debauched by the vices of the white people" (*Manners*, 258–59).

Throughout this group of narratives, captives speak with special fondness about their adopted Indian families. Jemison says that she loved her adopted sisters as much, if not more, than if they had been her sisters by birth: "The warmth of their feelings, the kind reception which I met with, and the continued favors that I received at their hands, riveted my affection for them so strongly that I am constrained to believe that I loved them as I should have loved my own sister had she lived, and I had been brought up with her" (*MJ*, 54). According to Jemison, "I was very fortunate in falling into their hands; for they were kind good natured women; peaceable and mild in their dispositions; temperate and decent in their habits, and very tender and gentle towards me. I have great reason to respect them, though they have been dead a great number of years" (*MJ*, 40). Decades after her death, Hunter speaks with deep emotion about his love for his Indian mother: "I sincerely and deeply felt the bereavement; and cannot even at this late day, reflect on her maternal conduct to me, from the time I was taken prisoner by the Kansas, to her death, without the association of feelings, to which, in other respects I am a stranger. She was indeed a mother to me; and I feel my bosom dilate with gratitude at the recollection of her goodness, and care of me during this helpless period of my life" (*Manners*, 34–35). Tanner expresses similar sentiments about his Indian "grandmother": "Though Net-no-kwa was now decrepid and infirm, I felt the strongest regard for her, and continued to do so while she lived" (*JT*, 117).

Another example of the fondness captives showed for their adopted families appears in Alexander Henry's *Travels and Adventures in Canada and the Indian Territories* (1809). Captured in 1763 by the Chippewas at Fort Mickilmackinack in Michigan, Henry was adopted by an Indian named Wawatam, in whom he found a "good" man and a true "friend and brother."[43] The bond of friendship between Henry and Wawatam is depicted as strong and sincere. At one point in the narrative, Wawatam explains their relationship: "'I adopted him as my brother. From that moment, he became one of my family, so that no change of circumstances could break the cord which fastened us together'" (*Travels*, 101). Wawatam, notes Henry, was "always watchful of my safety" (*Travels*, 110), and he taught Henry how to hunt and fish: "While we thus hunted along our way, I enjoyed a personal freedom of which I had been long deprived, and became as expert in the Indian pursuits, as the Indians themselves" (*Travels*, 127).

Eventually, circumstances beyond Henry's control force him to return to white society, but he does so only with extreme regret about having to leave behind his "father and brother." About his departure, Henry writes, "My father and brother, (for he was alternately each of these,) lit his pipe, and presented it to me, saying, 'My son, this may be the last time that ever you and I shall smoke out of the same pipe! I am sorry to part with you. You know the affection which I have always borne you, and the dangers to which I have exposed myself and family, to preserve you from your enemies; and I am happy to find that my efforts promise not to have been in vain'" (*Travels*, 161–62). Henry and Wawatam then "exchanged farewells, with an emotion entirely reciprocal." According to Henry, "I did not quit the lodge without the most grateful sense of many acts of goodness which I had experienced in it, nor without the sincerest respect for the virtues which I had witnessed among its members" (*Travels*, 162–63).

Indian marriages are depicted as particularly warm and caring. According to Hunter, "No state of society is, in my opinion, more exempt from strife and contention between husband and wife, than that of the Indians generally" (*Manners*, 46). This view is almost universally supported by transculturated captives, most of whom express a deep love for and commitment to their spouses. Among Indian spouses, states Slocum's son-in-law, "'there are instances of very great devotedness. An Indian who had a sick wife in a time of great scarcity of food, has been known to go an hundred miles, sell his pony for a hat full of corn, and carry it all the way back on foot for his sick wife! Can many white men shew stronger proof of sincere attachment?'" (*Sister*, 148–49). Twice married to Indian men, Jemison admired both of her husbands. She first married an Indian named Sheninjee. Initially unhappy about the thought of marrying this man, Jemison soon grew to admire and love her husband: "The idea of spending my days with him, at first seemed perfectly irreconcilable to my feelings; but his good nature, generosity, tenderness, and friendship towards me, soon gained my affection; and, strange as it may seem, I loved him!—To me he was ever kind in sickness, and always treated me with gentleness; in fact, he was an agreeable husband, and a comfortable companion. We lived happily together till the time of our final separation" (*MJ*, 44–45). Jemison expresses similar attitudes about her second husband, Hiokatoo. "During the term of nearly fifty years that I lived with him," states Jemison, "I received, according to Indian customs, all the kindness and attention that was my due as his wife.—Although war was his trade from his youth till old age and decrepitude stopt his career, he uniformly treated me with tenderness, and never offered an insult" (*MJ*, 104).

In sexual matters, Indians are seen as more virtuous than whites. "Children, born out of wedlock," states Henry, "are very rare among the Indians," whose courtship practices he considers "precisely similar to the *bundling* of New-England, and other countries; and, to say the least, as not more licentious" (*Travels*, 301). According to Rusoe d'Eres, Indians were generally faithful to their spouses: "Adultery is not known among them; jealousy therefore, is a stranger" (*d'Eres*, 141). Hunter blames contact with white society and ethnological misinterpretation as the reasons why whites considered Indians less virtuous in their sexual behavior than actually was true:

. . . we find chastity as common a virtue among those Indians who have not been corrupted by an intercourse with the whites, as it is, or ever has been, among any people on earth. Indeed, the reason why travellers, who have visited the Indians, so liberally accuse their females of an opposite trait of character, is, not because they are less virtuous than the females of civilized life, but, because their innocence and artlessness render them more liable to become the dupes of accomplished villains; and because when they have transgressed, they do not become outcasts; but retain their standing in society; thus inducing the appearance that the practice is generally tolerated. . . . Seduction is regarded as a despicable crime, and more blame is attached to the man, than to the woman, when instances of the kind occur; hence, the offence, on the part of the female, is more readily forgotten and forgiven, and she finds little or no difficulty, as before noticed, in forming a subsequent matrimonial alliance when deserted by her betrayer, who is generally regarded with distrust, and avoided in social intercourse. (*Manners*, 241–42)

Indeed, what vices Indians possess are usually seen as a consequence of the corrupting influences of white society. "Formerly, if what the Indians say may be relied on," explains Hunter, "illegitimate births seldom occurred in any of the tribes. But, since the white people have appeared among them, the character of their females has suffered a modification, and instances have become more frequent" (*Manners*, 243). Drunkenness is acknowledged as a prominent Indian vice, but it, too, is blamed on the efforts of white society to corrupt the Indian: "The use of ardent spirits amongst the Indians and the attempts which have been made to civilize and christianize them by the white people, has constantly made them worse and worse; increased their vices, and robbed them of many of their virtues; and will ultimately produce their extermination" (*MJ*, 48).

Stealing is another vice that Indians are said to have learned from whites: "It is seldom that Indians do steal anything from one another; and they say they never did, until the white people came among them, and learned some of them, to lie, cheat and steal" (*JS*, 42). According to Tanner,

Indians who live remote from the whites, have not learned to value their peltries so highly, that they will be guilty of stealing them from each other; and at the time of which I speak, and in the country where I was, I have often known a hunter leave his traps for many days, in the woods, without visiting them, or feeling any anxiety about their safety. It would often happen, that one man having finished his hunt, and left his traps behind him, another would say to him, "I am going to hunt in such a direction, where are your traps?" When he has used them, another, and sometimes four or five, take them in succession; but in the end, they are sure to return to the right owner. (*JT*, 65)

Even the Indians' supposed cruelties toward captives are said to have been aggravated and encouraged by white society: "The Indians are also often provoked by . . . frauds and thefts practised upon them, which provoke to retaliation and aggression; consequently, innocent and guilty, indiscriminately suffer. Such conduct, mutually practised by them and the whites, along the whole extent of the conceived, though arbitrary boundary, is the cause of the inveterate hostility that exists between them, and leads to all the scenes of Indian cruelty that are practised on the frontier settlers" (*Manners*, 17–18). As Henry further explains, "The Five Nations, and others, are known to have treated their prisoners with great cruelty; but, there is too much reason to believe, that the exercise of this cruelty has been often encouraged, and its malignity often increased, by European instigators and assistants" (*Travels*, 274).

According to Jemison, Indians were the happiest people in the world before they were introduced to "spirituous liquors" by the whites:

No people can live more happy than the Indians did in times of peace, before the introduction of spirituous liquors amongst them. Their lives were a continual round of pleasures. Their wants were few, and easily satisfied; and their cares were only for to-day; the bounds of their calculations for future comfort not extending to the incalculable uncertainties of to-morrow. If peace ever dwelt with men, it was in former times, in the recesses from war, amongst what are now termed barbarians. The moral character of the Indians was (if I may be allowed the expression) uncontaminated. Their fidelity was perfect, and became proverbial; they were strictly honest; they despised deception and falsehood; and chastity was held in high veneration, and a violation of it was considered sacrilege. They were temperate in their desires, moderate in their passions, and candid and honorable in the expression of their sentiments on every subject of importance. (*MJ*, 64)

Like most transculturated captives, Jemison views Indian culture as essentially more innocent and benevolent than white culture, and she blames most of the problems of her adopted culture onto the corrupting influences of the European, whom she is quick to indict as dishonest, lascivious, greedy, and violent.

Narratives by and about transculturated captives, then, reveal an image of the American Indian that stands in marked contrast to that presented in the anti-Indian captivity narratives. In fact, it is almost diametrically opposite. Though far fewer in number than the anti-Indian narratives, they present an almost idyllic view of life among a pastoral people whose vices were few and whose virtues many. While often overlooked by readers and students of the captivity narratives, these works provide an important corrective to the stereotypical view of Indian captivity as an unmitigatingly horrific experience that pitted the so-called civilizing forces of European society against the seeming barbarism and perceived savagism of the Indian. In these narratives, the

American Indian is seen as the moral superior of the European usurper, and life among the Indians as far preferable to that among whites. While it should be remembered that transculturated captives also had their biases and that they, like the anti-Indian captives and the authors of the propaganda narratives, filtered the experience of captivity through their own cultural perspective, it should nonetheless be noted that, despite editorial efforts to dilute their essentially positive image of Indians, captivity narratives that depict Indians favorably do exist and form a significant dimension of the historical and literary record.

Ethnocentrism and the Image of the Indian

Because most captivity writers approached the subject with strong biases, either negative or positive, toward Indians, obtaining a realistic image of Indians from the captivity narratives is extremely difficult. Ethnocentric in their perspectives, captivity writers filtered virtually everything they recorded through the lens of their prejudices and mis-understandings. Nonetheless, if the captivity narratives are read carefully and interpreted within a larger ethnological context, ambivalences about Indians usually emerge. These ambivalences reveal that, whether their manifest objective is to vilify or valorize Indian culture, the captivity writers are at bottom uncertain about their response to the Indian. More often than not, for example, the anti-Indian propaganda narratives contain information encoded within the texts that contradicts or at least calls into question the validity of the writers' manifest intent to depict the Indian in ways that their readers are likely to find threatening or dangerous. This information appears in essentially four different ways: 1) forthrightly favorable comments about Indians in narratives that other-wise portray Indians negatively; 2) individual Indians who appear in these narratives as exceptions to the negative stereotype the author consciously wishes to promulgate; 3) ethnocentric misunderstandings about Indians and their culture; and 4) subconscious self-revelations by the author that indicate conflicting emotions about the experience. When collectively analyzed and assembled, the data that the captivity narratives provide reveal what captivity writers from the start were unable to recognize about Indians: namely, that Indians possessed a culture essentially different from their own but with an integrity of its own that the captive was, at a manifest level, usually incapable of seeing or appreciating.

Throughout many of even the most blatantly propagandistic of the captivity narratives, for example, there exist counterimages of Indians that undercut surface propaganda. Often this information appears in the form of kindnesses captives begrudgingly admit to having received while among the Indians. Vituperatively unrelenting, for instance, in her condemnation of her captors, Hannah Lewis nevertheless feels compelled to include some favorable comments about them. Immediately after describing, in a typically propagandistic fashion, the torture and murder of several captives, Lewis mentions the kind treatment that her son received from the same Indians just depicted as incapable of mercy: "My more fortunate son, after his fate was determined, was taken by the hand and led to the cabin of the chief, into whose family he was to be adopted, where he was received with all imaginable marks of kindness. He was treated as a son, and apparently they loved and regarded him as if he had been one of their own children" (*HL*, 15). Like Lewis, John Davenport, a soldier captured by Indians along with Elias Darnall in 1813, admits inconsistencies in his vision of his captors. On one page of his narrative, Davenport describes Indians as "the most hideous of all animals that ever roamed over the forests of North America," but on the next page he states that "notwithstanding my disobedience," namely his refusal to wed an Indian woman, "the Indians treated me as well as was in their power, especially my mother who was very kind to me."[44]

In like manner, Robert Eastburn, whose *Faithful Narrative* is replete with anti-Indian propaganda, also reveals inconsistencies in his attitudes toward his captors. In the same paragraph that Eastburn describes the murder and scalping of a wounded prisoner, he speaks of the care the Indians took to minister to his own needs: "On my return, the *Indians* perceiving I was unwell, and could not eat their coarse Food, ordered some Chocolate (which they had brought from the *Carrying-Place*) to be boiled for me, and seeing me eat that, appeared pleased" (*RE*, 10). Later in the narrative, when Eastburn is given to an Indian family as their slave, he mentions that when he was unable, because of fatigue and stress, to perform the hard tasks given him, the attitude of his Indian master changed from brutality to concern: "Here I tried to reconcile to this Employ, that they might have no Occasion against me, except concerning the Law of my God; the old Man began to appear kind, and his Wife gave me Milk and Bread when we came Home, and when she got Fish, gave me the *Gills* to eat, out of real Kindness; but perceiving I did not like them, gave me my own choice, and behaved lovingly!" Thus, concludes Eastburn, "cruel Enemies" showed themselves capable of being "Friends," whose hearts exhibited "Love and Tenderness," despite the fact that they were still his enemies (*RE*, 23–24).

Yet another way that captivity writers reveal an ambivalent image of Indians involves the inclusion of specific Indian individuals who possess characteristics that run counter to the propagandistic stereotype the writers attempt at a surface level to promulgate. Such individuals are usually presented as "exceptions to the rule" and often appear as kindly grandmothers or Pocahontas-like sister-rescuers. Typical in this regard is Sarah Ann Horn's description of the Indian family who claimed her as their slave:

In the family to which I belonged, there were five sons and daughters. It was my task to dress the buffalo skins, to make them up into garments and moccasins; to cut up and dry the buffalo meat, and then pound it for use, and to do all the cooking for the family. I spent a considerable part of my time with the old woman. She was a merciful exception to the general character of these merciless beings, and greatly did she contribute, by her acts of kindness and soothing manners, to reconcile me to my fate. But she had a daughter, who was the very reverse of everything that is amiable, and it was not her fault that I enjoyed a moment's repose; indeed, she never appeared at ease unless actively employed in inventing some means to indulge her ill humor on me; but, (as though by the interposition of heaven,) it was not long before I had gained the mother's confidence to such an extent, that, in all matters of controversy between myself and this imp of darkness, my testimony was admitted, and the verdict rendered accordingly. (*Horn and Harris*, 36–37)

The language that Horn uses to describe these two Indian women reveals the extent to which she accepted and wished to encourage the racist stereotype of Indians as degenerate and dangerous. Within the rhetoric of the narrative, the younger Indian, depicted as an "imp of darkness" and "the very reverse of everything that is amiable," is presented as typifying the Indian character. Her mother, on the other hand, whose "kindness and soothing manners" helped to "reconcile" Horn to her "fate," is presented as "a merciful exception to the general character of these merciless beings." In this way, as markedly prejudiced toward Indians as she is, Horn nevertheless introduced an "exception" that undercuts her more negative claims about her captors.

Many of the anti-Indian narratives also describe younger Indian women who exhibit kindly characteristics that the captivity writer often presents as atypical Indian behavior. Like Pocahontas in the Smith captivity, these women usually protect captives from the harm that their less kindly brothers and fathers would inflict. Henry Grace is among those otherwise anti-Indian captives who begrudgingly admit that "if it had not been for the Kindness of the Squaws we must have been all killed" (*HG*, 22). More explicit is Josiah Mooso's account of the young Indian woman who saved him from death at the stake:

Among those who crowded around looking at us critically was a young Indian girl about sixteen years of age, who watched me curiously, coming close to me and retreating a few steps then returning again and finally going to the chief—who was her father—and saying something which I could not understand, but I noticed he made that peculiar guttural noise signifying his approval; she then came to me and commenced untying my hands, then proceeded to unfasten my feet and signed to me to dismount which I did. She next led me into a lodge and gave me the simple garments of the Indian which I donned, my own clothing being carried away.[45]

Indeed, while the parallel is clear, Indian women like those who saved Grace and Mooso are sometimes actually likened to Pocahontas herself. In *The Life and Adventures of William Filley*, for example, a young Indian woman is described as "a second Pocahontas": "The kindness of his Indian sister, who, like a second Pocahontas, took unwearied pains to mitigate his sufferings, made his captivity more endurable" (*WF*, 27).

Yet another way that the captivity writers reveal ambivalence toward Indians involves ethnological misinterpretation of Indian culture. Trapped by their biases, captivity writers frequently misunderstood the intention behind their captors' behavior, often perceiving malign motives when in fact what might appear to the writer as cruelty was in reality intended as a kindness or at least an act of justice. Such, for instance, was the case regarding the running of the gauntlet. Shortly after arriving at an Indian village, most captives expected to undergo this ritual, which involved forcing the captives to run between two rows of Indians who beat them, sometimes with sticks, clubs, and even tomahawks. From the captive's perspective, the gauntlet was, of course, seen as a wanton and cruel torture that indicated even more brutal activities to come. It also reinforced culturally conditioned fears of Indian savagery. It was, in fact, fear of the gauntlet that prompted Hannah Dustan to butcher her Abenaki captors. As Cotton Mather explains, Dustan and the other captives with her were told that when they arrived at their destination "they must be Stript, & Scourged, and Run the *Gantlet*, through the whole Army of *Indians*. They [the Indians] said, This was the

Fashion, when the Captives first came to a Town; and they derided, some of the faint hearted English, which, they said, fainted and swooned away under the *Torments* of this Discipline." It was immediately after this fearful disclosure, Mather tells us, that Dustan "took up a Resolution, to Imitate the Action of *Jael* upon *Sisera*" and murder her abductors (*Humiliations*, 46).

Widely practiced by both Eastern and Western Indian tribes, the gauntlet was never intended as the torture captives interpreted it to be. Instead, as ethnological research into Native American culture has revealed, the gauntlet was most likely a stage in an initiation rite practiced for receiving captives into the tribe (Axtell, "White Indians," 70–72). If the captive was severely beaten, such treatment did not necessarily stem from cruelty. Rather, these ordeals had a clearly defined ritualistic purpose as tribally accepted acts of justice through which the spirits of slain warriors were ceremonially appeased. As William Walton explains in his account of the eighteenth-century captivity by Senecas of Benjamin Gilbert and his family, Indians who used the gauntlet to inflict beatings on captives did so only "by way of Revenge for their Relations who have been slain" (Axtell, "White Indians," 71). Such treatment was normally reserved only for adult male captives who had participated in acts of warfare. Women and children were rarely brutalized, and almost everyone who was intended for adoption was allowed to run unmolested between rows of Indians who merely tapped them on their backs and shoulders. Captured in Pennsylvania during the French and Indian Wars for purposes of adoption, Marie Le Roy and Barbara Leininger report that their experience with the gauntlet consisted of "three blows each, on the back" which were "administered with great mercy." "Indeed," they stated, "we concluded that we were beaten merely in order to keep up an ancient usage, and not with the intention of injuring us" (Axtell, "White Indians," 71).

Fully expecting a severe beating, William Scudder fails to even recognize the dreaded gauntlet when he runs it. After Scudder arrived at the village of his captors, he explains that "each Indian who had his prisoner, set off running and pulling his prisoner with him as fast as possible to the council house, and all the rest of the Indians after them yelling and screaming with all their might." Scudder then explains that after an hour or so of "yelling and screaming" and "dancing," "each Indian took his prisoner home with him, without being the least abused or hurt, and gave them plenty of provisions." "What a happy circumstance for this!" concludes Scudder, "for instead of being bound in thongs, and suffering the most excruciating tortures, by having the finger nails torn out, and pine knots drove into the flesh and set on fire, with many other unheard of tortures, we were all treated like Christians, not even having been compelled to run what is termed the gantlet, although it is customary for the Indians to form two lines, about six feet apart, between which the prisoners must run and receive blows with fists, clubs, and sometimes tomahawks, and are frequently killed" (*WS*, 53).

Often the narratives of transculturized captives provide important ethnological insights that call into question what other captivity writers perceive as cruelty. Mary Jemison explains that her captors killed her parents not for revenge or cruelty but because they were being pursued: "In the course of the night they made me to understand that they should not have killed the family if the whites had not pursued them" (*MJ*, 30). According to Frances Slocum, revenge and cruelty had absolutely nothing to do with the reasons why Indians captured the children of their enemy. Instead, Slocum offers the following explanation: "When the Indians thus lose all their children, they often adopt some new child as their own, and treat it in all respects like their own. This is the reason why they so often carry away the children of white people" (*Sister*, 135). Admitting that Indians sometimes engage in activities that would appear "abhorrent to the feelings of civilized men," Tanner indicates that such practices must be understood within an ethnographic context:

But as the destitution of natural affection manifested in the conduct of many of the American tribes, towards their relatives in sickness and decrepitude, is undoubtedly that among their vices, which is most abhorrent to the feelings of civilized men, so we shall find the instances of rare occurrence, except where the rigour of the climate, or other natural causes, impose of them a necessity, to which we ourselves, in the same circumstances, should probably yield, as they do. The horrid practices to which men of all races have been driven in besieged cities, in cases of shipwreck, and other similar emergencies, should admonish us that the Indians, as a race, deserve no peculiar detestation for crimes growing unavoidably out of their situation. (*JT*, 293)

Among those actions frequently singled out as indications of Indian cruelty is the practice of separating captive children from their parents. From the point of view of white society, cruelty and vindictiveness could be the only reasons for what was perceived as a total disregard for the basic bonds between parents and children. Hunter, however, provides insight into this behavior from the Indians' point of view: "The practice no doubt originated more with a view to hasten a reconciliation to their change, and a nationalization of feelings, than with any intention of wanton cruelty" (*Manners*, 13).

Finally, captivity writers, while overtly anti-Indian, often reveal, usually without full conscious awareness, a positive image of Indian culture that undercuts the racist image they manifestly project. To Scudder, for instance, Indians are "infernal fiends" (*WS*, 36), but when given the opportunity to sleep near his fellow captives or with the Indians, he states, "I thought it best for me to go and lodge with my chief" (*WS*, 50). Earlier in his narrative, Scudder mentions that after the Indians first showed him some small kindnesses, he "slept that night very comfortably" (*WS*, 43). Despite his protests to the contrary, Scudder thus indicates a certain respect, if not liking, for his captors, for he reveals through these passages that he feels more secure with them than he does with other captives.

Even more significant, however, are Johnston's comments about the "intended bride" (*CJ*, 56) his captors chose for him. As Johnston himself states, he was "bred up with an instinctive horror of Indians" (*CJ*, 18). It thus comes as little surprise that he expresses consternation and horror at the prospect "of leading to the altar of Hymen an Indian squaw" (*CJ*, 54). Ransomed before his marriage, Johnston never had the opportunity to meet his betrothed. Nonetheless, at two points in his narrative he expresses a pronounced "curiosity" about the woman he was supposed to marry: "The matrimonial connexion, which had been designed for me, without my consent, occupied my mind, and I entertained an earnest curiosity with respect to the female, the place of whose husband I was to supply, and with whom I was to be allied by the ties of marriage. Whether she was old or young, ugly or handsome, deformed or beautiful, were questions not without their interest to me" (*CJ*, 55). Later in the narrative, when Johnston receives word that his "intended" was passing through a town where he was staying, he writes, "I felt an irresistible curiosity to have a view of this female, and it was my determination to find her dwelling, and see her there, if no other opportunity should occur." Upon finally viewing this woman, Johnston states, "I could not help chuckling at my escape from the fate which had been intended for me. She was old, ugly, and disgusting" (*CJ*, 71). Johnston's continued fascination with this woman, his desire to see her for himself, and his relief that he found her unattractive all indicate that he considered the lifestyle and culture of his Indian captors more appealing than he would consciously allow himself to admit. As Johnston clearly indicates, sexu-

ally, at least, Indian women and the possibility of marriage into the tribe
were not without their attractions.

Mary Rowlandson indicates a similar respect for Indians through her
description of their foods. Early in her narrative, Rowlandson describes
her initial response to Native American cuisine: "The first week of my
being among them, I hardly ate any thing; the second week, I found my
stomach grow very faint for want of something; and yet 'twas very hard
to get down their filthy trash: but the third week though I could think
how formerly my stomach would turn against this or that, and I could
starve and die before I could eat such things, yet they were pleasant and
savoury to my taste" (*MR*, 9). As time progresses, Rowlandson's appetite
for the unfamiliar foods of her captive culture increases: "There came an
Indian to them at that time, with a basket of *Horse-liver*: I asked him to
give me a piece: (what sayes he) can you eat Horse-liver: I told him, I
would try, if he would give a piece; which he did: and I laid it on the coals
to rost; but before it was half ready, they got half of it away from me; so
that I was fain to take the rest and eat it as it was with the blood about my
mouth, yet a savoury bit it was to me" (*MR*, 10). Eventually, Rowlandson
even develops a liking for the flesh of wild animals such as bear: "I have seen
Bear baked very handsomely amongst the *English*, and some liked it, but the
thoughts that it was Bear, made me tremble: but now that was savoury to me
that one would think was enough to turn the stomach of a bruit-Creature"
(*MR*, 13).

Perhaps the most significant indication of Rowlandson's growing
preference for Indian food appears toward the end of her narrative when
she describes a meal of boiled horse hoofs:

Then I went into another Wigwam, where there were two of the *English
Children*; The Squaw was boyling horses feet, then she cut me off a little piece,
and gave one of the *English Children* a piece also. Being very hungry, I had
quickly eat up mine: but the Child could not bite it, it was so tough and sinewy,
but lay sucking, gnawing, chewing, and slobbering it in the Mouth and Hand,
then I took it of the Child, and eat it my self; and savoury it was to my
taste. . . . Thus the Lord made that pleasant and refreshing, which another
time would have been an Abomination. (*MR*, 18)

Indoctrinated by her Puritan background to hate Indians, Rowlandson
had difficulty consciously admitting a certain respect and even liking for
her Indian captors. She therefore displaces her gradual acceptance of
Indian culture onto her description of Indian foods. At first unable to

"stomach" their meals, Rowlandson eventually finds them so "savoury" that she is literally willing to steal food from "the Mouth and Hand" of "one of the *English Children*," thus revealing the extent of her growing subconscious identification with her captors.

In many ways the image of the American Indian contained in captivity narratives is as complex and multifaceted as the tradition itself. Biased and ethnocentric in their perspectives, captivity writers usually had a point to make when writing about Indian captivity and rarely did this point favor the Indian. Consequently, what the captivity narratives say about the American Indian often reveals more about the prejudices and hostilities of the writers themselves and the culture they represented than about the realities of Indian culture, and while generalizations can be made, any image of the Indian that emerges from the captivity narratives is more a matter of historiography than historical reality.

Chapter Four
Mary Rowlandson's Captivity Narrative

The portion of some is to have their Affliction by drops, now one drop and then another: but the dregs of the Cup, the wine of astonishment, like a sweeping rain that leaveth no food, did the Lord prepare to be my portion.

—Mary Rowlandson, *A True History* (1682)

Mary Rowlandson's Indian captivity narrative, titled *The Soveraignty & Goodness of God* in the 1682 Boston and Cambridge editions and *A True History* in the 1682 London edition, has many claims to fame (see Fig. 5). It was the earliest full-length account to be published as a single book, it became a best-seller overnight, it contained all the structural elements that eventually characterized the captivity narrative, it established itself as the first indigenous American literary form, it was a rare example of a publication by a Puritan woman (especially in prose, rather than in poetry), and it rapidly obtained a reputation as a perennially popular classic. Even before much attention was paid to minority writings and nontraditional literary forms, Rowlandson's narrative continued to be reprinted (a dozen times in the eighteenth century, several dozen in the nineteenth, and a dozen or so in this century) and to be anthologized.[1] It is no coincidence that despite the publication of thousands of captivities since Rowlandson's, readers have singled out her particular text as a great work of narrative nonfiction, eloquent and dramatic in its timeless appeal.[2] This chapter explores the background, aesthetics, and influence of arguably the most significant example of the captivity narrative form.

Rowlandson's account is the most widely available of all Indian captivity narratives, so only a brief review of the plot is necessary here. The initial attack was sudden and brutal, as Rowlandson's gripping opening shows: "On the tenth of *February*, 1675. came the *Indians* with great numbers upon *Lancaster*. Their first coming was about Sun-rising. Hearing the noise of some Guns, we looked out; several Houses were

A TRUE HISTORY

OF THE

Captivity ⨍ Restoration

OF

Mrs. *MARY ROWLANDSON,*

A Minister's Wife in *New-England.*

Wherein is set forth, The Cruel and Inhumane Usage she underwent amongst the *Heathens,* for Eleven Weeks time : And her Deliverance from them.

Written by her own Hand, for her Private Use : And now made Publick at the earnest Desire of some Friends, for the Benefit of the Afflicted.

Whereunto is annexed,

A Sermon of *the Possibility of God's Forsaking a People that have been near and dear to him.*

Preached by Mr. *Joseph Rowlandson,* Husband to the said Mrs. *Rowlandson:* It being his Last Sermon.

Printed first at *New-England :* And Re-printed at *London,* and sold by *Joseph Poole,* at the *Blue Bowl* in the *Long-Walk,* by *Christs-Church* Hospital. 1682.

Title page from *A True History of the Captivity & Restoration of Mrs. Mary Rowlandson* (1682). This popular and much anthologized text was the earliest captivity account to become a best-seller. *Courtesy of the Edward E. Ayer Collection, the Newberry Library.*

burning, and the Smoke ascending to Heaven. There were five Persons taken in one House, the Father, and the Mother, and a sucking Child they knock'd on the head; the other two they took, and carried away alive" (*MR*, 1). Indeed, this method of beginning in the midst of the action became typical of the form, especially in its shorter versions. In the Rowlandson garrison house, the author claims that the Narragansetts and Nipmucks killed or captured at least 36 people who had taken refuge there (*MR*, 2). Because total casualties in Lancaster that day were no more than 55, Rowlandson's house took the brunt of the attack (Diebold, lxvii). Rowlandson was wounded and captured along with her three children: Joseph, 14; Mary, 10; and Sarah, 6, who sustained a serious gunshot wound that proved fatal within days. Separated from Joseph and Mary and emotionally and physically weakened, Rowlandson endured 20 forced "removes"—as she called them—in the dead of winter. She was exposed to further abuse, especially at the hands of her sachem (chief) mistress, Weetamoo, but because she was a minister's wife likely to bring a large ransom, she probably observed more violence than she actually experienced. Added to her other hardships was an unfamiliar and irregular diet that included acorns, lily roots, horses' hooves, frogs, and snakes. Rowlandson was so traumatized she even contemplated suicide, certainly a sin for any good Puritan. Yet through God's providence, as she believed, her life was spared, and she and her two remaining children were ransomed and reunited. Rowlandson's captivity lasted "eleven weeks and five days" (*MR*, 29)—her narrative records the length to the day—and her children's a month or so longer.

To better understand Rowlandson's text, we must know something of her origins. She was almost certainly born in England between 1637 and 1638, shortly before her parents, John and Joan White, sailed for Salem in 1639.[3] Contemporary records show that by 1653 the White family had settled in Lancaster and that John White was the wealthiest landowner there with an estate valued at £389. In 1654, Joseph Rowlandson, an unordained Harvard graduate, became Lancaster's first minister, and around 1656, he and Mary White married. Their first child, Mary, was born in 1657 but died at age three in 1660; Joseph was born in 1661; a second Mary in 1665; and Sarah in 1669. Joseph Rowlandson was ordained in 1660 and became a prominent New England clergyman (Diebold, lxii–lxiii).

As a frontier community, Lancaster was especially vulnerable when relations between the settlers and the Nipmucks deteriorated and when King Philip's War led to an alliance among the Wampanoag, Nipmuck, and Narragansett Indians. The town felt so threatened in the first months of 1675 that Joseph Rowlandson and his brother-in-law, Henry Kerley, left for Boston to beg help from the Massachusetts General Assembly. In their absence, the American Indian alliance attacked Lancaster. Because of Mary Rowlandson's social standing, her capture attracted considerable attention in the community and prompted special efforts to ransom her.[4] Once reunited, the family moved temporarily to Boston (their home in Lancaster had been razed to the ground), and then in 1677 to Wethersfield, Connecticut, where Reverend Rowlandson became pastor. But on 24 November 1678, he died unexpectedly, only three days after delivering a powerful fast-day jeremiad whose text was published and bound with the early editions of his wife's narrative. He left his widow and family a substantial estate and a large library (significantly, the latter must have been collected in the few years after all their possessions were lost in the attack on Lancaster).

Until recently, scholars simply lost sight of Mary Rowlandson after March 1679 and assumed—rather conveniently—that she must have died shortly after her husband. But recently examined genealogical records show that on 6 August 1679, eight months after Joseph Rowlandson's death, she married Captain Samuel Talcott, a Harvard graduate and respected community leader.[5] Thus she disappeared as Mary Rowlandson only because she took her second husband's surname.[6] Samuel Talcott died in Wethersfield on 11 November 1691, but Mary Rowlandson Talcott outlived both her spouses by decades and died on 5 January 1710. Unfortunately, we know very little about her life during this time, except that in 1707 she testified in a notorious court case involving her son. Joseph Rowlandson, Jr., and David Jesse were accused of getting Nathaniel Wilson, their brother-in-law, drunk in June 1702 and putting him onto a ship bound for Virginia, where he was sold into servitude. Presumably, their motive was that they stood to benefit from his estate if he were declared dead by law. In 1707, a man claiming to be Wilson reappeared just as the estate was to be settled, but within months he apparently suffered a mental breakdown and was unable to either unequivocally establish his identity or claim his due. The irony of Joseph Rowlandson, Jr., himself a ransomed Indian captive, later selling his brother into slavery would have been overwhelming to his contemporaries, as would the typological parallel with that most famous story of slavery from the book of Genesis, the selling of Joseph. If Mary Rowlandson Talcott left written references to this case, they have not been found, so we can only speculate on her reaction as violence and captivity followed her family down the decades.[7]

Rowlandson's only literary work is her autobiographical narrative, which reveals the physical, spiritual, and psychological terrain she reluctantly traversed in her journey across "the vast and desolate Wilderness" (*MR*, 4). Historian Douglas Leach estimates she travelled 150 miles while a prisoner, from Lancaster to Menamaset; north to Northfield and across the Connecticut River to meet with King Philip himself, sachem of the Wampanoags; next up into what is now southwest New Hampshire; south again to Menamaset; and finally north to Mount Wachusett, where she was released for £20 at a local landmark now called Redemption Rock.[8] Rowlandson divides her ordeal into 20 stages, or "removes," paralleling the number of forced marches she made (one remove for each pound of her ransom, perhaps). Her unusual word choice seems deliberate: the *Oxford English Dictionary* (*OED*) lists among several definitions current at the time the following one that conveys her literal and symbolic intent: "The space or interval by which one person or thing is remote from another in time, place, condition, etc." Like the fine seamstress she was, Rowlandson quilted into her basic narrative a complex design of physical data, spiritual regeneration, and psychological insight.

It has not been possible to establish exactly when Rowlandson composed her text; however, internal and external evidence suggests she wrote it within several years of her release in May 1675 but did not publish it then.[9] Like many later captives, Rowlandson seems to have been induced by others to publish her private story for very public reasons—in her case, both political and spiritual ones. Introducing her work in all four 1682 editions was an anonymous preface to the reader, signed only "Per Amicum" ("By a Friend"), but almost certainly written by Increase Mather. In 1681, Mather had proposed to a group of Puritan ministers that they collect stories of "special providences" concerning New England to be evaluated, sorted, and eventually anthologized. Quite probably Rowlandson's narrative was among the providential accounts he received, but owing to its length, local currency, and intrinsic worth, he may have suggested separate publication and agreed to help. Certainly Mather was in a position to facilitate the work's appearance as a book because he had many connections at the Boston press which published the first edition. And of course, as a woman, Rowlandson herself could not initiate publication (nor could her predecessor, Anne Bradstreet, whose brother-in-law, John Woodbridge, carried the manuscript of *The Tenth Muse* to England to arrange for its publication). Her own account and the accounts of later women captives sold better when the voyeuristic public thought it was hearing "the untold story" published only at the request of friends.

Whether Mather editorialized Rowlandson's text is open to question. It has been suggested, for example, that the sheer number of biblical insertions must indicate ministerial involvement. However, we do not believe it was editorialized to any great extent—if at all—by either Mather or Joseph Rowlandson. Puritans were steeped in the Bible, and as a minister's wife from an affluent and educated background, Mary Rowlandson would have been quite able to edit her own work. Moreover, if we compare the tone and voice of *A True History* to that of Reverend Rowlandson's humiliation sermon published with his wife's text and to the retellings of captivities by both Increase and Cotton Mather, a distinctive, individual voice emerges—that of the captive-composer herself.

Again establishing a pattern that was to become commonplace for later captivities, Rowlandson's story was so popular that no complete copies of the first edition remain: passed from one person to another, it was read to shreds. Hurriedly, second and third editions, full of errors, came out from the already antiquated Colonial press in Cambridge, and the book was considered such a sure seller that a fourth edition was published the same year in London, set either from the manuscript itself or, more likely, from the first edition. However, either the English readership was not interested in the story or it had lost its sales and novelty potential after three previous editions in such a short time; at any rate, it was not republished until 1720, after which it acquired the status of a classic. Rowlandson's narrative was like many others in its mass appeal but unlike them in its additional specialized, even academic, appeal. We saw in chapter 2 that in his study of popular versus elite culture, David D. Hall distinguishes between "extensive" and "intensive" reading practices.[10] The extensive, or novel, world of print catered to the general public's insatiable appetite for change, but the intensive, or traditional, world of print furnished steady sellers with tried-and-true forms and subjects to a much smaller elite. The best of the seventeenth- and eighteenth-century American best-sellers, like Rowlandson's, combined both patterns to reach many different kinds of readers. A number of elements contributed to the lasting popularity of Rowlandson's text including structure, point of view, style, characterization, and emotional impact. While most captivity accounts are relatively artless in terms of literary craft, the Rowlandson story has distinctive narrative tensions indicating its author's skill.

First, Rowlandson's overall mythic structure of capture-initiation-return became the norm for the form. Specifically, the structural elements included a sudden attack, casualties, a forced march, sale or trade, and eventual ransom, release, or escape. Almost invariably the early narratives open *in medias res*, so readers can vicariously experience the individual's own terror and surprise (late eighteenth- and nineteenth-century narratives, because they are often longer, may have extensive background information in an introduction and not begin so abruptly). Also, such openings stress that the attack was a radical turning point in the person's life, a technique that allows for ironic contrasts between the past and present. So, for example, in her first remove, Rowlandson describes how she felt bereft of everything familiar, particularly of her place within an established social and familial unit: "All was gone, my Husband gone (at least separated from me, he being in the Bay; and to add to my grief, the *Indians* told me they would kill him as he came homeward) my Children gone, my Relations and Friends gone, our house and home, and all our comforts within door, and without, all was gone (except my life) and I knew not but the next moment that might go too" (*MR*, 3). Rowlandson's literary talent imbues this extract with enormous emotional power, compared to what was to become a cliched opening in many later captivities.

We have already noted how *A True History* is arranged in 20 removes. These highly structured stages seem virtually unique to Rowlandson (when they are present elsewhere, they were probably derived from Rowlandson's text): other captives (or their editors) tended to see their experiences as part of a more cohesive plot, indicating the rapidity with which the form moved away from fact toward fiction, from individual recollection to editorial intervention. But for Rowlandson, each remove "removed" her further from all she knew, so even though progressive marches eventually brought her physically closer to home, she remained distant from it psychologically and spiritually.

Yet another device used in early captivity narratives with a strong religious dimension is a sandwich structure alternating the story line with biblical commentary.[11] But Rowlandson's position was a little different from that of most other prisoners because her biblical interpretations were not just inserted after the narrative episode to bolster its ideological credence. After some days in the wilderness, an American Indian gave her a Bible taken as plunder, so that often she quotes a passage she says she actually looked at while a captive. For example, just after accepting the Bible, she states:

In that mellancholly time, it came into my mind to read first the 28 *Chapter* of *Deuteronomie*, which I did, and when I had read it, my dark heart wrought on this manner, that there was no mercy for me, that the blessings were gone, and the curses came in their room, and that I had lost my opportunity. But the Lord helped me still to go on reading, till I came to *Chap*. 30. the seven first verses: where I found there was mercy promised again, if we would return to him, by repentance: and though we were scattered from one end of the earth to the other, yet the Lord would gather us together, and turn all those curses upon our Enemies. I do not desire to live to forget this Scripture, and what comfort it was to me. (*MR*, 7)

Later on, Rowlandson claims that one of her reasons for writing is to thank God for "his goodness in bringing to my hand so many comfortable and suitable Scriptures in my distress" (*MR*, 11). Her access to a Bible while a captive makes for an unusually dense account with plausible transitions from plot to quotation and back. One of the literally countless narrative examples occurs when a distraught captive, Goodwife Joslin, tells Rowlandson that she wants to run away. Rowlandson advises her not to, then turns to her Bible for support: "I had my Bible with me, I pulled it out, and asked her, whether she would read; we opened the Bible, and lighted on *Psal. 27*. in which Psalm we especially took notice of that, *ver. ult. Wait on the Lord, be of good courage, and he shall strengthen thine Heart, wait I say on the Lord*" (*MR*, 7).

Yet the presence of such pronounced narrative shifts, however well integrated, has resulted in a great deal of critical attention to Rowlandson's point of view, specifically to the dichotomy between the voice telling the plot details and the voice interpreting them. David L. Minter, for example, refers to the "curious and double present-mindedness"[12] of the text, while Robert K. Diebold describes the styles of the two voices as "the energetic 'colloquial' style . . . found in the bulk of the narrative, in her renditions of persons, places, and events," and "the 'biblical' (and the use of biblical quotations) when she tries to elicit their significances" (Diebold, cvi). To use different terms, *empirical narration* (the "colloquial" style) defines the author's role as participant, while *rhetorical narration* (the "biblical" style) defines her role as interpreter and commentator. However, the narrative's duality arises not merely from this contrast between participant and observer but additionally from a clash of codes between Rowlandson's psychological and religious interpretations of her experience.[13] During and immediately after her captivity, Rowlandson seems to have suffered from trauma akin to what is now termed the "survivor syndrome," but to have minimized the symptoms to conform to the Puritan doctrine of providential affliction. The blend of religious and psychological commentary in this archetype of the captivity narrative gives the work a distinctive texture, and the tension between these two forces—the known and the conventional against the unknown and the unconventional—underlines the narrative's powerful appeal.

Much of Rowlandson's spiritual commentary is concerned with the significance of her captivity, and on that level the work functions as a spiritual autobiography.[14] Again, this is typical of many early narratives by Puritans, Catholics, Quakers, and members of other denominations, where the prisoners strove to see their experiences as providential. Captives must have used strategies similar to those of the nineteenth-century Anglican Andrew Murray (not a former captive), who was incapacitated by a back injury, and who tried to come to terms with the role of affliction throughout his life by saying the following to himself, and advising others to do the same:

In time of trouble, say, "First, he brought me here. It is by his will I am in this strait place; in that I will rest." Next, "He will keep me here in his love, and give me grace in this trial to behave as his child." Then say, "He will make the trial a blessing, teaching me lessons he intends me to learn, and working in me the grace he means to bestow." And last, say, "In his good time he can bring me out again. How and when, he knows." Therefore, say "I am here (1) by God's appointment, (2) in his keeping, (3) under his training, (4) for his time.[15]

For a Puritan, then, the autobiographical act sought constantly to persuade both writer and reader of God's favor toward that one individual. In *A True History*, Rowlandson deepened her religious sensibility and recovered her conviction that she was one of the Elect.

However, counteracting the religious commentary—the autobiography of the soul—is the psychological undercurrent of a deeply troubled person—the autobiography of the psyche. This psychological commentary exists throughout the work, but it is especially evident at the end, where Rowlandson includes a long interpretive section reviewing her past and present spiritual and emotional states. From internal evidence in her work, Rowlandson reveals classic symptoms of the *survivor syndrome*, a term coined after the Holocaust to describe "a type of traumatization of such magnitude, severity, and duration as to produce a recognizable clinical entity."[16] The following symptoms constitute a textbook profile of this condition: depression, "emotional anesthesia," chronic anxiety, insomnia, hypermnesia and amnesia, survivor guilt, unresolved grief, and identity change. Rowlandson suffered from them all.

Throughout, *A True History* contains information about its author's emotional bleakness and fragility, though she frequently masks these signs with spiritual interpretations. When little Sarah died, for instance, Rowlandson was so distracted she considered suicide; almost shuddering at the memory, she comments, "I have thought since of the wonderful goodness of God to me, in preserving me so in the use of my reason and senses, in that distressed time, that I did not use wicked and violent means to end my own miserable life" (*MR*, 5). Also, when the Indians retraced their steps along an English path, she recalls becoming so depressed that she felt she "could there have freely lyen down and died" (*MR*, 10).

After Rowlandson was first captured, she fell into a state of shock that numbed her against the physical, emotional, and spiritual dislocation. In her text she refers to her psychological denial of her experience as she actually underwent it, "And here I cannot but remember how many times sitting in their Wigwams, and musing on things past, I should suddenly leap up and run out, as if I had been at home, forgetting where I was, and what my condition was" (*MR*, 16). This state continued for approximately one month, after which tears melted away her "emotional anesthesia": "Then my heart began to faile: and I fell a weeping; which was the first time to my remembrance, that I wept before them. Although I had met with so much Affliction, and my heart was many times ready to break, yet could I not shed one tear in their sight; but rather had been all this while in a maze, and like one astonished" (*MR*, 11). Here and in the epigraph to this chapter, Rowlandson uses several now obsolete meanings of the word *astonish*; according to *OED*, it means both "to deprive of sensation, as by a blow; to stun, paralyse, deaden, stupefy" and "to stun mentally; to shock one out of his wits; to drive stupid, bewilder." Equally significant is *OED*'s entry under "astonishment," where the biblical phrase "Wine of astonishment" is defined as "stupefying wine." During her captivity, Rowlandson is emotionally stunned, or turned to stone, like a person who is dead drunk; hence her reference to affliction as "the wine of astonishment, like a sweeping rain that leaveth no food" (*MR*, 36). Yet wine, a spirit, not only intoxicates a person physically; more important, it has spiritually transforming powers when taken at Communion (called, in Puritan phraseology, "the Lord's supper").

Chronic anxiety forms "a prominent symptom among survivors and is associated with fears of renewed persecution" (Niederland, 415). Rowlandson's distress comes out most clearly in the final section where, while she strives to convince herself of the providential role of suffering, her fear of facing future tests is so intense it reveals the human side of affliction. Hasn't this single gruelling test been enough, she wonders, even for a soul that once craved trials as signs of God's confidence in her spiritual stamina? And she implies in the following quotation that even if her spirit could bear more anguish, her flesh probably could not:

The portion of some is to have their Affliction by drops, now one drop and then another: but the dregs of the Cup, the wine of astonishment, like a sweeping rain that leaveth no food, did the Lord prepare to be my portion. Affliction I wanted, and Affliction I had, full measure (I thought) pressed down and running over: yet I see when God calls a person to any thing, and through never so many difficulties, yet he is fully able to carry them through, and make them see and say they have been gainers thereby. And I hope I can say in some measure, as *David* did, *It is good for me that I have been afflicted*. (*MR*, 36)

Rowlandson's anxiety also manifests itself in nightmares and insomnia. She strikingly draws attention to these symptoms near the end of *A True History*, where she reflects: "I can remember the time, when I used to sleep quietly without workings in my thoughts, whole nights together: but now it is otherwise with me. When all are fast about me, and no eye open, but his who ever waketh, my thoughts are upon things past . . . Oh the wonderful power of God that mine eyes have seen, affording matter enough for my thoughts to run in, that when others are sleeping mine eyes are weeping" (*MR*, 33). Night after night, she suffers from sleeplessness as the obsessive "workings" in her thoughts revive the past and make her cry.

This tendency to merge past and present suggests the disorientation and alienation haunting Rowlandson on her return. She also was prone to hypermnesia, in which certain details of the trauma are so immediate they seem tangible. In fact, this symptom may explain the story's strong narrative support and clear structure. Patients with hypermnesia do not necessarily recall their entire experience with equal vividness: particular incidents may stand out more than others. In this case, some of the indelible events included the initial attack, Sarah's death, and the series of struggles to stave off starvation.

Among the most characteristic symptoms of the survivor syndrome are intense grief and unresolved guilt at having escaped when other people did not. These feelings are especially acute in survivors whose family members have died. During Rowlandson's captivity, her instinct for self-survival prevented her from being overwhelmed by guilt, but after her release, she repeatedly admitted her trouble in coming to terms with being alive when so many were dead or untraced. "Yet I was not without sorrow," she confessed, "to think how many were looking and longing, and my own Children amongst the rest, to enjoy that deliverance that I had now received" (*MR*, 32). Predictably, she thought far more about Sarah than about her other children who were still alive: "That which was dead lay heavier upon my spirit than those which were alive amongst the *Heathen*: thinking how it suffered with its wounds, and I was no way able to relieve it" (*MR*, 33). Further difficulty, even denial, is evident by Rowlandson's inability to use "she" and "her" for Sarah, merely the impersonal "that" and "it."

Perhaps the most convincing evidence that Rowlandson underwent severe trauma during her captivity is that she changed as a result. In the thirteenth remove, she claimed that one immediate difference was her awareness of previous spiritual negligence: "I saw how in my walk with God, I had been a careless creature," she admits (*MR*, 18). Her increased spiritual responsiveness and responsibility also enable her to discipline herself and resist some undesirable worldly habits—pipe smoking, for example: "*I* remember with shame," she writes, "how formerly, when I had taken two or three Pipes, I was presently ready for another, such a bewitching thing it is: But I thank God, he has now given me power over it; surely there are many who may be better imployed, than to lye sucking a stinking Tobacco-pipe" (*MR*, 11). Further, her devotional development lays the foundation for a permanent reversal of values described at the very end of her narrative that helps her "to look beyond present and smaller troubles, and to be quieted under them" (*MR*, 36).

Although the psychological dimension of *A True History* suggests its author suffered from many typical survivor syndrome symptoms, the text lacks evidence of two other usual signs: psychosomatic illness and inability to verbalize. The reasons she does not display these latter symptoms may be related. Many survivor syndrome victims cannot articulate their experience; like Kurtz in Joseph Conrad's *The Heart of Darkness*, "the horror"

of experienced evil has stunned them into silence. Yet for others, the will to
survive becomes the will to testify. In Rowlandson's case, Puritan ideology
strongly encouraged her to memorialize her experience, and in so doing, she
may have decreased her likelihood of developing the psychosomatic com-
plaints typical of many survivors. Certainly Rowlandson does not admit to
any of them in her work where the emphasis is appropriately on spiritual and
emotional signs, not physical ones. Moreover, Rowlandson herself becomes
an individual example of survival while her text becomes a communal
exemplum.

Rowlandson's dual point of view as participant and commentator
obviously determines the style and the evidence—or not—of "stylization." Roy Harvey Pearce originally defined stylization as the progressively cliched overlay of propagandist or literary messages in accounts
written, or "improved" as the title pages often claim, by an editor rather
than by a captive (Pearce, "Significances," 3). Pearce believes that the
earliest narratives of captivities such as Rowlandson's are superior because they are direct, genuine documents of an individual's disintegrated, then reintegrated, spiritual and physical self. Revising this
definition, David Minter argues that even the religious aspects of early
narratives constitute a kind of stylization that contradicted their so-
called spontaneity and individuality (Minter, 336–37). Certainly it is
true that if one reads many captivity accounts, they tend to merge
together stylistically because, like formula fiction today, distinctive style
was commercially risky. Once again, though, *A True History* is probably
an exception because it was the earliest full-length example of the form
and its author's individual experience was not diminished by religious,
propagandist, sensational, or literary intentions. A few other captivities
show evidence of individual style and trauma—for example, Emeline L.
Fuller's *Left by the Indians* (1892), Mary Schwandt-Schmidt's *The Story of
Mary Schwandt* (1894), Urania White's *Captivity among the Sioux* (1901),
and Minnie Buce Carrigan's *Captured by the Indians* (1907)—but they are
unusual.[17]

Whatever her precise combination of education, experience, and skill,
Rowlandson is a superb stylist. Take, for example, the extended description of Sarah's death:

My child being even ready to depart this sorrowful world, they bad me carry it
out, to another Wigwam. . . . Whither I went with a very heavy heart, and
down I sate with the picture of death in my lap. About two hours in the Night,
my sweet Babe like a Lamb departed this life. . . . I cannot but take notice,

how at another time I could not bear to be in the room where any dead person was, but now the case is changed: I must and could lye down by my dead Babe, side by side, all the night after. (*MR*, 5)

Rowlandson presents here a verbal pieta of tremendous emotional force, a combination of biblical echoes, precise observation, and lucid expression.

Another example of Rowlandson's stylistic ability occurs in her riveting account of the death of Goodwife Joslin, who, after deciding against escape, had then begged the Indians to let her go because she had one babe in arms and was about to give birth to another. But the Indians were so "vexed with her importunity," they "stript her naked, and set her in the midst of them: and when they had sung and danced about her (in their hellish manner) as long as they pleased: they knockt her on the head, and the child in her arms with her: when they had done that, they made a fire and put them both into it" (*MR*, 8). The significance of this extract—the full description is longer—is that Rowlandson did not even witness Joslin's death but fictionalized it from other captives' eyewitness accounts. She provides drama, sensation, victimization, and propaganda in the figure of the helpless woman—stereotypical elements of the captivity narrative form that soon became exploited and clichéd but that must have reached their original readership undiluted and that retain considerable impact even today.

Rowlandson's skill as a stylist is also evident in her use of metaphor, and the most dominant image cluster concerns food. In a double irony, while she is physically well fed before her capture, she is spiritually malnourished, and while she is poorly fed and almost always hungry during her captivity, she is spiritually replete. As a prisoner, Rowlandson continually searches for food to ensure her physical survival; indeed, she is obsessed with this activity. Yet she recognizes the simultaneous typological significance of her religious renewal. Her clearest use of the food metaphor occurs in this observation: "I cannot but think what a Wolvish appetite persons have in a starving condition: for many times when they gave me that which was hot, I was so greedy, that I should burn my mouth, that it would trouble me hours after; and yet I should quickly do the same again. And after I was throughly hungry, I was never again satisfied. . . . And now could I see that Scripture verified (there being many Scriptures which we do not take notice of, or understand till we are afflicted) *Mic. 6. 14. Thou shalt eat and not be satisfied*" (*MR*, 19–20). While she finally ate, and even relished, unfamiliar food when famished, she realized that it was only because "to the hungry Soul every bitter thing is sweet" (*MR*, 10). Apart from these quotations, a random glance at any page indicates Rowlandson's preoccupation with the daily details of food gathering and its symbolic overtones.

Near her conclusion, although Rowlandson understands the theoretical connection between physical deprivation and spiritual growth among Christians, she still marvels at God's design to feed the Indians so they can continue to harrass the Puritans, but thereby bring the Elect to eternal life. Included in this section is a long, negative, ethnocentric description of Indian food and its preparation. Later captives, especially women, focused similarly on the food's unfamiliarity and unavailability or, in the nineteenth century, treated the topic pseudoanthropologically by including supposedly authentic Indian recipes, often as a sales gimmick (one of the best examples occurs on the title page of Mary Barber's narrative, which exclaims, "*A valuable feature of this work is the INDIAN RECEIPTS*").[18] This change indicates different readership expectations, emphasizing the shift from education to edification and entertainment.

A True History also illustrates the use of characterization in early captivities. Quite properly in the largely autobiographical and spiritual accounts written by the captives themselves, the strongest characterization to emerge is usually that of the captive-composer. As such, Rowlandson reveals a wealth of physical, spiritual, and emotional data about herself. She is a woman of many roles: victim, mother, sinner, slave, and survivor, but she is also a character who changes and develops. In eighteenth- and nineteenth-century narratives, as the form moved closer to fiction or anthropology, a larger cast of characters became more important. Rowlandson's narrative contains only fleeting character sketches of other captives such as Goodwife Joslin, John Gilbert, and Robert Pepper. Predictably, many of the Indians receive scant and stereotyped attention; they are often "hell-hounds" (*MR*, 3) and "merciless and cruel *Heathen*" (*MR*, 32). Yet in this early text, before the form was overtaken by anti-Indian propaganda, the author is honest enough to reveal ambivalence toward her captors, who behaved inconsistently toward her, and to document the kind acts as well as the unkind ones: "Sometimes I met with Favour, and sometimes with nothing but Frowns" (*MR*, 14), she admits, puzzled.

However, two American Indians receive extended characterization: Quannopin, Rowlandson's master, the Narragansett sachem, and his chief wife, Weetamoo (or Wettimore), sister-in-law of the powerful

Wampanoag sachem King Philip. While Rowlandson reached some understanding with Quannopin—even calling him "the best Friend that I had of an *Indian*" (*MR*, 15)—she and Weetamoo clashed constantly as they tried to outmanoeuver each other. Although similar in nature, they held opposite values, for Weetamoo was as worldly as Rowlandson was otherworldly, a contrast made plain in one of several descriptions of the Indian princess: "A severe and proud Dame she was; bestowing every day in dressing her self near as much time as any of the Gentry of the land: powdering her hair and painting her face, going with her Neck-laces, with Jewels in her ears, and bracelets upon her hands" (*MR*, 22). Although initially Weetamoo slapped Rowlandson and tried to beat her with a stick, the prisoner eventually rebelled, thereby gaining respect from her captor.

Rowlandson's narrative ability in delineating the relationship between herself and Weetamoo is best revealed in two parallel episodes. The first few days of Rowlandson's capture were dominated by her daughter Sarah's slow death and her mother's distraction and disbelief, especially when the Indians removed the dead child and later showed Rowlandson the shallow grave: "I saw the ground was newly digged, and there they told me they had buried it, there I left that child in the Wilderness, and must commit it, and my self also in this Wilderness condition, to him who is above all" (*MR*, 6). The thought of Sarah buried alone, without a Christian ceremony, in an unmarked grave continued to haunt Rowlandson, so that when Weetamoo's child died some weeks later, Rowlandson could only respond coldly, "My Mistresses *Papoos* was sick, and it died that night; and there was one benefit in it, that there was more room. I went to a Wigwam, and they bad me come in, and gave me a skin to lye upon, and a mess of Venison and Ground-nuts; which was a choice Dish among them. On the morrow they buried the *Papoos*: and afterward, both morning and evening, there came a company to mourn and howl with her: though I confess, I could not much condole with them. Many sorrowful days I had in this place" (*MR*, 18). Compared to the pages she devotes to her own child's death, the few sentences on Weetamoo's unnamed child are brief and brusque. Moreover, as a contrast to Weetamoo's unkindness, Rowlandson describes the kindness of the other Indians who fed her choice food. She is aware of her hard-heartedness but believes her afflictions warrant such a stony response. Thus this common experience does nothing to improve relations between the two women, and each is left with her own separate grief.

Apart from some well-drawn characterization, *A True History* is also unusual for its strong emotional impact. This must have been true when it was first published—Rowlandson's capture being newsworthy and even notorious before she published her own version of events—but it continues to hold true today. For like a small group of other Colonial writers including William Bradford, Anne Bradstreet, Samuel Sewall, and Sarah Kemble Knight, Rowlandson's text was and is popular in the best sense; namely, it is emotionally accessible even for the general reader. Specifically, Rowlandson appealed to the archetypal human experience of cultural and personal integration, followed by disintegration, and succeeded by a sense of frail reintegration. Because her individual experience is always uppermost, her intense emotional force is rare within the form. The narrative's length and placement as the earliest full-fledged example of the form also support this contention.

Yet even though the text's emotional honesty is beyond question, Rowlandson does seem nascently aware of strategies within the form that later writers exploited, specifically, religious, propagandist, and pseudo-literary emphases. But to illustrate the relative mildness of Rowlandson's editorializing, it is useful to compare her brief negative references to Indians to an extended pejorative reference in "The Preface to the Reader," a letter prefacing her text in the 1682 editions and giving some background on Rowlandson and on the political situation. Such prefatory material became common and it served several functions: it induced the reader to continue reading by various advertising ploys; it excused the writer, especially if female, from any accusation of impropriety in writing and publishing; and it endorsed the work's quality because it was often written by an influential person with name-recognition. The preface to Rowlandson's text recognized and exploited the story's propagandist potential far more than the story itself. The following quotation from the preface is the most blatant example of propaganda there: "*None can imagine, what it is to be captivated, and enslaved to such Atheistical, proud, wild, cruel, barbarous, brutish, (in one word) diabolical Creatures as these, the worst of the heathen*" (*MR*, n. p.). Already present are the stereotypes of the Native Americans that would recur again and again, until the captivity narrative form lost any residual connection to reality and became wholly fictional.

Rowlandson's text has rightly received a great deal of attention in the three centuries since it first appeared. It should not, of course, be given pride of place in the canon merely on the basis of tradition and longevity;

many other captivity narratives warrant attention—some still buried in archives, others out of print, yet more available only in specialized collections. But *A True History* retains its literary significance because it is one of those rich, rare texts that seem capable of constant reinterpretation and renewed relevance.

Chapter Five
Images of Women

We had Husband and Father, and Children and Sisters, and Friends and Relations, and House, and Home, and many Comforts of this life: but now we might say as *Job, Naked came I out of my mothers womb, and naked shall I return, The Lord gave, and the Lord hath taken away, blessed be the Name of the Lord.*
— Mary Rowlandson, *A True History* (1682)

To seperate the Husband from the Wife, and the Child from the Mother . . . [is] murder of the most henious Degree[.]
— Jean Lowry, *Journal* (1760)

What a mysterious tie is that of the family relation! How strong the cords which bind the heart of parents and children, of brothers and sisters.
— John Todd, *The Lost Sister of Wyoming* (1842)

Introduction

Statistics on the number of women captured vary, and any attempt at an accurate assessment is complicated by incomplete information on the total number of both male and female captives and by uneven attention to particular regions and timeframes. The statistics become even more suspect if we consider the muted or absent voices of transculturated women, of black and Mexican women, of women who simply disappeared.[1] Thus the documented experiences of captive women are largely synonymous with white women of European—mostly English—background. However, we do know that a large number of the several thousand captivity narratives known to exist are by or about women (using "women" to mean both girls and goodwives).

The experience of women captives is far more complex and ambivalent than often recognized, but, as the three opening epigraphs to this chapter illustrate, their narratives stress that captivity's main metonymy was the dramatic and decisive fracturing of the original family unit. Family, of course, symbolized not only individual households but society at large and the greater social chaos caused by American Indian incursions. What Carol F. Karlsen says about the significance of family for the Puritans applies also to later times: family was "crucial as a symbol of a hierarchical society. Functioning as both 'a little Church' and 'a little Commonwealth,' it served as a model of relationships between God and his creatures and as a model for all social relations."[2] For no matter how strong those ties, things could never be the same again. Typically, in the women's captivity literature, a husband and/or teenage sons died during the initial attack; a mother was either pregnant or had just given birth; an infant or newborn child might be killed at any time—but usually early on; surviving siblings were often deliberately separated to harden them for servitude or slavery, to increase their individual ransom, or to hasten their assimilation as substitute adopted children; and women always ran the risk of sexual harassment or abuse.

Once disintegrated, the family unit could not be reintegrated physically, spiritually, emotionally, or economically without great difficulty, and often not at all. For some of the family were dead; others remained scattered, sometimes by choice; the home base was almost certainly destroyed; and possessions were rifled or removed. Women especially faced realigned roles as they attempted to relocate themselves within new networks, whether they remained with the American Indians—as some did—or eventually returned to their culture of origin. In *Women's Diaries of the Westward Journey*, editor Lillian Schlissel concludes, "In the face of all of the forms of dislocation that commonly accompanied emigration, these women determined to maintain the family as an integral unit."[3] From the seventeenth through the nineteenth centuries, women captured on different frontiers reacted with the same urge documented by the nineteenth-century diarists included in Schlissel's study. Hannah Swarton's *Narrative* (1697)—one of the earliest to be published—epitomizes the theme of family dislocation in its moving introduction and conclusion:

Introduction: I was taken by the *Indians*, when *Casco* Fort was taken, (*May*) 1690. My husband being slain, and Four Children taken with me. The Eldest of my Sons they killed, about two Months after I was taken, and the rest Scattered from me[.]

Conclusion: Mr. *Cary* was sent with a Vessel, to fetch Captives from *Quebeck*, and when he came, I among others, with my youngest Son, had our Liberty to come away: And by Gods Blessing upon us, we Arrived in Safety, at *Boston*, in *November*, 1695. our Desired Haven. And I desire to *Praise the Lord for His Goodness, and for His Wonderful Works to me*. Yet still I have left behind, Two Children, a Daughter of *Twenty* Years old, at *Mont Royal*, whom I had not seen in Two years before I came away; and a Son of *Nineteen* years old, whom I never saw since we parted, the next morning after we were taken. I earnestly Request the Prayers of my Christian Friends, that the Lord will deliver them. (*HS*, 51, 71–72)[4]

Here Swarton is suddenly thrust into the role of sole parent reporting her household's dispersal. Moreover, as the ending illustrates, even though she and her youngest son eventually returned to Boston, she had to live with the guilt and uncertainty of not knowing what might happen to her daughter in Canada and what had happened to her 19-year-old son, whom she last saw the day after the initial attack.

While some female captives such as Swarton recorded the story of family fragmentation themselves, many female captives allowed (male) editors to either ghostwrite, revise, or sponsor their stories for publication, for reasons ranging from imputed impropriety to inadequate literary skill or downright illiteracy. Sometimes the editor's name appeared on the title page or in the introduction; sometimes it did not. In certain narratives editors did more than simply write the basic plot: they had their own agenda and substantially reoriented the narrative; sometimes, they created it. This editorializing was present from the seventeenth century, most notably in Increase and Cotton Mather's propagandist recastings of Puritan women's captivities. A particularly complex case study showing the intervention of a series of male editors concerns the nineteenth-century narrative *Regina, the German Captive; or, True Piety among the Lowly* (1856), whose editorial apparatus further distances its authentic basis and exploits its propagandist potential.[5] The story centers on a German emigrant family who settled in the Pennsylvania wilderness in the early 1740s. In 1755, Regina and Barbara Leininger were captured by Allegheny Indians after an attack on the family homestead. The sisters were separated, and Barbara and another companion, Marie Le Roy, escaped to freedom in 1759. In the same year, Barbara's story was published simultaneously in German and English editions.[6] Regina, however, did not return for nine years; she was one of a group of captives whom Colonel Henry Bouquet forced the American Indians to relinquish. She had forgotten virtually all her native German and spoke and looked like an Indian, but she was able to recall fragments of German hymns and prayers, by which her mother identified and claimed her. In 1765, mother and daughter—both devout Lutherans—visited Reverend Melchior Mühlenberg and told him Regina's story, which he published originally in German in *Hallische Nachrichten* (*Hallean Annals*).

Decades later, another Lutheran clergyman, Reuben Weiser, expanded and translated parts of Mühlenberg's book to produce *Regina, the German Captive*, in which Regina Leininger appears as the quasifictional Regina Hartman.[7] In his preface, Weiser attempts a generic definition of his volume: "It is no novel, nor is it a myth, nor an allegory, but it is a true narrative of well-authenticated facts,—somewhat enlarged and embellished, we admit;—but, nevertheless, all the main facts are true, and recorded by Rev. Dr. H. Melchior Mühlenberg" (*Regina*, 5). But later, Weiser admits to having prepared the book "for our Lutheran Sabbath-schools" (*Regina*, 7). Throughout the narrative he uses pleas and ploys to the Lutheran youth he designates as his readers: "Oh, what happy children they were!" he says of Regina and her siblings, then cautions, "Would that all the children that read this book were like them" (*Regina*, 57). In addition to pro-Lutheran and anti-Catholic propaganda, he repeatedly inserts literary references and embellishments. Thus, the facts of Regina Leininger's captivity have been diluted and distanced by various layers of male editorializing in two different languages and by overt retelling in the third person. The gap between this portrayal of women and that in wholly fictional accounts is virtually nonexistent.

As with much popular culture, we might ask whether the public taste and pocket determined what got published and how it was packaged, or whether the print media manipulated information according to what it thought the public really wanted. Yet whether written by men or by women, whether mediated or unmediated, whether single-layered or multilayered, the narrative voice presents the following images of women, reinforced by the controlling theme of family dislocation: (1) victims and virgins, (2) victors and vanquishers, (3) mothers, daughters, and sisters, (4) traumatized women, and (5) transculturated women. These categories provide a way of accessing dominant motifs while simultaneously showing the depth and variety of women's experience.

A Case Study

We can obtain a preview of the complex interrelationships in these categories by considering how three women captives taken during the

1862 Sioux Uprising in Minnesota wrote up their accounts from much the same basic information. The differences lie in the background, age, and reactions of Jannette De Camp Sweet, Nancy McClure-Huggan, and Mary Schwandt-Schmidt, all of whom were invited to compile and publish their recollections 32 years later in volume six (1894) of *Minnesota Historical Society Collections*.[8] The stories can be read independently or together, but they were probably meant to be read one after another because they appear consecutively; each gets progressively shorter (26, 22, and 13 pages), relying on previous information; Sweet, author of the first, had the most education and status; and Schwandt actually cut short her narrative by referring readers to Sweet: "As she has so well described the incidents of that dreadful night and the four following dreadful days, it seems unnecessary that I should repeat them; and, indeed, it is a relief to avoid the subject" (*Schwandt*, 468). Sweet's account shows her in the role of mother; McClure portrays herself as a vanquisher, and, because she was half-Indian—through her mother—and married to a "mixed-blood," as a transculturated woman too; Schwandt-Schmidt, the most traumatized of the three, presents herself as a victim, someone with permanent psychological scars.

Jannette De Camp—as she was in 1862—lived at the Red Wood Sioux Agency where her husband was in charge of the lumber mill. She ascribes her relatively good treatment while a captive to her husband's previous kindness to the Dakotas. Therefore, the usual link between the roles of victim and mother is largely absent from her narrative. Her dominant role is maternal as she tries to protect her three (soon to be four) children during their monthlong imprisonment. Some Christianized Indians helped the family escape, but when they reached the Fort Ridgely garrison, she learned that her husband—in St. Paul at the time of attack—had died. As she recalls her reaction to this sad news, it is not in terms of her own loss of a husband but in terms of her children's loss of a father: "Every hope seemed blotted out from the horizon of my existence, and life and liberty bought at such a price seemed worthless as I looked at the future of my fatherless children" (*Sweet*, 378). However, they were not fatherless for long, as she married Reverend Joshua Sweet, the man who brought her news of her first husband's death. Thus, she reunified the family by providing a second father for her sons and bonding the old De Camp family within a new network.

Nancy McClure-Huggan's narrative is quite different in tone because she accentuates her ability to overcome misfortune and also to unify her dual white/Native American background, though not—as in most of the examples in the section on transculturated women—as a white adopting American Indian culture, but as a "poor little half-blood 'chincha'"—as she calls herself—embracing as much of white culture as she can (*McClure*, 441). The Sioux did not kill her because she and her husband trusted the tribe with goods. At several points in her brief narrative, McClure-Huggan rebelled against being a prisoner and asserted herself. By assuming an active role, she became a vanquisher. For example, when she recognized her horse, Jerry, in Little Crow's camp, she grabbed him from the Indian who had stolen him. When an American Indian woman insulted what she called cowardly "half-breeds," McClure-Huggan retaliated but then apologized to her readers, explaining, "Perhaps it was not a very ladylike thing to do, but I was dreadfully provoked" (*McClure*, 455).

McClure-Huggan endured the hardships of captivity as she had earlier endured and overcome her mixed ethnic background. Yet in dealing with Native American matters—perhaps to conform to white readers' expectations—she stereotyped Indians in general, recalling, for example, her "first 'Indian scare'" as a schoolgirl in a mission school (*McClure*, 443), and claiming, "I was always more white than Indian in my tastes and sympathies" (445). What real or wished-for acculturation made McClure-Huggan reveal such a double standard? Or were there, in truth, two acculturations: mixed-blood/American Indian in real life, mixed-blood/white in print? Certainly, Mary Schwandt–Schmidt refers to her as "Mrs. Huggan, the half-breed woman" (*Schwandt*, 469) in her narrative. Perhaps McClure-Huggan's printed text revised and embellished the text of her life.

Born in Germany, Schwandt and her family immigrated to America in 1858, when she was 10. Four years later, as a mature 14-year-old, she asked to work as a domestic for the nearby Reynolds family. Her reasons had less to do with the wages than with the opportunity to mix with two other girls of her age in the household. When the Sioux attacked Schwandt's family home less than a month later, only her brother August escaped, and she recalls how her brief goodbyes on leaving home were, in fact, final farewells to all but August. The Reynolds farm was also attacked, and the family and their servants captured. Mary Anderson, the other servant girl, was badly wounded and lingered several days before she died. Apparently, in the initial attack, some braves tried to assault Schwandt, for Jannette De Camp Sweet states in her narrative, "Mary Swandt [*sic*] had fled to me for protection from their indecent assaults" (*Sweet*, 362).

Several elements combined to make the tone of Schwandt-Schmidt's account that of the victimized and traumatized survivor: lingering guilt at not being with her own family when they died; helplessness at seeing her sister-servant's suffering, death, and hurried burial; and terror at the "indecent assaults"—whatever they were (neither Schwandt-Schmidt nor Sweet elaborates). When she realized her family had died, she fell into a deeply depressed state in which her eyes were "always red and swollen from constant weeping," she was barely able to talk, and she moved "like a sleep-walker" (*Schwandt*, 469). She was rescued from the Sioux by General Sibley's forces and was reunited with her brother, but they were just "two little orphans" (*Schwandt*, 473), sundered from, and sole survivors of, a "peaceful and happy household" (*Schwandt*, 463). As late as 1894, while detailing her story, her profound scarring surfaces in the conclusion to her account: "The memory of that period, with all its hideous features, often rises before me, but I put it down" (*Schwandt*, 474).

Victims and Virgins

> But we ought not to pass over the marvellous Display of the Powers of God, in supporting and preserving the poor *Captives*, when they travelled thro' the horrid Wilderness, oftentimes much more than a score of miles in a day, & thro' very deep Snows, and with vast Loads on their backs; & grievously pinched with Hunger, having scarce one bit of any Refreshment, for whole Days together. Poor, weak, sick *Women* have done so!
> —Cotton Mather, *Good Fetch'd Out of Evil* (1706)

In this statement about how special providences saved Puritan captives, Cotton Mather irrevocably yokes together the two italicized words "*Captives*" and "*Women*." By doing so, he established a metonymy that later accounts—factual and fictional—simply took for granted: one central defining image of captivity was the victimized woman. As we know, this is not the only image of women in captivity, but it is a dominant one, and it has remained dominant throughout the form's many metamorphoses. Scholars share this one icon, even when they differ on other important images of women in the captivity literature.[9] For example, Annette Kolodny's observations on the significance of Indian captivity for the Puritans can also apply to later texts in which the seventeenth-century spiritual emphasis is replaced by mythic resonance that reinforces the victimization: "In the Puritan sermon's rhetorical emphasis upon this Americanized Babylon, the captivity story—*especially when its protagonist was a woman*—proved repeatedly useful. For nowhere in American experience would the authors of these jeremiads find a more affecting image of New England as *Judea capta* than in the languishing figure of a Puritan woman held captive in the wilderness retreats of the Indian" (Kolodny, *Land*, 21). Dawn Lander Gherman's "From Parlor to Tepee: The White Squaw on the American Frontier" takes a similar starting point: that the traditional image of the white frontier woman was that of "a victim and, at the same time, a vindictive and castrating avenger of her own victimization" (Gherman, vii). She adds, "Victimization and martyrdom are the bone and muscle of every statue, picture and word portrait of a frontier woman" (3). It is hardly surprising that this view of woman as victim should prevail because she embodied—the pun is deliberate—a range of potential perils. The images we are about to examine of woman's physical, sexual, and spiritual exploitation all have particular relevance for her role within the family. This is also true for emotional victimization, which will be examined later in the section on traumatized women.

The most significant images of women's physical victimization concern abuse or torture, slavery, and food deprivation. In virtually every instance, women captives were torn from a cohesive family unit. Very few examples can be found either of single women being taken or of women being taken without at least some of their kinfolk. Thus remaining family members watched as relatives were wounded or killed, and because one standard narrative pattern was for American Indians to take hostage more women and children than men, it was the women who usually saw their menfolk being slain and who experienced the actual shattering of the household. Therefore, descriptions of tortures they either endured personally or observed were filtered through extreme subjectivity, bias, editorialization, or ethnocentrism.

Sometimes the sensationalism was so excessive that the tortures seem to have been fabricated, even in the fact-based accounts. For example, Marie Le Roy and Barbara Leininger really were captured by Alleghenies in 1755, but the gratuitous violence in one particular scene was almost certainly fictionalized with propagandist intent. Both the German and English editions of their captivity describe how the Indians first scalped an Englishwoman who had tried to escape (scalping itself did not always result in death; there are instances of people who were scalped and who later recovered—August Schwandt, for example). Next, they laid burning wood splinters on her body; then cut off her ears and fingers, forced them into her mouth, and made her swallow them. After she was dead, an Englishman who had joined the French cut off part of her body to eat. Finally, the corpse was cut in two and left for the dogs (*Le Roy and Leininger*, 4–5). The narrative is not in the first person, so it is unclear whether the two German girls really observed and wrote this graphic, gruesome incident or whether an anti-Indian, anti-British editor created and inserted it (most likely the latter).

Ironically, there was often no need to fabricate violent acts in authentic accounts because the facts of captivity were grim enough. According to J. Norman Heard, "The Indians' favorite method of attack was to surround a cabin during the pre-dawn hours and to rush the family when the father came outdoors at first light. They would massacre men, old women, and children too small to travel, take the young women and the older children captive, and be well on their way back to their villages before neighbors could organize for pursuit."[10] Mary Rowlandson's description of the initial attack's brutality is echoed in many subsequent narratives, where the physical violence is dramatized by the difference between ordered family life and its sudden disruption. For example, we can see a similar narrative strategy to Rowlandson's in the opening to a much later work, Minnie Buce Carrigan's account of the Sioux Uprising, in which her father was putting up hay and her mother was sewing when the attack began:

How painfully distinct are all the memories of this dreadful afternoon. While my mother was being murdered I stood about ten feet away from her, paralyzed with fear and horror, unable to move. The Indian began loading his gun and was looking significantly at me and my sister Amelia, who sat by my side. Suddenly I regained my self-control and believing that I would be the next victim, I started up and ran wildly in an indefinite direction. Accidentally I came to where my father lay. He had on a checked shirt, the back of which was covered with blood, the shot having passed clear through his body. (*Captured*, 9)[11]

The initial attack was just the start because harsh treatment and primitive living conditions generally characterized the forced march that followed. Remaining family members were usually separated, food was scarce, communication was difficult, and physical stamina among the wounded and stunned women captives was not great. Again and again, the narratives stress how alien the wilderness experience was for the stereotypical victimized woman. Rampant ethnocentrism blinkered captives of both genders, but especially females, and rendered cultural differences even more threatening. Therefore, accounts of torture cannot be taken at face value: sometimes the captive may have misjudged or misremembered what she saw; at other times, the figure of an injured or tortured woman was exploited for propaganda.

While most references to physical torture among women see the American Indians as the perpetrators, a smaller number show the indirect victimization and privation of women as they tried to evade, or escape from, the Indians. A clear instance occurs in *An Authentic Narrative* (1836) by Mary Godfrey who, when attacked by Seminoles in Florida, fled into a swamp with her four daughters.[12] After four days in hiding, they made some noise that attracted the attention of an escaped slave fighting with the Seminoles. He was about to tomahawk them, but Godfrey begged him to spare her children (significantly, all girls):

. . . the negro dropped his axe, and after contemplating the sad spectacle for a few moments, appeared much affected, and broke silence by assuring Mrs. G. that she had nothing to fear, that neither herself or her children should be hurt—that he had two children who were held in bondage by the whites, that to enjoy his own liberty he had left them to their fate, and something now seemed to whisper him, that if he should destroy the lives of her innocent children, God would be angry, and might doom his little ones to a similar fate by the hands of the white men in whose power they were! (*MG*, 10)

He brought food to the family, but they underwent great privations as long as they were forced to remain in the swampy area. Later and longer fictional accounts sometimes introduced exotic wild animals—including panthers—as additional dangers beyond the elements.

The Godfrey narrative, whether fact or fiction, is also significant because the slave, called "'the humane African (our deliverer)'" (*MG*, 12), is the agent by which five females are spared bondage and family dispersal. Like the African slaves, Indian captives could be bought and sold and families could be separated and lose their identity. Captivity and slavery are linked in evil precisely because they sacrificed the family for economic ends. Thus a very real fear especially for women captives was that they would be physically victimized as slaves. Many women's captivities make explicit references to enslavement. In the related Horn/Harris/Plummer narratives discussed in chapter one, Sarah Ann Horn, for example, calls herself "a lonely exile, in the bonds of savage slavery," in her *Narrative* (1839), while Caroline Harris refers at the end of her *History of the Captivity* (1838) to the forthcoming publication by her "unfortunate friend and late companion in misery" in these words: "The narrative of Mrs. Plummer, (which is now preparing for the press, and will be issued in a few days,) will comprise a faithful, although sorrowful detail of her sufferings from the day of her capture to that of her liberation from savage bondage" (*Horn*, 41; *CH*, 22–23).

Another well-known instance of enslavement concerned Olive and Mary Ann Oatman, the daughters of a Mormon farmer from Illinois. In 1851, the family set off westward to help establish a renegade Mormon (Brewsterite) community on the Colorado River. While crossing the Arizona desert, they were attacked by Yavapai raiders, who took 13-year-old Olive and her younger sister, Mary Ann, captive. The rest of the family died, except the girls' brother Lorenzo, who survived his wounds. Their story "provides perhaps the best account of female prisoners by Indians of the Southwestern deserts" (Heard, 85). After marching more than 200 miles in three days, Olive and Mary Ann reached the village where they would stay for one year. The first edition of their story, *Life among the Indians* (1857), was told to editor Royal B. Stratton, who states that the Indian women "were *the* laborers, and principal burden-bearers, 'and during all of our captivity,' says Olive, 'it was our lot to serve under these enslaved women, with a severity more intolerable than that by which they were subjected to [*sic*] their merciless lords.'"[13] A third, revised, edition in 1858, *Captivity of the Oatman Girls*, clarifies this particular passage regarding Olive and Mary Ann: "Their fate was clear. They were now slaves."[14] Indeed, they were slaves to slaves. After the first year in captivity, during which the Yavapais relaxed their extreme discipline somewhat, the two sisters were sold to Mohaves, who treated them more humanely. But for reasons that remain unclear—whether to dissuade the girls from escaping, or to hasten their assimilation into the tribal culture as slaves, initiates, or wives—the Mohaves tattooed their faces. Written information on this ritual was omitted from the first edition, and a print of Olive with tattoos on her chin did not appear until the concluding chapter; the second edition described the tattooing in some detail and published the same print of Olive as a frontispiece.[15] Ultimately, only Olive rejoined white culture in 1856; Mary Ann had starved during a famine (see the photograph of Olive Oatman after her return to white society, Fig. 6).

A final manifestation of physical victimization beyond torture and slavery concerned food deprivation. Most obviously, many captives had to face either eating what was to them culturally unacceptable food or starving. Puritan Hannah Swarton could not eat anything at first, and by

Photograph of Olive Oatman after her forcible return to white society in 1856 showing the facial tattoos she received while living among the Mohaves. Oatman's Indian name was Aliutman. *Courtesy of the Arizona Historical Society/Tucson.*

the time she had regained her appetite, the English food was gone, so she ate whatever was available: acorns, purslain, hogsweed, dog flesh, moose liver, and bear (*HS*, 52). During a forced march, little time was allowed for regular eating because speed was needed to outpace pursuers. If the captives remained in an American Indian camp for any time, they realized that many tribes did not, or could not, lay up stores of food, so that food gathering was a continual activity and starvation an ever-present possibility for all. In frontier white and Indian culture, women were largely responsible for gathering and preparing (but not hunting for) food, and this may explain the constant references to food pathways in many women's accounts. Quaker Elizabeth Hanson mentions in *God's Mercy Surmounting Man's Cruelty* (1728), "But the greatest Difficulty that deserves the first to be named, was Want of Food, having at Times nothing to eat but Pieces of old Beaver-Skin-Match Coats . . . and they were used more for Food than Rayment" (*EH*, 12).

Another agonizing aspect for many women, especially mothers, was how food should be allotted during lean times. Some tribes were loath to feed weak captives who might die anyway, and these were usually women and children. Additionally, there may have been other tribal practices concerning women's food allowance. For instance, the Oatman narrative specifies that tribal culture did not allow young women to eat meat unless starving, "which, considering their main reliance as a tribe upon game, was equal to dooming their females to starvation" (*Oatman 2*, 115). While some mothers deprived themselves of food in the short term to provide for their captive children, they realized that they needed to remain alive to provide long-term protection. Mothers particularly were caught in this dilemma: how to sacrifice enough for their children without starving themselves to death and orphaning those who depended on them?

The effects of inadequate food on mothers finds expression in detailed information on breast-feeding. Elizabeth Hanson clarifies the connection between lack of food and the resulting lack of breast milk: "My daily Travel and hard Living made my Milk dry almost quite up, and how to preserve my poor Babe's Life was no small Care on my Mind" (*EH*, 13). Many narratives include the detail that a woman was captured as she was nursing her baby, and the child-at-breast/child-in-arms motif recurs throughout the captivity literature. Yet a surprising number of eighteenth- and nineteenth-century narratives include even more intimate information on the difficulties of breast-feeding. For example, in House's edition of Sarah Ann Horn's captivity, there are literally numerous references to the "broken breasts" (*Horn*, 16) of Horn's sister captive, Caroline Harris. Horn as narrator continues, "Poor Mrs. H. suffered extremely with her breasts" (*Horn*, 21), and a few pages later, "I begged and obtained leave to pay some attention to Mrs. Harris' breasts. I found they had broken and were in a wretched condition" (*Horn*, 23), and so on, and so on. Why should narratives include such intimate information on painful breasts?

One example of the theme of "outraged maternity" concerns William Hubbard's seventeenth-century account of a young woman killed by Indians while breast-feeding an infant. Although the mother was dead, "they nayled the young Child to the dead body of its mother, which was found sucking in that rueful manner, when the People came to the Place" (quoted in Ulrich, 173–74). Yet although this theme is potentially significant in all of the women's captivity literature, there may be another reason why it is especially emphasized in the eighteenth- and nineteenth-century accounts. Traditionally, breast-feeding has been practiced not only for nourishing a baby, but also for its contraceptive effect. (We now know that if it is carried out frequently, it can cause hormonal changes that delay ovulation until after the child is weaned. Though highly unreliable, it was one of the only birth control methods available in early times.) In the seventeenth-century New England captivities, breast imagery receives relatively little attention because rape by Native Americans in that region was rare. In later accounts involving other tribes that were more likely to rape captive women, foregrounding this motif may have triggered an unstated (perhaps prurient) assumption among readers: if the women were raped while they were lactating, at least conception would not occur, but with interrupted lactation and stopped milk flow, then conception could occur. The earlier narratives merely toyed with the possibility of rape, but the later ones were more likely to deal with the greater probability of rape and subsequent childbirth.

While inadequate and unfamiliar food resulted in physical distress, and while this may have contributed to difficulties in breast-feeding, two other food-related areas involved taboos for many women: eating dog flesh and human flesh. (These were taboos for both men and women, of course, but particularly for women who symbolized the more "genteel" of the two genders.) Typical of the received response to killing and eating dogs is Minnie Buce Carrigan's recollection of Sioux preparations for a dog feast: "On investigation I saw a most disgusting spectacle. Side by side, with their throats cut and their feet in the air, lay a number of dogs.

I returned to the tent sickened by the sight, but in a little while my curiosity got the better of my sensations and I went out again. By this time the Indians were singeing the hair off the dogs with burning hay. I recognized our little white poodle among the carcasses" (*Captured*, 16). She says she would rather starve than eat dog. Carrigan partly excuses her ethnocentrism by adding that she has since found out that "they were religious feasts and indulged in only by warriors, who on this occasion were preparing for battle" (*Captured*, 16). But the image that haunts the (white) reader is the pet poodle about to be eaten in a three-day ritual; indeed, perhaps it was the ritualistic aspect of the dog feast that was particularly repugnant. Faced with starvation, however, captives and survivors were more willing to compromise. So Emeline Fuller, who at age 13 fled an Indian attack and led into the wilderness an infant and four other children, plainly states that after three days without food, "we killed our faithful family dog, that had shared our hardships through all that long journey" (*Left*, 21). The little band also killed a neighbor's dog, prudently saving some of the meat for the onward journey instead of eating it all at once. Fuller's survivalist history also suggests that if the women were in charge, they would take responsibility for their actions, but they would not be coerced by Indians into violating a taboo.

A still deeper taboo—but one that could also be broken *in extremis* by the victimized woman—concerned cannibalism. Ritual slaughter is not a factor in the women's captivity literature, but occasionally—especially in the factual accounts—descriptions of the captives eating human flesh to avoid death from starvation are found. For example, after eating dog, then horse, Emeline Fuller and the other survivors ate the bodies of those who died, including Fuller's little sister. Equally—if not more—horrifying is the well-known story of the California emigrants known as the Donner party, whose cattle and other provisions were raided by Indians. The group was forced to winter in a remote mountain camp and to splinter off into smaller expeditionary parties—some guided by friendly native inhabitants—to seek help. Ironically, one emigrant, Mr. Foster, killed two of these Indians for food. When survivors were finally discovered in some of the primitive cabins at the Mountain Camp, "parts of human bodies were found prepared for eating," and at a further camp aptly called Starved Camp, a married couple, the Brinns, survived by repeated cannibalism of two children and a woman.[16] A man called Kiesburg had come to prefer human flesh "even when other food was to be obtained" (Frost, 261). The retelling of this and 39 other stories in John Frost's *Heroic Women of the West* (1854) bears out his stated claim in the preface that "The heroism of woman is the heroism of the heart" (iii). Accordingly, amidst the grim details of the Donner story, he foregrounds unselfish acts by women and concludes, "Amidst events almost too frightful for thought, the wife was found ready to sacrifice herself for her husband, and the mother for her children," and "when to save themselves from death, men became brutes, woman's true nobility shone forth in all its splendor" (Frost, 266–67). Frost's Victorian mentality blinkers him to his inconsistencies, for example that some of the women (including Mrs. Brinn) did resort to cannibalism. Instead, he prefers to stress their familial role as all-giving wives and mothers.

Yet physical victimization in the form of abuse, slavery, and starvation was only part of the story. Another serious fear concerned the sexual victimization of captive women. An objective assessment of the reality, rather than the myth, of rape would require information over several centuries about many different tribes, which may now be irretrievable.[17] But as we know, women captives of the Southern Plains Indians had more to fear than their earlier Northern sisters. Lonnie J. White's article "White Women Captives of Southern Plains Indians, 1866–1875" examines letters, oral statements, newspaper clippings, public records, diaries, and government reports to survey the cases of many Plains women captives (White, 327–54). While media sensationalism was certainly a factor in the nineteenth century, these other kinds of external evidence also support the conclusion that rape did occur. A *Leavenworth Daily Times* article on the Box Massacre in Texas in August 1866, and the women survivors' capture by Kiowas, reports: "'The mother and the two eldest daughters were subjected to the most unheard of cruelties and outrages by their brutal captors'" (quoted in White, 332). During their ten-week captivity, the women had apparently been repeatedly raped; after her rescue, the eldest daughter, Margaret, reportedly gave birth to a child fathered by an Indian (White, 332). Major General Philip J. Sheridan, in his personal memoirs, recalls an incident on Spillman Creek, in Kansas, where a woman named Mrs. Shaw and her sister "were raped by thirty Indians 'until long after they had become senseless'" (quoted in White, 335).

An interesting, though inconclusive, perspective can be gained by considering the story of the German family, first as reconstructed from documentary evidence in White's article, and second as retold by Grace E. Meredith, Catherine German's niece, in *Girl Captives of the Cheyennes* (1927).[18] The German family was attacked by Cheyennes near Fort Wallace, Kansas, on 11 September 1874, en route to Colorado. Five family members—including both parents—were killed; the four remaining daughters, Catherine, age 17; Sophia, age 12; Julia, age seven; and Addie, age five were captured. After a few days, the Indians left the two youngest girls on the prairie after pursuit by soldiers. Frightened and weak after wandering for several weeks, they were rescued. Catherine and Sophia were not freed until February 1875 when the Cheyennes under Stone Calf and Grey Beard, among others, surrendered to General Nelson A. Miles (White, 349). In a letter to the Commissioner of Indian Affairs, Indian Agent John D. Miles mentioned specific Indians who had either raped the girls themselves or who had acted as their pimps. White says that according to two newspaper stories, Catherine was pregnant when she was freed (350).

Grace Meredith, Catherine's niece by marriage, claims to correct previously inaccurate accounts of the nationally publicized captivity by access to "first-hand, definite and accurate information" (v) from all four sisters and from other reliable sources. She tells the story through Catherine as narrator. Yet her audience is children (she refers to them directly on page 40, for example, where she says, "To you children who think your faces have to be washed too often, I will say that the Indians never asked me to wash my face"), and the closest she comes to mentioning anything sexual is when she says Catherine almost becomes the wife of a young brave (51–52). In this area at least, Meredith ignores or omits the very real sexual harassment, if not actual rape, that the sisters faced, in order to sanitize the story for children.

As might be expected, many Victorian women in the West were loath to admit that they themselves had been sexually abused; instead, they tried to claim that while other women had been harmed, they had been (miraculously, inexplicably) spared. In the case of the wife and daughter of M. C. Meeker, the Ute agent, both of them "reluctantly acknowledged that they had been raped the night following the attack on the agency" (Heard, 101). Women who returned from captivity presumably downplayed evidence of sexual abuse. If pregnancy occurred before rescue, some women chose to remain with the American Indians either because they would be outcasts if they returned or because they had formed genuine bonds. The personal price of such a choice is evident in the poignant story of a Mexican woman among the Comanches, found in 1838 by the Santa Fe trader Josiah Gregg. Kidnapped from the home of her father, the Governor of Chihuahua, she refused to return even after he offered a substantial reward: "'She sent word to her father that they had disfigured her by tattooing; that she was married . . . and that she would be made more unhappy by returning to her father under these circumstances than by remaining where she was'" (story quoted in Heard, 101). This woman may never have been more than acculturated into Comanche culture; more willing captives became transculturated. But whether raped then rescued, or raped and remaining with her abductors, the abused wife, daughter, or mother would never have the same relationship with her family of origin.

To stress victimization, the two classes of females most often mentioned in connection with rape were adolescents and mothers still of childbearing age (either pregnant and/or nursing at time of capture). The image of "outraged virginity" was a powerful propagandist tool, and the crime gained added dimensions from the underlying belief that the American Indians were despoiling the future mothers of a generation of whites, not merely the present ones, by either traumatizing or transculturating them. Thus, in the white popular imagination, family life was disrupted, perhaps destroyed, over the very generations that were supposed to be peopling the West—a point that June Namias stresses in her work on captivity narratives.

The frontispiece to *Narrative of the Capture and Providential Escape of Misses Frances and Almira Hall* (1832) is captioned, "Two Young Ladies Taken Prisoners by the Savages, May 1832," and the title page contains a plot summary describing them as "Two respectable young women (sisters) of the ages of 16 and 18." Based on the purported captivity of Sylvia and Rachel Hall by Sauk and Fox Indians in Illinois, this account is nevertheless highly sensationalized and romanticized: the Hall sisters learn that their lives have been spared so they can marry two young chiefs, who, to their surprise, treat them chivalrically and hand them to the Winnebagos for return to their home. This publication also quotes the text of a broadside circulated to publicize the plight of the real Hall sisters: "WAR! WAR!! WAR!!!" it begins; the second line continues, "WOMEN AND CHILDREN BUTCHERED!" and the third line explains, *"Two young ladies taken by the Savages"* (*Hall*, 17). Lest the reader not grasp the significance of the third, italicized, line, the broadside elaborates in its opening paragraph, "Two highly respectable young women of 16 and 18 years of age, are in the hands of the Indians, and if not already murdered, are perhaps reserved for a more cruel and savage fate" (*Hall*, 18).

With the move to outright fiction, phallic symbolism and overt description sometimes became sensationally overwritten. For example, the faked atrocity story titled *An Affecting Narrative of the Captivity and*

Sufferings Mrs. Mary Smith (1815) contains details of the death of Smith's two daughters, ages eleven and nineteen, taken virtually verbatim from the fictitious Manheim narratives, first published in 1793 (Levernier and Cohen, 64). The two girls were stripped, tied hands above head to saplings, pierced with pine splinters dipped in turpentine (described in rape imagery as "standing erect on the bleeding victims") that were then set on fire. The girls are termed "ill fated females" (*MS*, 10), "forlorn girls" (*MS*, 10), "bleeding victims" (*MS*, 11), and finally—significantly—"helpless virgins" as they sank "down in the arms of their deliverer, Death" (*MS*, 11). The phallic imagery of the stake and the "erect" pine arrows, the arrows' multiple violation of the girls' flesh, the copious bleeding recalling the (believed) breaking of the hymen with the loss of virginity, the orgasmic fire, and the screams not of ecstasy, but of agony, provided a permissibly prurient variation of the offstage rape scene in domestic and sentimental novels and dramas. While the trope of the adolescent virgin is present throughout all the captivity literature, it is most evident in those late eighteenth- and early nineteenth-century narratives heavily influenced by sentimental fiction. In the seventeenth- and early eighteenth-century accounts, the American Indians are devils, and it was the devil, in Calvinist belief, who tempted women's souls to eternal bondage (God, however, encouraged women's and men's souls to join Him in an eternal marriage). In the less spiritual, more secular, accounts of the late eighteenth and early nineteenth centuries, the American Indians have become the villains of melodrama, and the young women they torture and rape the "helpless virgins" of sentimental fiction who are deflowered and then die.

A third area of victimization concerns the spiritual, whose earlier counterpart among male captivities showed Jesuit priests' martyrdom. The aspect of women's spiritual abuse is obvious primarily in the stories where Puritan prisoners not only suffered for their faith but were coerced to adopt Catholicism by American Indian converts or, once in Canada, by French clergy and laity. While the women's physical safety initially concerned them the most, their spiritual survival was rarely far from their thoughts: captivity in this life by native inhabitants viewed as devils was harsh, but temporal; whereas in the life to come, damnation brought eternal captivity in hell. Cotton Mather says as much in *Humiliations Follow'd with Deliverances*, exhorting a congregation that included the recently delivered captive Hannah Dustan and her two cohorts, Mary Neff and Samuel Lennardson, "You are not now the Slaves of *Indians*, as you were a few days ago; but if you continue *Unhumbled*, in your sins, you will be the Slaves of *Devils*; and, let me tell you, A Slavery to *Devils*, to be in *Their* Hands, is worse than to be in the Hands of *Indians*!" (*Humiliations*, 49). Or as Hannah Swarton stated after finally reaching relative safety in Canada in 1690:

Here was a great and comfortable Change, as to my *Outward man*, in my *Freedom* from my former Hardships, and Hard hearted Oppressors. But here began a greater Snare and Trouble to my Soul and Danger to my *Inward man*. For the Lady my Mistress, the Nuns, the Priests, Friars, and the rest, set upon me with all the strength of *Argument* they could, from *Scripture*, as they interpreted it, to perswade me to Turn *Papist*; which they pressed with very much Zeal, Love, Intreaties, and *Promises*, if I would Turn to them, and with many *Threatnings*, and sometimes Hard Usages, because I did not Turn to their Religion. (*HS*, 62–63)

Swarton was torn between the difficulty of maintaining a faith she believed and the ease of adopting a faith she did not believe. That spiritual victimization was a particular peril of women is evident in Swarton's wry observation that it was pointless to write down the arguments she used in combating the Catholics because she was a mere woman (and by inference, since her largely male readership would not be interested in hearing those arguments): "But its bootless for *me* a poor Woman, to acquaint the World, with what Arguments I used, if I could now Remember them; and many of them are slipt out of my memory" (*HS*, 64). Therefore, women were at double risk because their inferior intellect first, would not let them defend their beliefs very convincingly, and second, would allow them to be more easily swayed by others' arguments. But Swarton's obstinacy paid off: when it was clear she would not convert, the French backed off and left her alone.

In *Good Fetch'd Out of Evil* (1706), Cotton Mather's collection of "certain *Memorables* occurring to these *Children of the Captivity*" (*Good*, 1), he warns his readers that "The *French* use all the means imaginable, to Seduce their *Captives* unto the Idolatries and Superstitions of the Church of *Rome*. Their *Clergy* especially, are indefatigable in their Endeavours to *Captivate* the Minds of these Poor People, unto the *Romish* Religion" (*Good*, 21). His rhetoric of seduction and his wordplay (captive/captivate) again suggest the special temptation for women. Some pages later, Mather includes a poem by the captive Mary French, age 16 or 17, urging her captive sister to resist "the Popish Delusions" (*Good*, 29). In a series of 26 verses, French begs her sister to keep the faith and remember the role of affliction in strengthening the spirit:

Let us be Silent then this day
under our Smarting Rod.
Let us with Patience Meekly say,
It is the Will of God. (11. 65–68, *Good*, 32)

To convert to Catholicism inevitably meant transculturation and further
fracture of the original family unit. Small wonder, then, that Mather
included Mary French's plea.

Victors and Vanquishers

> One of these women took up a Resolution, to Imitate the Action of *Jael*
> upon *Sisera*, and being where she had not her *own life* secured by any *Law*
> unto her, she thought she was not forbidden by any *Law*, to take away
> the *Life*, of the *Murderers*, by whom her *Child* had been butchered. She
> heartened the *Nurse*, and the *Youth*, to assist her, in this Enterprise. . . .
> But cutting off the Scalps of the *Ten Wretches*, who had Enslav'd 'em, they
> are come off; and I perceive, that newly arriving among us, they are in
> the assembly at this Time, to give Thanks unto, *God their Saviour*
> —Cotton Mather, *Humiliations Follow'd with Deliver-
> ances* (1697)

> The heroism of woman is the heroism of the heart. Her deeds of daring
> and endurance are prompted by affection. While her husband, her
> children, and all the other objects of tenderness are safe, her heroic
> capabilities repose in peace, and external troubles have little power to
> disturb her serenity. But when danger threatens the household, when the
> lurking savage is seen near the dwelling, or the war-whoop is heard in
> the surrounding woods, the matron becomes a heroine, and is ready to
> peril life, without a moment's hesitation, in the approaching conflict.
> —John Frost, *Heroic Women of the West* (1854)

This section examines those women who fought against the odds not
only to save themselves but to keep the family together and to avenge its
destruction—in other words, those women who became victors and
vanquishers. Although victimization is the most common image of
women in captivity, victory forms "the aggressive inversion of that
image" (Gherman, 34). As victims, women remained passive and reinforced age-old stereotypes; as vanquishers, they became active and challenged those stereotypes. Unlike their passive sisters, who believed their
lives were out of control during, and even after, captivity, the victors and

vanquishers retaliated: they took matters into their own hands, made certain choices, and thus exerted some control over their fate. Almost always, the catalyst arose from their response to their role as protectors within the family, especially when husbands, fathers, sons, or brothers were absent or immobilised. The captivity literature presents various strategies by which women outwitted their (male) oppressors: through physical, intellectual, and spiritual means. When the accounts are documentary, the narrator generally justifies her actions as self-defense, but when an editor retells the story, or when it is fictional, the mediator's own ethics color his or her view. In the first scenario, the ends always justify the means; in the second, this is not necessarily the case.

The story of Hannah Dustan dramatically exemplifies the complexities of the three aspects of women as victor (or victrix).[19] It first appeared in Cotton Mather's *Humiliations Follow'd with Deliverances* (1697), which contains four parts: the text of a sermon on humiliation as a necessary step to conversion; the story of Dustan's captivity and escape, titled "A Narrative of a Notable Deliverance from Captivity," and told in the third person; Mather's interpretation (in his seventeenth-century terminology, his "improvement") of the narrative; and an appendix containing the first-person account of Hannah Swarton's captivity and release. When Mather first preached parts one, two, and three, Dustan was in the congregation, listening as the famous minister used her story for its typological significance.

Just having given birth to a child in spring 1697, Hannah Dustan was lying in tended by her nurse, Mary Neff, when the house was attacked by Indians. Dustan's husband shepherded the other seven children to safety; the infant was killed; and Dustan, Neff, and others were captured. The two women, later joined by an English youth named Samuel Lennardson, were marched toward a location where they would have to run the gauntlet. En route, while the Indians were in a *"Dead Sleep*, ('twill presently prove so!)" Mather cannot resist adding, the three prisoners carried out a plan conceived by Dustan and killed 10 of their captors with hatchets (*Humiliations*, 46). Only a squaw and a young boy escaped.

The English were now free to canoe back down the Merrimack River. Why, then, did they risk precious time to stop and scalp all 10 corpses? Lennardson had been a captive for 18 months, and Samuel Sewall says in his diary that Lennardson's American Indian master had shown him how to scalp, yet apparently he was not the ringleader.[20] Mather unequivocally states that Dustan "heartened the *Nurse*, and the *Youth*, to assist her, in this Enterprise" (*Humiliations*, 46). Did they scalp out of revenge, out of fear their story would not be believed, out of a sense of righteousness, or out of greed? In 1694, the Massachusetts Bay Colony had established the huge bounty of £50 per Indian scalp; this was reduced to £25 in 1695; and it was repealed altogether in December 1696, only a few months before Dustan's capture. Nonetheless, Thomas Dustan successfully petitioned the Legislature to offer his wife and her accomplices a special bounty, reasoning thus:

That the wife of ye petitioner (with one Mary Neff) hath, in her late captivity among the barbarous Indians, been disposed & assisted by Heaven to do an extraordinary action, in the just slaughter of so many of the barbarians, as would by the law of the Province which a few months ago would have entitled the actors unto considerable recompense from the Public. . . . that the merit of the action still remains the same; & it seems a matter of universal desire thro' the whole Province that it should not pass unrecompensed. And that your petitioner having lost his estate in that calamity wherein his wife was carried into her captivity, render him the fitter object of what consideration the Public bounty shall judge proper. . . .[21]

In other words, Thomas Dustan claimed that Hannah's action was so "extraordinary" it was Heaven-directed; that the slaying was "just"; that only a few months before, the death of 10 "barbarians" would have made Hannah a very wealthy woman; that despite legal formalities (such as the law actually changing), the "merit" of the action remained the same; that public pressure demanded an exception in this case; and that therefore any money deemed appropriate would help the Dustans recover from their financial losses. The arguments worked: from a total of £50 the public treasury gave £25 to Hannah Dustan and £12–6s each to Neff and Lennardson. The settlement was made in June 1697, three months after Mather delivered his sermon.[22] Such a public attestation to Old Testament ethics could have helped sway the Legislature (a scalp for a scalp, or actually, 10 scalps to avenge the death of Dustan's baby). Dustan was feted in Boston and plied with gifts, including a pewter tankard from the Great and General Court of Massachusetts.

Hannah Dustan's maiden name was Emerson, and *Emerson* was also a household name in Massachusetts because Elizabeth, Hannah's unmarried sister, had been accused of infanticide and hanged after an infamous trial only four years earlier (Ulrich, 184–86). In 1693, Mather had preached Elizabeth's execution sermon, decrying her guilt and seeing her as the individual blot on the community; in 1697, he preached a humiliation sermon, praising Hannah's bravery and using her individual accomplishment as a special providence for the entire community. Mather, the Emersons, and the Dustans must have understood only too well the inherent ironies of their family affairs. Ulrich reminds us, "The two sisters touch opposite margins of a larger fabric of female violence in northern New England" (185), but because they acted in different contexts, their cases were rather a cause for marvel than for meditation on a predisposition toward family violence. Elizabeth's act of rending the family fabric by suffocating her twin babies was evil; Hannah's act of avenging her newborn baby's death by murdering its murderers was heroic. The crucial criterion by which both examples of violence were judged concerned a private (individual) and a public (communal) response to family. And within that framework, context was all.

Elizabeth was hanged in June 1693, still protesting she was innocent of infanticide, though in a written confession she acknowledged that her sin lay in disobeying her parents by being rebellious and becoming pregnant out of wedlock (Ulrich, 201). Hannah slipped back into the obscurity of daily routine after her temporary fame faded. But unlike most women captives whose postcaptivity life remains unknown, a fascinating document provides us with a coda to Dustan's narrative. Dustan was 40 when she was captured, and despite her presence in the congregation at Cotton Mather's North Church in Boston, she was not a church member at the time. However, in 1724, at age 67, she applied for admission to the church at Haverhill by submitting—as required—a brief conversion narrative (see Fig. 7). The most important parts of this letter are reproduced below:

I Desire to be Thankful that I was born in a Land of Light & Baptized when I was Young: and had a Good Education by My Father, Tho I took but little Notice of it in the time of it:—I am Thankful for my Captivity, twas the Comfortablest time that ever I had: In my Affliction God made his Word Comfortable to me. I remembered 43d ps. ult—and those words came to my mind—ps. 118.17. . . . I have had a great Desire to come to the Ordinance of the Lords Supper a Great while but fearing I should give offence & fearing my own unworthiness has kept me back; reading a Book concerning +'s Suffering Did much awaken me. . . . I desire the Church to receive me tho' it be at the Eleventh hour; & pray for me—that I may hon'r God and obtain the Salvation of my Soul. (quoted in Kilgore, 13–14)

What on earth did she mean by calling her traumatic experience "the Comfortablest time that ever I had" and in repeating that God had made

her affliction "Comfortable" to her? Certainly Dustan was using an
archaic meaning of these words as in the *OED*'s definition of *comfortable* as
"strengthening or supporting (morally or spiritually)." Twenty-seven
years after her captivity, she still identified it as the central experience of
her life, but in this document she wisely emphasized its private aspect,
namely, its role in strengthening her faith, rather than its public aspect.
For her public role had led to notoriety and material gain, hardly model
qualifications for one of the Elect. Dustan was mistaken in thinking she
was at "the Eleventh hour" in 1724; she lived another 12 years and died
in 1736 at the advanced age of 79. According to local lore, Dustan was
buried in an unmarked grave for fear of Indian retaliation.

As Rowlandson is the prototype of woman as victim, Dustan is the
prototype of woman as victor. Her conquest covers physical superiority
(she overpowered the Indians), intellectual superiority (she outwitted
them), and spiritual superiority (her Puritanism proved more powerful
than her captors' tribal religion or their adopted Christian denomina-
tion, Catholicism). Moreover, Mather at once sensed the mythic resonance of Dustan's story, which many later retellings have reinforced
either as avenged motherhood acting *in extremis* or as perverted motherhood exceeding the bounds of respectability. Thus Hawthorne and
Thoreau, in their recastings, see her as a mythic, but nonmaternal, figure,
and Hawthorne twists the family roles further by presenting Thomas
Dustan, who after all led seven of his children to safety, as far more
stereotypically maternal than his wife.

The logical extension of the Dustan story is perhaps the sketch "Sal
Fink, the Mississippi Screamer: How She Cooked Injuns," an example of
Old Southwest Humor first published in the *Crockett Almanac for 1854*[23]
(see Fig. 8). Sal is the daughter of Mike Fink, the historic figure whose
"extravagant, sometimes virtually mythic accomplishments" made him,
like Davy Crockett, into a legend (Levernier and Cohen, 186). Sal
"fought a duel once with a thunderbolt, an' came off without a singe,"
but "the greatest feat she ever did, positively outdid anything that ever
was did" (Levernier and Cohen, 188). Captured by 50 Indians and carried
to "Roast flesh Hollow," Sal "burst all the ropes about her like an apron
string!" and extracted a suitably grisly revenge: "She then found a pile o'
ropes, took and tied all the Injun's heels together all round the fire,—
then fixin a cord to the shins of every two couple, she, with a sudden-
achous jerk, that made the intire woods tremble, pulled the intire lot o'
sleepin' red-skins into that ar great fire, fast together, an' then sloped like
a panther out of her pen, in the midst o' the tallest yellin, howlin,

The comic figure Sal Fink, daughter of the legendary folk-hero Mike Fink, taken from the *Crockett Almanac for 1854*. This illustration accompanied an account of her exploits titled, "Sal Fink, the Mississippi Screamer. How She Cooked Indians," which is an example of Southwest frontier humor. *Courtesy of the American Antiquarian Society.*

scramblin and singin', that war ever seen or heerd on, since the great burnin' o' Buffalo prairie!" (Levernier and Cohen, 188). The exclamations, the righteousness, the vengefulness, the sensationalization, the glee—these are all in keeping with the tradition of the woman victor established by Cotton Mather in his retelling of Dustan's exploits. While Mather would not have approved of the fictional basis of "Sal Fink," even he might have cracked a smile of recognition at the exaggeration and—as he would perceive it—the justness of the conclusion.

Many narratives contain an instance of a woman's bravery but still define her as essentially victimized. Fewer narratives define a woman as the victimizer and recount her deeds. Those women who are defined as vanquishers tend to be either matrons (mothers) or virgins (unmarried, young, teenage girls). As physical and sexual victimization are the most pronounced images in section one, so victory over those potential perils forms the most important element in this section. With the traditional de-emphasis of women's mental capabilities, physical self-reliance brought on by crisis is more evident than intellectual strategizing, though sometimes women win in the captivity literature through a combination of both.

Many of Frost's 40 retellings of women's captivities in *Heroic Women of the West* (1854) show a violent line of descent from their progenitress, Hannah Dustan (though whether directly influenced by Mather as source is another matter). In his introduction, Frost stresses that female aggression arises from a threat to family and that this response defines female heroism: "Captured and dragged away from her home, she endures fatigue, braves danger, bears contumely, and sometimes deals the death-blow to the sleeping captors, to save the lives of her children" (iv). Sometimes, however, the captors were very much awake when such women acted in self-defense.

During Pontiac's Rebellion, Mrs. Porter, for example, was alone at her house on the Pennsylvania/Virginia border when it was attacked. Because her husband was a militia captain, sword and rifle were readily available, so she grabbed them. She hacked two of the Indians to death with the sword and shot the third. After she ran to safety, other Indians burned the house "partly from revenge, and partly to conceal the evidence of their discomfiture by a woman," says Frost (21). In another story, the Merril family of Kentucky found itself under attack in 1787, and when Mr. Merril was wounded, his wife fended off seven Indians. "A perfect Amazon," Frost editorializes (79), she axed four of them; emptied the feathers from a mattress to stoke the fire when others tried to come down the chimney; and used the axe again to wound the last man, who ran off to report "the fierceness, strength, and courage of the 'long knife squaw!'" (Frost, 80). Another woman, Experience (Elizabeth) Bozarth, defended her home in Pennsylvania when it was stormed in 1779. She too wreaked vengeance by wielding an axe and wounding or killing at least three Indians. Frost's fidelity to his often vaguely identified sources and their fidelity to fact are of course open to question. Writing in the midnineteenth century, Frost's editorializing seems aimed at rationalizing how "the Angel in the House" could become "the Avenging Angel on the Homestead."

Frost's "twice-told tales" remove even the fact-based stories (for example, his account of the women in the Donner Party, which he titled "Wonderful Fortitude of Female Emigrants," and which took place only eight years before he published his book) into a semifictional realm. In the wholly fictional *An Affecting Narrative of the Captivity and Sufferings of Mrs. Mary Smith* (1815), Smith's two adolescent daughters were presented in stereotypically victimized images. The story of Smith herself shows the mother reacting violently to the deaths of her husband and daughters when she is faced with having to form a new family bond by forced marriage to a chief. Initially feigning compliance, she waited until they were alone and then stabbed and tomahawked him to death. She escaped into the wilderness, climbing trees to avoid detection and travelling by day so she was not endangered by the nocturnal "wild beasts" (*MS*, 14). Unable to hunt, she fortuitously found wild turkey eggs. At about this point, the narrative—as well its narrator—loses its way and relinquishes all credibility, for responding to voices she believed came from "some christian settlement" (*MS*, 17), Smith instead found herself recaptured by Kickapoos. This time there were more than 100 captors, so she dared not risk escape a second time. The only satisfactory resolution can be rescue by a large number of white males, which indeed is what happens, as Smith abruptly ends her narrative, "I was fortunately rescued from their merciless hands by Lieut. Brown and his brave little company of soldiers! FINIS" (*MS*, 18). A *deus ex machina* is thus the only way to finish the story and facilitate Smith's grateful reentry into a male-dominated society.

The above examples all concern matrons, but rape was a constantly perceived threat for all women, regardless of their marital status, and the impetus for escape might be attempted rape or talk of forced marriage. If the woman does not retaliate or escape (that is, if she remains passive), she is a stereotypical victim; if she acts, she may become a vanquisher. Some women in the captivity literature respond at the critical moment of sexual aggression. For example, in *A Surprizing Account of the Captivity of Miss Hannah Willis* (1799), almost certainly propaganda fiction, the protagonist is a young unmarried woman—a virgin—who is at risk of rape from two men: a Cherokee and his ally, a British soldier.[24] Willis was about to be burned at the stake when she fainted; as she regained consciousness, a British officer told her that he had rescued her by promising the Cherokees that she would marry a young chief the next day. But through political pressure, he thought he could release her from "'this cruel alternative, provided you will promise to allow me two things,—1st that you will permit me to take what liberties I please with you while I remain in this country, and 2d, on my leaving it that you will go with me—'" (*HW*, 9–10). Pretending to agree, she stabbed him at night, and before he died, he admitted that his intentions were dishonorable because he had intended to ruin her and then hand her back to the Cherokees. Even worse, he confessed that he had done the same thing twice before, so that Willis's action prevented catastrophe for her but also meted out just punishment for her two unlucky predecessors. His last words include the admission that his death was warranted, and that thereby "Injured innocence had obtained vengeance" (*HW*, 10). The brief 12-page narrative concludes as Willis meets her father at the ransacked house and is reabsorbed—unviolated—into her family.

The price young women paid for rebelliousness against the will of the family could be extreme, and one critic cites the case of Jane MacCrea, and the extensions and adaptations of her story, proving a political and sociological thesis (Namias, 234–82). In the eighteenth and nineteenth centuries, titles and title pages overtly draw attention to the marital status of the female protagonist. Thus, the titles of Willis's and Mac-Crea's narratives clearly designate "Miss," while examples of narratives using "Mrs." are legion. For example, the titles of 27 of Frost's 40 stories in *Heroic Women of the West* designate marital status somehow, either by "Miss" or "Mrs." or by some other clue, such as "The Wife and Daughters of Daniel Boone" or "The Widow Scraggs."

Apart from the women who overcame physical and sexual aggression by payment in kind, there were others who used their wits to effect an equally decisive victory. These women let their heads, not their hearts, rule them, and their methods were strategic rather than reactive. Thus Frost praises a number of his female protagonists for their coolness and calmness. Mrs. Neff, for instance, an eighteenth-century homesteader on the Pennsylvania/Virginia border, pretended to be resigned to her captivity, but, ever watchful for the right moment, she slipped away at night and evaded pursuit because she used her knowledge of the land so effectively. Frost comments on her "cool, determined spirit" (18) and "many good qualities of head and heart" (19). Another significant tale concerns Mrs. Clendennin, surprised in West Virginia in 1763 by Shawnees who first pretended friendship, then set upon the Greenbriar settlements. Clendennin, who witnessed the death of her husband and friends, remained levelheaded, refused to be intimidated, and lashed out with her tongue: "Indignant at the treachery and cruelty of the Indians, she loudly abused them, and taunted them with lacking the hearts of great warriors, who met their foes in fair and open conflict. The savages were astounded" (Frost, 24).

A Narrative of the Sufferings and Surprizing Deliverance of William and Elizabeth Fleming (1756), based on a true event and written to provide the destitute couple with funds, is interesting for its narrative approach. It tells the stories of husband and wife, captured and then separated by a hitch in their escape plans, and uses italics in parts of Elizabeth's narrative that seem like sentimentalized interpolations that contrast with the down-to-earth details in the nonitalicized, factual parts (*Fleming*). Throughout her portion of the narrative, Elizabeth Fleming shows her deductive abilities and survival instincts prevailing over the physical weakness of pregnancy. She begins her section recalling her fears of wolves, bears, and panthers, like an eighteenth-century fictional heroine, but she quickly adds, *"Yet I was not so lost and overwhelmed as to be incapable of Reflection; I remembred there was a just, a merciful and an Almighty Power who saw my Miseries"* (*Fleming*, 20). However, her reflectiveness does more than remind her of God: it reminds her she can choose between panicking or being levelheaded. Her ingenuity leads her to hide in an oven, a gum tree, and a pile of fodder to escape detection. But the clearest example of her mind winning over her emotions occurs as she wishes, in vain, for her husband to suddenly appear and help her, but then pulls herself together and finds her own solution: *"But I was now forlorn in the Wilderness, and had no other comfort than to sit down on the cold Earth, indulge my usual melancholic Reflections, and bathe my bleeding Feet with my Tears. This being done, I* tore off a few of the remaining Rags (for the Bushes had nigh deprived me of most of them) that my merciless Ravagers thought not worth taking from me, and with the Hem of my tottered [*sic*] Petticoat (for Gown I had none) tied them around my Feet, and returned the same way . . ." (*Fleming*, 26). We note the effective use of the italicized and nonitalicized portions. She and her husband are reunited, and her bravery saves herself and also (presumably) her baby, so the family unit, though battered, survives.

One factual and one fictional narrative indicate another way women could minimize harm and maximize their privileged position to save themselves and their children: by drawing on their knowledge—in these two cases, their knowledge of healing. In *The Story of My Capture and Escape* (1904), Helen Tarble describes how she and her husband became the first white family to live in Beaver Creek, Minnesota, and how she learned the Sioux language and socialized with the Sioux.[25] The principal medicine man befriended her and she became his assistant: "I was a ready and willing pupil," she observes (*Capture and Escape*, 20). When the Sioux Uprising began, she was shielded from harm for some time because she "was practically an adopted child of the Sioux and had the special protection of their great medicine man" (*Capture and Escape*, 22). Even after she escaped to Fort Ridgely, her knowledge of herbal remedies helped her and her children recover from starvation followed by overeating when more conventional treatment by the Fort physician failed. In the wholly fictional *Gertrude Morgan: Or, Life and Adventures among the Indians of the Far West* (1866), the heroine pretends to have healing knowledge and through ingenuity and luck succeeds in curing the wounded chief The Buffalo Horn, her captor.[26] As a result, "They now looked upon me as a being specially favored by the Great Spirit, and in short, to use their own expressive language, 'Great Medicine.' A portion of the lodge of *The Buffalo Horn* was devoted to my exclusive use; no one, not even that chieftain himself, ever intruding upon my privacy" (*GM*, 24). Her escape plans went awry even though she found—but apparently did not use—a compass, and she circled back to the very village she was trying to escape from. However, putting on a brave face, she rode into camp and found the tribe "looked upon my journey as '*Medicine*,' or '*a great mystery*'" (*GM*, 34). Still other narratives, including Mary Rowlandson's, show how women could "buy" privileges by drawing on domestic skills such as sewing and cooking.

In the earliest fact-based, generally Jesuit or Puritan, accounts, spiritual victory was ultimately more important than than any other victory. If we leave Jesuit narratives aside in this chapter because their narrators were male, one of the challenges for female captives, since they were considered the most likely to forget, was the message conveyed in Paul's Second Letter to the Corinthians, quoted here from the Geneva Bible—the version the Puritans used: "Therefore we faint not, but thogh our outwarde man perish, yet the inwarde man is renewed daily. For our light affliction which is but for a

moment, causeth unto us a farre moste excellent & an eternal waight of
glorie: While we loke not on the things which are sene, but on the things,
which are not sene: for the things which *are* sene are temporal: but the things
which are not sene, *are* eternal."[27] Ministers such as Cotton Mather and his
father, Increase Mather, were not likely to forget, and they very quickly
applied the typological significance of the true accounts to the state of the
Colony. Indeed, because the captives themselves as laity were limited in the
amount of spiritual interpretation they could grant their experience, they
needed a clerical editor or mentor to point it out. In *Good Fetch'd Out of Evil*,
Cotton Mather claims that "Astonishing Deliverances have been sent from
Heaven, to many of our Captives" (33), includes several brief accounts, then
adds, "We will supersede them all, with a Relation of what befel, Mrs.
Bradly of Haverhil. *Ab una Disce omnes*" (*Good*, 37–38). Indeed, the community of Haverhill had apparently been marked for special providences to two
of its women inhabitants: Hannah Dustan, whose exploits we have already
discussed, and Hannah Heath Bradley, who was captured twice within eight
years. Mather retells both these stories in the third person. Bradley's first
captivity lasted two years, after which her husband ransomed her from
Canada and they resumed their life together for six years. But in 1703,
Bradley was at home with her sister, some children, and only one man when
they were again attacked by Indians. Initially, she reacted violently by
pouring boiling soap over several of the attackers; she then bravely stepped
forward and accepted captivity to save her sister and a child, who had not
been detected. Bradley was pregnant, and the forced march brought on
labor. The child was born alive, but because she was not allowed to tend to
it and because it was abused by her captors, it "Starv'd, and dy'd" (*Good*, 42).
Eventually, she arrived in Quebec where a priest recognized her from before
and prevailed upon the Indians to sell her to a French family. There,
sometimes joined surreptitiously by a network of other Puritan women, she
prayed and became convinced that she would again be released and "*See the
Goodness of God*, in this land of the Living" (*Good*, 44). Indeed, her husband
brought her home a second time. The point of this remarkable story is not
that the individual bewailed her misfortune, but that she glorified God for
His mercy in rescuing her twice. Mather thus concludes the account by
saying that Bradley "affectionately calls upon her Friends, *O magnify the Lord
with me, and let us Exalt his Name together*!" (*Good*, 44). Thus Bradley's story
becomes a call to the faithful to endure affliction.

Hannah Swarton, whose first-person story Mather had included in
Humiliations Follow'd with Deliverances, was haunted during her captivity
by her previous spiritual lapses and her inability to pray in the face of

physical danger. Nevertheless, she found herself reminded of various scriptural passages, especially from Psalms, Job, and Jeremiah—those biblical books of trial—when she was threatened with death, when she learned of her son's death, and when she felt sorry for herself: "And by many other Scriptures, that were brought to my Remembrance, was I instructed, directed and comforted" (*HS*, 59). When the French pressed her to convert to Catholicism, several passages from the Second Letter to the Corinthians helped her keep her resolve.

Finally, Jean Lowry's *Journal* (1760) shows her spiritual triumph over the French in Canada by an appendix after the narrative proper titled "Several Disputes between the said Mrs. LOWRY, and the French," which comprises a third of the total work. This is a series of religious arguments she used as a Calvinist against Catholics who tried to persuade her to convert. Predictably, the arguments become a vehicle for anti-French and anti-Indian propaganda. In this later work, Lowry is allowed the last word, and she indeed emerges victorious as the narrative ends with her dispelling the points of a Frenchwoman trying to persuade her of the necessity of praying to the Virgin Mary: "This is the case with the Blessed King *Jesus*, who has Commanded to ask of him, who giveth liberally, and upbraideth none, and there is no other Mediator or Daysman: Another who was present answered, she has you now, so they added no more. FINIS" (*JL*, 31).

Mothers, Daughters, and Sisters

The mother's heart, doubled in wedlock, multiplied in children, stands but the broader mark for all the mischiefs that rove promiscuously abroad, and widens and dilates to wide dimensions its sad capacity of pain.
> —E. House, *Narrative of the Captivity of Mrs. Horn with Mrs. Harris* (1839)

My daughter, Captive, still keeps the dress she appeared in . . . and often refreshes my memory with past scenes when showing it to her children. These things yield a kind of melancholy pleasure.
> —Susannah Johnson, *A Narrative of the Captivity of Mrs. Johnson* (1796)

The terrible stories of your being tortured and finally murdered, outraged the feelings of the whole civilized world, and while men swore to avenge your wrongs, women mourned you, as sisters.
> —Theresa Gowanlock, *Two Months in the Camp of Big Bear* (1885)

The epigraphs above suggest that women were often cast into roles in
the captivity literature and that the roles most often foregrounded were
mother, *daughter*, and *sister*. With fathers, sons, and brothers in the
background, the fragmented family's main hope of maintaining its
identity and continuity was through its womenfolk. In the first edition
of Sarah Ann Horn's narrative, the protagonist defines herself precisely in
terms of her old and new roles: "Here, then, was the once happy English
girl—the wife of an affectionate and loving husband! but now, the
bereaved and disconsolate widow of the murdered father of her orphan
and captive babes!" (*Horn*, 35). This extract from the Horn narrative also
shows that the role of mother is the foremost one, and that many accounts
focus on the relationship between mother and child(ren). As early as
Mary Rowlandson's narrative, we find the moment of attack defined by
maternal/filial reactions: "Now might we hear Mothers and Children
crying out for themselves, and one another, *Lord, what shall we do!*"
Rowlandson says in her second paragraph (*MR*, 1). Often the relationship
between mother and daughter(s) is presented as particularly pathetic
because female frailty is multiplied by several figures. The image of
sisterhood has several different strands. In cases where siblings were
separated from parents, as with Olive and Mary Ann Oatman, and in
cases where two women were captured together, as with Fanny Kelly and
Sarah Larimer, the protagonists became sisters-in-adversity. But sometimes there were systematic networks of captive women; moreover,
women's experiences could spread out further to include and affect their
nonparticipant reader-sisters, as the third epigraph shows.

The earlier sections of this chapter have dealt implicitly with many
women who were mothers. However, one explicit reference to woman-
as–mother occurs at the beginning of a significant number of accounts—
especially the earlier ones—with the information that a woman is either
pregnant or recovering from childbirth. Certainly, the birth rate in the
seventeenth, eighteenth, and nineteenth centuries, as well as the atten-
dant dangers of pregnancy, was high. Between 1650 and 1750 alone,
"fully one fifth of adult female captives from northern New England
were either pregnant or newly delivered of a child" (Ulrich, 205). The
literature itself suggests a higher number. Elizabeth Fleming and Jean
Lowry, for example, were pregnant when taken, while Hannah Dustan
and Elizabeth Hanson had just given birth to a child. Both situations
draw attention to the woman's increased physical and emotional vulnerability, perhaps best exemplified by Goodwife Joslin, who was pregnant

but also nursing a two-year-old when taken. Rowlandson embeds Joslin's story into her own account as she describes meeting the hysterical woman and advising her not to try to escape. They are separated shortly afterward, and Rowlandson conveys secondhand, in an extract quoted in the previous chapter of this book, what happened to "that poor woman" (*MR*, 7). Joslin, her babe-in-arms, and her unborn child symbolize the outrage against women as mothers and the death of several generations.

In other accounts, pregnant women sometimes gave birth during the captivity itself. Two of these women indelibly marked their daughters by naming them "Captivity" and "Captive" to memorialize both the mother's and the child's bondage. John Norton, in his famous account *The Redeemed Captive* (1748), includes this entry for Thursday, 21 August 1746, "Mrs. *Smeed* was taken in travail: . . . she was graciously delivered of a Daughter, and was remarkably well. The Child also was well."[28] His entry for the next day, Friday, 22 August, begins, "This morning I baptised *John Smeed's* child. He called its name CAPTIVITY." And Susannah Johnson (Hastings), captured in Massachusetts in 1754, went into labor after a few days. On reaching Canada, she agreed to name her baby daughter "Louise," after a Canadian benefactress, Mrs. Du Quesne, "to which," Johnson says, "I added the name of Captive."[29] Once released, Johnson referred to her daughter only by the name Captive, and in the revised, enlarged edition of her narrative in 1814, she talks of the especially close bond between herself and her daughter owing to their providential salvation from the Indians and from the dangers of childbirth.[30] Both editions contain this reflection in their penultimate paragraph: "INSTANCES of longevity are remarkable in my family. My aged mother says to me, arise daughter and go to thy daughter, for your daughter's daughter has got a daughter; a command which few mothers can make and be obeyed" (*SJ*, 144). With its biblical reverberations, this passage shows longevity to be reckoned matrilinearly, as Johnson's spared life literally engenders the lives of her daughter, granddaughter, and great-granddaughter.

Not so lucky was Mrs. Dary, whose story appears in the 1825 edition of Massy Harbison's propagandist *Narrative of the Sufferings*, and who saw "the appalling and heart rending sight, of an Indian's taking her own child, of eighteen months old, and knocking its brains out against the head of her mother, by which means her mother was also killed. Thus by one inhuman act of barbarity, she was deprived of a mother and a child!" (*MH*, 10). The commentary clarifies the outrage against several generations of women whose line of descent is irrevocably cut: the past (Dary's

mother) and the future (Dary's child) disappear, leaving the present—
Dary herself—contextless.

The story of Jennie Wiley, part of William Elsey Connelley's *The Founding of Harman's Station* (1910), provides another variation on the image of woman-as-mother.[31] Captured by Cherokees and Shawnees in 1784 in Kentucky, Wiley and her youngest child of 15 months were the only survivors of the initial attack. During the forced march it became evident that she could not fend for both herself and her child, so a Cherokee chief seized it "by the feet and dashed out its brains against a big beech tree" and then scalped it (*Founding*, 46). But one reason she had difficulty keeping up was owing to pregnancy. Shortly after, she went into labor prematurely, but although deathly ill, both she and her son lived. However, adopted by a Shawnee chief, the boy apparently failed his first initiation rite at three months and was tomahawked and then scalped (50). Despite the impact of the deaths of two babies, Wiley was resourceful and resilient, and she eventually escaped after a premonition in a dream. In the initial attack and during her captivity, Wiley lost all five of her children, yet the editor, Connelley, felt the need to state in his preface, "*Mrs. Wiley has many descendents living in Kentucky and West Virginia. After her return from captivity to her husband there were five children born to them—Hezekiah, Jane, Sarah, Adam, and William*" (n. p.). The intergenerational information continues as Connelley states that these children, in turn, all married and left families. For some women, then, Indian captivity was a traumatic interruption to their family lives, but not necessarily an endpoint. Life could continue afterward, and in the case of the Wiley family, although five children died, another five became symbolic replacements.

The fate of Wiley's 15-month-old child is echoed throughout the captivity literature. So, for example, Cotton Mather describes in almost identical language the death of Dustan's baby: "But e're they had gone many Steps, they dash'd out the Brains of the *Infant*, against a Tree" (*Humiliations*, 43). The constants in this stock propaganda folk motif are a *mother*, at least one male *Indian*, and a *child*, usually held by the *heels*, whose *brains* (or *head*) are *dashed* against a *tree*. Heard points out that "Most children were treated brutally at the time of capture. Babies and toddlers usually were killed immediately," and other small children were killed if they gave trouble and hindered retreat (Heard, 97). Certainly the particular method of death described in the three examples was rapid and brutal, but the identical language and cast of characters may have touched deeper, mythic, unstated and unstateable associations. Traditionally, at birth, a newborn was held upside down to force it to breathe. Perhaps the ritualistic description of the killing of captive babies—even if it truly was part of some tribal cultures—was described so often by writers and deemed so shocking by (white) readers because instead of being part of birthing, where the man (father) and woman (mother) were life-giving, the man (Indian-aggressor) was the agent of death, and the woman (mother-victim) was a helpless onlooker. Rather than taking its first breaths when held upside down, in these cases the baby breathed its last.

Earlier in this chapter we saw how descriptions of a mother's milk drying up triggered underlying fears of sexual abuse as well as more obvious evidence of food deprivation. A few (presumably propagandist) narratives exploit the image of woman-as-mother even more by including descriptions of a woman's breasts being mutilated. One particularly extreme example occurs in Minnie Buce Carrigan's narrative, which includes the supposed eyewitness accounts of several other people, including a man named Emanuel Reyff. He describes the carnage at his brother's house during the Sioux Uprising in Minnesota, which turns out to be a catalogue of mutilations, culminating in this one: "Mrs. Smith's head was lying on the table with a knife and fork stuck in it. They had cut off one of her breasts and laid it on the table beside her head and put her baby nursing the other breast. The child was still alive, but the dog they had shot on the door step" (*Captured*, 26). In fewer than 60 words, as many gruesome elements as possible have been included to elicit a strongly negative response from both male and female readers: decapitation, cannibalism, mutilation, gratuitous violence, and dog killing. These gain added horror from their contrast with the child still trying to nurse at its dead mother's breast.

Elsewhere, we have seen the interaction between sisters when they were captured together. Whether factual or fictional, the plots of these narratives are particularly effective owing to the comparison or contrast of the sisters' fates and to the sense of multiple outrage against one family. Most often, only two sisters are either present or targeted for attention in the narrative. For example, within Royal B. Stratton's various editions of Olive and Mary Ann Oatman's stories, a great deal of pathos comes from the girls' double misery and Olive's fruitless attempts to protect Mary Ann. We also examined earlier the story of the Hall sisters, the fictional narrative based very loosely on the actual case of Sylvia and Rachel Hall, in which the girls suffer equally horrific abuse. Interestingly, in the embroidered experiences of the four German sisters, also discussed previously, the narrative follows them in pairs, as the youngest—Julia and Addie—were left in the wilderness after several days, while the eldest—Catherine and Sophia—endured a longer and harsher captivity.

Yet another perspective on sisters can be gained from Jemima Howe's *A Genuine and Correct Account* (1792), in which Howe as mother presents her difficulty in helping her two captive daughters from her first marriage, Mary and Submit Phipps.[32] These girls were the eldest of the seven children captured with Howe in 1755 in New Hampshire. They were taken to Canada, where Mary stayed with the St. François tribe while Submit went to a Catholic convent. On learning that Mary was to be married to an Indian, Howe enlisted the help of the Governor, de Vaudreuil, who succeeded in moving her to the same convent as her sister and who ordered that the girls be treated "as his adopted children" (*JH*, 17). When the Governor returned to France, he took Mary with him and married her to a French gentleman, Cron Lewis. Whether the marriage occurred with either Howe's or Mary's consent is not clear; the narrative implies, however, that this turn of events was preferable to Mary's previous marriage prospects. In contrast, Submit remained in the convent for so long that even though Howe was finally able to intervene when her daughter was to be sent to France, she resolutely refused to leave the convent until the Governor threatened to send soldiers to force her, as Howe says, "to submit to my parental authority" (*JH*, 18). True to her name, Submit apparently was given no option but to submit, and her mother describes the girl's anguish at leaving a life she had grown to prefer: she departed "with the greatest reluctance, and the most bitter lamentations . . . and wholly refused to be comforted" (*JH*, 18).

A final twist to the presence of sisters in the captivity literature occurs in Emeline Fuller's true survivalist narrative. With both her parents killed in an Indian attack, 13-year-old Emeline became a mother-substitute and led a babe-in-arms and four younger children into the wilderness, accompanied by the remnants of several other families. As starvation took hold, cannibalism was the last resort, and Fuller describes—guilty and grief-stricken—how having failed to preserve her younger sisters, she survived because of them: ". . . but the awful madness of hunger was upon us, and we cooked and ate the bodies of each of the poor children, first sister Libbie, then Mr. Chase's little boys, and next my darling little baby sister, whom I had carried in my arms through all that long dreary journey and slept with hugged to my heart, as though if possible I would shield her from all danger" (*Left*, 27).

But sisterhood could refer not only to siblings but also to women who clung together as sisters-in-suffering. If not kin, they felt themselves to be kindred, and their female bonding helped to temporarily counteract their sense of bondage. The narrative effect, as with biological sisters, reinforced the sense of women's vulnerability. A representative example can be found in the related Horn, Harris, and Plummer narratives. Plummer in her captivity account refers to Harris as "my suffering companion" (*CP*, 8); while Harris in her account describes how the Indian who forced Plummer to live with him invited Harris to see "'my sister,' his 'white squaw'" (*CH*, 14), whom Harris calls "my unfortunate companion in misery" (*CH*, 14), "my sister captive" (*CH*, 16), and "my unfortunate friend and late companion in misery" (*CH*, 22). In the Horn narrative, one extract significantly draws attention to the importance of having a confidante for psychic survival, as Horn and Harris part: "I could not but feel glad on her account that she was released from her sufferings; but I now felt, and that keenly, the truth of the saying, that 'misery loves company'; for though our meetings had been 'short,' and frequently 'far between,' still they had been seasons in which we would exchange sympathies, and mingle our tears" (*Horn and Harris*, 25). Even when the women did not know each other well, and did not even meet very often, common circumstances might throw them together as kindred sister spirits.

Captive women tended to polarize Indian women either as extremely cruel and primitive or as exceedingly kind and sympathetic. Of course, some captives became transculturated and stayed with the American Indians, but among those who always felt a sense of alienation and eventually returned to white society, a few could see that a sense of sisterhood might be able to cross cultures. Mary Schwandt, for example, describes how an old Indian woman, Wam-nu-ka-win, whose Anglicized name was Maggie, took pity on her and bought her: "Maggie and her mother were both very kind to me, and Maggie could not have treated me more tenderly if I had been her daughter. Often and often she preserved me from danger, and sometimes, I think, she saved my life" (*Schwandt*, 470–71). Many years later, as Schwandt-Schmidt writes her account, she indicates that through networking, she had kept up with information on Wam-nu-ka-win and publicly wants to acknowledge and address her: "I learn that she is somewhere in Nebraska, but wherever you are, Maggie, I want you to know that the little captive German girl you so often befriended and shielded from harm loves you still for your kindness and care" (*Schwandt*, 471). Sometimes the sense of sisterhood was tested in the face of stronger family and tribal ties. For example, when four braves claimed Helen Tarble, and Little Crow ordered that she should be killed for causing trouble among his best warriors, she approached an Indian woman for aid: "I appealed to the squaw as a woman and a mother to help me and my children to escape, but she said 'no,' and that she would do nothing to help me" (*Capture and Escape*, 34). That night, however, the squaw had a change of heart and was instrumental in the escape of Tarble and her children.

Sometimes, formalized networks of women captives evolved, most notably in eighteenth-century Montreal. For example, Grizel Otis Robitaille became assimilated into French faith and society and influenced other captives to stay, including her relative Abigail Willey. Thus, one transculturated woman could, through networking, hasten and soften the transition to full transculturation for other women. And as more New England women converted, their influence spread beyond Montreal, both as wives of French and Indian men and as nuns in Catholic convents (Ulrich, 209–11). At least some of these women must have made deliberate choices and not stayed merely out of passivity or powerlessness.

Although the nuclear family was threatened by Indian attack, the female survivors who returned to their culture of origin could derive comfort and support from a network of sympathetic women who had often been active on their behalf while they were still captives. As early as 1682, Rowlandson publicly identified in print the importance to her of a loving community of her own gender: "The twenty pounds, the price of my Redemption, was raised by some *Boston* Gentlewomen, and M. *Usher*, whose bounty and religious charity I would not forget to make mention of" (*MR*, 33). And Theresa Gowanlock, taken by Crees in Canada with Theresa Delaney, clarifies the interaction between the captive women and the women who heard or read about the incidents and vicariously participated in the prisoners' pain (*Bear*, 56). Gowanlock quotes a letter from a stranger, Mrs. C. F. Bennett, part of which is included in the third epigraph to this section. Later in the letter, Mrs. Bennett says, "'. . . your sufferings have given you a sister's place in every heart, and *every one* in Winnipeg would be deeply disappointed if you did not give them an opportunity of expressing their deep sympathy and regards'" (quoted in *Bear*, 56). Gowanlock and Delaney acknowledged "the kindness of strangers"—to use Blanche Du Bois's immortal words at the end of *A Streetcar Named Desire*—by including at the beginning of their work a dedication "to Our Sisters the Ladies of Canada," and Gowanlock in her introduction thanked the general public, but "especially the ladies" for "their kindness and sympathy in my bereavement, and their noble and disinterested efforts for my release" (*Bear*, 6).

As a last example, we can look at the end of Rachel Plummer's *Narrative* (1839). The daughter of Reverend James W. Parker and cousin to another famous captive, Cynthia Ann Parker, Plummer was captured by Comanches in 1836 in Texas and stayed with them for 21 months. When she was released, she lived for a while with Colonel and Mrs. William Donoho, and like other captives, she made a point of publicly thanking the efforts of a woman, in this case, Mrs. Donoho: "I have no language to express my gratitude to Mrs. Donoho. I found in her a mother, to direct me in that strange land, a sister to condole with me in my misfortune, and offer new scenes of amusement to me to revive my mind" (*RP*, 362).

Traumatized Women

> It was three months before the least colour of blood appeared in my
> hands or feet. But my mind appeared more impaired than even my body,
> and I remained in a kind of listless, unreflecting, and almost unconscious
> stupidity for more than nine months before the least sensible emotion of
> either love or hatred was felt in my stupid heart[.]
> —Anne Jamison, *An Interesting Narrative* (1824)

Earlier, we saw that the victimized woman is one of the standard images in the captivity literature and that victimization covers physical, sexual, and spiritual abuse. This section examines the fourth area, emotional abuse. Traumatized women are defined here in more or less the same specialized way they were defined in chapter four, that is, to refer to captives like Mary Rowlandson and Anne Jamison who suffered mental and psychological impairment. They survived the ordeal, but at great price.

As might be expected, survivors in this sense are found only in the factual accounts, and generally in the first person, unmediated ones where the captive cannot help but reveal this side of her experience. These captivities contain the most convincing, specific, and extended information. Perhaps, too, more women than men were willing to articulate this side of their experience. In the fictional or fictionalized narratives, if emotional battering is dealt with at all, it is in vague terms, as in Mary Kinnan's sentimentalized text, *A True Narrative* (1795), where she says, "The picture of my life was deeply, too deeply dashed with shade, and but a few faint strokes of light were intermingled with the numerous touches of the *sombre* pencil" (*MK*, 8). Comparatively few accounts deal with this aspect of captivity, perhaps because it was too painful and personal, because it was deemed inappropriate, or because it did not enhance saleability. In some captivities, though, especially in the nineteenth century, women did confess to the kind of experiences that led to emotional damage, and this image, while unusual, merits separate attention.

Anne Jamison's *An Interesting Narrative* (1824) is one of the earliest examples after Rowlandson's of the stresses of survival.[33] Her party was attacked in 1778 in the Mississippi Valley by American Indians; one person was captured, and the rest fled in seven boats toward Natchez. Jamison's boat held 19 people, of which the only men were her husband and a man named James Young. Sickness and inadequate food on this boat caused it to be abandoned by the other six vessels, and the weakened people began to die quickly with only animal skins, grass, and berries to eat. Jamison's husband was the first of her family to die; then her two-year-old son; and last, her baby girl, whom Jamison had tried to keep alive by parching and pulverising "about twelve grains of coffee" and then boiling the powder (*Interesting Narrative*, 4). Young insisted that cannibalism was the only way to stay alive, even when he pulled a straw with his daughter Mary's name; however, food erratically came from other sources. Nonetheless, "We were a disconsolate, heartless and helpless company 550 miles from Natchez," Jamison said (*Interesting Narrative*, 8). Eventually, after several months, they found a settlement from where they travelled to Natchez. As the epigraph shows, Jamison became severely depressed and stayed in Natchez for more than a year, until sufficiently recovered to function and fend for her remaining four children. An old friend found her and took her back to Philadelphia, from where she was able to return—significantly—to her mother's, but she was still, "somewhat like Naomi returning from the land of Moab, a bereaved and disconsolate widow" (*Interesting Narrative*, 12). Jamison's emotional response, then, arose only indirectly (and initially) from Indian attack and more directly from the trauma of basic survival.

Like Jannette De Camp Sweet, Nancy McClure, and Mary Schwandt-Schmidt, Urania White was captured in Minnesota during the Sioux Uprising and her recollections also appeared in *Collections of the Minnesota*

Historical Society (*Sioux Captivity*, 395–426). The attack on her home-stead occurred at the beginning of the war, on 18 August 1862, and White was released after 39 days. Her account is particularly noteworthy for its emphasis on the psychological effects during captivity. For exam-ple, on the first day of the march, White observes, "Members of families were separated and taken to different places, seemingly to add to our suffering by putting upon us the terrible agony of wondering where the other prisoners were and what was to be their fate" (*Sioux Captivity*, 403). White was given to an Indian and his wife, and more than 30 years later, she still cherished "with kindest feelings the friendship of my Indian father and mother" (*Sioux Captivity*, 404). Perhaps since her physical safety was not at issue, she deliberately focused more on her mental state. For instance, recalling how out-of-place she and the other captives thought Indian children looked wearing "rich laces and bedecked in many fantastic styles with silk fabrics," she said they laughed, until the "laugh died on our lips," as they thought, "Where did these things come from? What tales could they tell if power were given them to speak? . . . My heart was crushed, my brain reeled, and I grew faint and sick wondering, or rather trying not to wonder, what would be our own fate" (*Sioux Captivity*, 405–6). Believing that if she gave in to fright, she would be killed, she said her will sustained her, and she remembered one particularly telling detail: "I said to one of my neighbor captives, when we were first made prisoners, that I felt just like singing, so near did I in my excitement border on insanity. I have thought since many times that, had I given up to the impulse and sung, it would have been a wild song and I should have certainly crossed the border of insanity and entered its confines" (*Sioux Captivity*, 407). At other times, White talks about how she could not sleep and obsessively thought of her family, about bouts of weeping, and about feeling dazed. However, after a relatively short time, she was released and rejoined her husband and two of her three children, her eldest son having been killed in the initial attack; "My mind was now at rest," she concludes, "at least as to the whereabouts of my family, and we could begin to plan as to what we should do" (*Sioux Captivity*, 425). The family could begin to attend to its future, in other words, because only one member had died.

Minnie Buce Carrigan, captured with her brother and sister, was yet another casualty of the Sioux Uprising, but her account was published in a newspaper and then in book form, not as part of the *Collections of the Minnesota Historical Society*. Carrigan was only seven in 1862, but she claims that others have corroborated her story and observes convincingly, "The nature of these incidents impressed them on my youthful mind so deeply that I can never forget them" (*Captured*, 15). Her narrative is particularly significant for its apparently accurate reflection of the emotional effects of captivity on a small child. For example, she recreates her train of thought when the Sioux took her to her neighbor's place, the Boelter house. She recalls that Mrs. Boelter had a beautiful flower garden and that she had always wanted to pick some of the blooms. As she realized that Mrs. Boelter must be dead, she "gathered a handful and the next moment flung them back into the flower bed. I did not want them. Mrs. Boelter was dead; if I did not see her, I was sure of it, and was taking advantage of a dead person" (*Captured*, 9–10). As she looked into the house, she saw the mutilated body of Mrs. Boelter, and throughout her captivity was haunted by the sight. The three children often found themselves weeping helplessly, especially when they became the property of the same Sioux who killed both their parents and when they recognized their family's clothes and their father's hymn book. On one occasion, "the young squaw put on my mother's dress, a dark green woolen one, and it just about fitted her. I looked at her and then laid down on the ground and burst out crying; I could not bear to see her" (*Captured*, 12). The first Sunday after her capture, Carrigan took her father's hymn book, sang part of a familiar German hymn, but then "had the longest and bitterest cry since my parents had been murdered" (*Captured*, 13). Carrigan's account contains more information concerning emotional victimization as a result of both her parents being dead: when released, the three children were adopted by a legal guardian who misappropriated the $1,200 compensation for their father's property, of which, Carrigan says, "we never received one cent" (*Captured*, 24). Both Carrigan and her sister left their guardian at the ages of 15 and 14, respectively, to fend for themselves. Thus the initial attack, which deprived the children of their parents, had substantial, negative long-term effects. While the ending of her brief 25-page narrative is a little sentimentalized, it gains added pathos from Carrigan's memory of so many dead friends and relatives:

> The flowers that bloom in the wildwood
> Have since dropped their beautiful leaves,
> And the many dear friends of my childhood
> Have slumbered for years in their graves.   (*Captured*, 25)

We have already examined Emeline Fuller's narrative for its information on physical abuse, in the form of starvation and cannibalism, following an Indian attack on 9 September 1860 on the Snake River in Idaho, and for its portrayal of the 13-year-old becoming a mother-substitute to five younger children, all of whom died before rescue. Fuller was the only survivor of the Utter-Myers overland party to write up her account. She was so traumatized that even when she thought help might be close at hand, she could not feel relief: "I was alone in the world and had suffered enough in the past few months to change me from a light-hearted child into a broken-hearted woman, and my wish was that I might lie down and die, and join my kindred in a world free from cares and troubles like those I had passed through" (*Left*, 30–31). Also, it was an initiation into the worst of human nature, not only in terms of the American Indians, but more particularly in terms of the other family to escape, the Myers family. Fuller could not come to terms with the injustice of the entire Myers family surviving intact or with their offensive piety, which they used as an excuse for not pulling their weight but spending their time praying when Fuller and her siblings gathered food and fuel for both families.

When Mr. Myers was asked how he accounted for his whole family being saved when others were "entirely annihilated," he answered, "'It was prayer saved my family'" (*Left*, 33). Fuller concludes otherwise, "Perhaps the good Lord, who is the searcher of all hearts, heeded his selfish prayers, but I would quicker believe that shirking duty and stealing from others was what saved the Myers family" (*Left*, 33–34). Fuller infers that part of her family might still be alive if food and work had been divided more fairly and if the Myers adults had acted more responsibly, instead of exploiting the children whose parents were dead. She was treated well by her uncle in Oregon but was acutely aware of her isolation and lived a double life: at school, scenes from her past intruded and distracted her; during the day she played happily with her new friends, but at night, she prayed that her mother would come and take her away. Her first marriage was happy, but her husband died; her second marriage was not happy, so the couple separated. Among her last comments she says that she became a member of the Baptist Church in 1861, "Since then I have found Jesus to be a 'friend that sticketh closer than a brother'" (*Left*, 40). Fuller's entire account is marked by a curiously detached, factual tone and by a series of incidents that illustrate parting and sorrow. In the introduction, James Hughes talks about meeting Fuller and noting both her "careworn face" and her inability to kneel in church owing to residual health problems from her wilderness experience (*Left*, 3). Physical and mental reminders of her ordeal seem to have remained with Fuller all her life, and she makes a conscious decision to include them in her text.

Finally, we might look at the case of Anna Belle Morgan and Sarah C. White, two Kansas women captured by Cheyennes at the same time as the famous Clara Blynn and rescued by General Custer himself in 1869. Both women were reportedly pregnant when released, and Morgan gave birth to a child supposedly fathered by an Indian. White apparently lived a normal life afterward: she became a schoolteacher, married a Kansas farmer, and raised a family (no ready information is available on whether she had a part-Indian child nor not) (White, 342). However, although Morgan was reunited with her husband, she "never fully recovered from her ordeal, and in time her 'mind became weak' and she was placed in a home for the feeble-minded in Topeka" (White, 342). Thus readjustment and recovery were not always possible for the individual and her biological family, and we might wonder how many other families experienced emotional turmoil as a woman returned, with one or more half-Indian children, and what psychological adjustments were needed by both husband and wife under such circumstances. Certainly, another Minnesota captive, Helen Mar Tarble, admitted at the end of her account, "After my capture by the Indians there was discord between me and my husband, and at St. Peter we 'agreed to disagree'" (*Capture and Escape*, 49). They parted and went their separate ways. Thus the theme of family disunity sometimes extended to insoluble psychological problems even if husband and wife were both alive after the captivity.

Transculturated Women

> At every opportunity [Olive Oatman sought] to flee back to her Indian husband and children. . . . For four years she lived with us, but she was a grieving, unsatisfied woman who somehow shook ones' [*sic*] belief in civilization. In time we erased the tatoo marks from her face but we could not erase the wild life from her heart.
> —Susan Thompson Lewis Parrish[34]

In most of the captivity literature that deals with women's transculturation, it is a white woman who embraces the life of a particular American Indian tribe, or of a different culture such as French-Catholic Canada. Some accounts, such as those as Eunice Williams, Mary Jemison, and Frances Slocum, show the original captive staying with her adopted people until death within the strong kinship of Native American society. Others tell the story of a white woman unwillingly returning—or more accurately, being returned—to white society and experiencing tremendous emotional and cultural adjustments: Olive Oatman and Cynthia Ann Parker, for example. Still other narratives present a woman who adapted to Native American life but who returned to the culture of her birth without apparent difficulty, a woman who was flexible and resilient enough to accept transculturation several times. Finally, a few narratives consider the individual cases of non-Anglo or Indian women being transculturated.[35]

All these strands raise the complex question of what constituted captivity and for whom. For some captives, both male and female, it was white society that came to define the captive state, despite their white background.[36] An American Indian environment gave them a tribal identity, and their white birth was meaningless regarding that identity. These people became "white Indians" who looked and acted like Indians—indeed, were Indians to themselves and to their adopted culture, despite biological accidentals like blue eyes or blond hair. However, in the mind of white society, of friends and relatives who remembered the moment of captivity and always considered the family member as a captive who belonged forever to her culture of origin, captivity meant remaining with the American Indians, and rescue, even after many years, remained a priority. This view was especially true for women who were taken captive, and we see the pattern of a father, husband, or brother continuing to press for the release of his daughter, wife, or sister. Conversely, we see the woman within several new family circles: that of her foster family and eventually that of her own husband and children.

From 1675 to 1763, far more women than men were statistically likely to stay with their French or Indian captors; indeed, "The prime candidate for transculturation was a girl aged seven through fifteen" (Vaughan and Richter, 64). But we cannot underestimate the extent to which transculturation originated in habituation or coercion rather than in conscious choice, that is, in the replacement of old authority figures by new ones, especially for young girls. Transculturated women eventually lost their native language and established their own family ties by marrying Indians or Frenchmen, or remaining within the closed environment of a Catholic convent, so we must be especially wary of believing that their texts come to us undisturbed.

The life of Eunice Williams is a case in point, and we will take her as representative of other women who stayed in Canada, including Christine Otis, Esther Wheelwright, Thankful Stebbins, and Grizel Otis Robitaille.[37] Nowhere does Williams herself tell her own story: almost all the information comes from the two viewpoints of her minister-father, John Williams, in *The Redeemed Captive, Returning to Zion* (1707), and her minister-brother, Stephen Williams.[38] The image and reputation of Eunice Williams, like that of so many other transculturated women, was at the mercy of her storytellers. She herself remains shadowy and silent. The attack by Iroquois on Deerfield, Massachusetts, began on 29 February 1704; almost 40 people died and 112 were captured, including both of seven-year-old Eunice's parents, her sister, and her three brothers. Her mother died before reaching Canada, but her four siblings and her father were redeemed. In his captivity narrative, John Williams talks of his attempts to release Eunice and the resistance from both the Maquas who owned her and the Catholics. Through Jesuit intemediaries, he is told *"if I came that my labour would be lost; and that the Macqua's would as soon part with their hearts, as my Child"* (*Zion*, 29). Was there reciprocal love between the little girl and the Maquas, or were the Indians and the Jesuits trying to force the Puritan minister's child to stay and convert to Catholicism? When the governor of Canada finally intervened and allowed John Williams to meet with Eunice, Williams claimed she was "very desirous to be redeemed," though one of his prime concerns was that she be released before she could "forget her *Catechism*, and the *Scriptures*" (*Zion*, 29).

In 1713, John Schuyler, an intermediary from Reverend Williams, attempted once again to have Eunice released and left in a state paper an account of his interview with Eunice, her Indian husband, and several interpreters.[39] On the basis of this letter, one of the many myths about Eunice Williams evolved: namely, that she was *unwilling* to return to Deerfield. Yet the most noticeable aspect of her behavior is not so much her refusal as her silence (Gherman, 78). Schuyler claims that she was "bashfull in the face but proved harder than Steel in her breast," yet elsewhere in the letter he says he and others "could not gett one word from her" (Baker, 145), until finally, after two hours, she simply said in her Indian language, *"zaghte oghte* which words being translated into the English Tongue, their Signifycation is *may be not*; but the meaning thereof amongst the Indians is a plaine denyall" (Baker, 146). Perhaps rather than "No" she simply meant, "It cannot be," because she had replaced her role as dutiful daughter in the Williams family with her new role as dutiful Indian wife, and because she had been part of Catholic/

Indian culture for longer than she had lived in Puritan New England. One other official attempt to release Eunice was made by her father, but she did not return to New England until August 1740, after his death, and then only as a visitor.

Stephen Williams continued to hope that his sister would reconvert to Puritanism and rejoin her white relatives throughout all three of her visits—August 1740, July 1741, and June 1761—but after this seems to have stopped trying. Certainly, Eunice's visits created quite a stir and gave rise to several myths that available data do not support: legend has it that (1) she eventually visited Deerfield (she didn't; she visited Longmeadow, where Stephen lived); (2) she would not enter the house but camped with her family outside (there is no evidence of this); (3) she insisted on wearing Indian dress (there is no specific information about her dress in the primary sources); and (4) the Massachusetts legislature offered her land if she would return to white culture (again, there is no specific evidence of this in the eighteenth-century sources) (Gherman, 82–89).

An extant letter from Eunice to Stephen dated 12 March 1771 shows that she still cared for her brother and valued her kinship to him,[40] even though by this time he had stopped communicating with her, since she mentions his last letter was 10 years old, dated 19 September 1761: "We are Verey desirous of hering from you . . . I am now growing old and Can have but little hopes of Seeing you in this world," she says, and ends, "your Loving Sister until death Eunice Williams." This final word, as it were, does belong to Eunice herself, and it shows her able to bridge the two cultures, white and Indian, and psychologically merge the two families, even if her brother was unable to do so.

Both Mary Jemison, "the white woman of the Genesee," and Frances Slocum, "the lost sister of Wyoming," also remained with their original Indian captors and established a new family network. (The tags given these women by whites insist on seeing them as still part of white culture, when in fact they had become thoroughly Indianized. Jemison was not "the white woman of the Genesee," she was a Shawnee named Dehgewanus; and Slocum certainly did not define her identity as that of a "lost sister," since she had become first the wife of a Delaware and subsequently the wife of a Miami Chief, and had been given the name We-let-a-wash many years previously by her adoptive parents.) Each married and gave birth to children, claimed to be content with her life, had a prestigious position within her tribe, and was adamant about not wishing to return to white society. In each case, too, the woman told her story to a male editor, yet although there is considerable editorializing, Jemison and Slocum have more of a narrative presence than Williams. After only four years of captivity, Jemison states that her wish to escape from the Shawnees had almost gone, because "With them was my home; my family was there, and there I had many friends to whom I was warmly attached in consideration of the favors, affection and friendship with which they had uniformly treated me, from the time of my adoption" (*MJ*, 46).[41] At the end of her account, she stresses the continuity of her family as evidenced by her eight children, 39 grandchildren, and 14 great-grandchildren, all living close by (*MJ*, 143), and she concludes, "Thus situated in the midst of my children, I expect I shall soon leave the world, and make room for the rising generation" (*MJ*, 144). Slocum was accidentally discovered living among the Miamis 59 years after she had been captured, and she admitted that she had deliberately kept her identity secret for fear that her white relatives would force her to leave. Her brothers visited her and tried to persuade her to return to the Wyoming Valley of Pennsylvania. Being thoroughly transculturated, she refused, saying: "'I cannot. I cannot. I am an old tree. It cannot move about. I was a sapling when they took me away. It is all gone past. I am afraid I should die and never come back. I am happy here. I shall die here and lie in that grave-yard, and they will raise the pole at my grave with the white flag on it, and the Great Spirit will know where to find me. I should not be happy with my white relatives'" (*Sister*, 143). Slocum's degree of transculturation extended even to Indian religious belief, and she was not willing to risk dying while away visiting blood-relatives she had not seen for almost six decades.

Another interesting, but very brief and unsubstantiated, story of transculturation is embedded in Fanny Kelly's *Narrative* (1871), where Kelly talks of meeting Elizabeth Blackwell, from Salt Lake City (*FK*, 238). Blackwell, her mother, and sisters escaped from their "brute of a father" (*FK*, 238) when he took another wife in accordance with his Mormon faith. Left wandering in the mountains, all the women died of exposure except Elizabeth, who was found by American Indians and restored to life. When she was well enough, Blackwell went East for further medical attention and had both legs amputated. However, she had no wish to stay among whites because "The treatment received from the Indians so attached her to them that she prefers to live a forest life, and when she gave me her narrative, she was on her way from the States to her Indian home," apparently accompanied by her Indian husband (*FK*, 239).

Williams, Jemison, and Slocum were able to live with the American Indians yet still maintain some contact with their white relatives. However, other transculturated women such as Cynthia Ann Parker and Olive Oatman were unwillingly returned to a society which they considered unfamiliar and unacceptable and which also tore them away from their American Indian families. At age nine, Parker was captured in Texas in 1836 by Comanches, Kiowas, and Wichitas. In 1860, during a raid that killed her husband, the Comanche chief Peta Nocona, she was recognized as white because of her blue eyes and was returned with one of her children to her uncle, Colonel Parker. James T. DeShields, who wrote up the narrative called *Cynthia Ann Parker* (1886), briefly indicates the different responses of her white relatives and of Parker—whose Indian name was Preloch—herself: "But as savage-like and dark of complexion as she was, Cynthia Ann was still dear to her overjoyed uncle, and was welcomed home by relatives with all the joyous transports with which the prodigal son was hailed upon his miserable return to the parental roof. As thorough an Indian in manner and looks as if she had been so born, she sought every opportunity to escape, and had to be closely watched for some time" (*Parker*, 71). For her relations, Parker remained the nine-year-old who had been torn away from them and whose return was cause for joy. To them, the intervening years counted for nothing, while Parker, of course, sought to escape from this new captivity to her Indian family and to her two sons—to what she saw as freedom. Her daughter, Topsannah, was her only link to her previous life, and when Topsannah died in 1864, Parker starved herself to death. Unable to admit unequivocally that Parker never did readjust to white society, DeShields concedes that "The ruling passion of her bosom seemed to be the maternal instinct" (72) and that concern for her two sons may have hampered her reassimilation. Significantly, DeShields includes a photograph of Parker as a frontispiece showing a woman who looks like a pure-blood Indian cradling a child who is breast-feeding: "maternal instinct" is the only reason DeShields can acknowledge that would stop her from wanting to embrace white culture.

After five years among the Yavapai and Mohave Indians, Olive Oatman was, in the words of Royal B. Stratton's preface to her story, "purchased and restored to civilized life" in 1856 (*Oatman 1*, iii).[42] "Civilized life" it may have been to her relatives, which included her brother, Lorenzo, but not at first to Olive herself, who had become transculturated to Indian society, who had been renamed Aliutman or Spantsa, and who, as the epigraph to this section suggests, desperately tried to return to her Mohave family. That transculturated women loved, married, and had children by American Indian men was an issue that the editors of their narratives found difficult—if not impossible—to deal with. Stratton omits the information on Oatman's marriage entirely, despite the fact that her infamous facial tattoos sometimes signified marriage for Mohave women.[43] But the knowledge that Oatman probably did marry a Mohave and have children places the following extract from the first edition of her story in a completely different light. Told in the first person as though by Olive herself, this extract must be seen instead as ethnocentric editorializing over which Olive presumably had no control: "Friends or kindred to look after or care for me, I had none, as I then supposed. . . . I considered my age, my sex, my exposure, and was again in trouble—though to the honor of these savages, let it be said they never offered the least unchaste abuse to me" (*Oatman 1*, 149). But Olive did apparently have American Indian "friends and kindred" to whom she tried to return, and while it might be true that the Indians "never offered the least unchaste abuse" to her, that was not tantamount to saying she was a virgin, for she apparently had children.

The epigraph to this section comes from Susan (Thompson) Parrish, whose parents and family were with the Oatman party until Royce Oatman, Olive's father, decided to branch off alone and try to reach Fort Yuma with his family, at which point they were attacked. It was with the Thompson family that Olive Oatman lived for a while after her return, and the information in Susan Parrish's personal correspondence may therefore be more trustworthy than the information in Stratton's book. Stratton says Olive was "restored to civilized life"; Parrish says her adjustment difficulties made her so "grieving" and "unsatisfied" that she "shook ones' [*sic*] belief in civilization." Eventually, Olive went to relatives in Oregon, and Susan Parrish adds, "She must have forgotten as the years went by for in time she married a Mr. Fairchild, a banker from Texas" (quoted in Schlissel, 69). Thus, the best information we have is that after some years of renewed exposure to white society, Olive Oatman was able to transculturate herself a third time. Captured as an adolescent and returned alone to white society five years later, she was presumably still young and resilient enough to readjust when it became clear that she would not be allowed to resume Mohave life.

Two other women forcibly returned to white society, Elizabeth Studebaker and Elizabeth Hawkins, succeeded in escaping to rejoin their tribes. Studebaker had been captured in 1775 in Pennsylvania and was delivered up to Colonel Henry Bouquet in 1784. After 10 days of marching, she evaded the close guard and went back to the Delawares. Hawkins was also taken in Pennsylvania in 1781 and married a Shawnee warrior: "Restored to her white family when the Indian wars ended in the Old Northwest in 1795, she was never able to rebridge the gap between civilizations. After a short stay among the familiar scenes of her childhood she returned to her Indian husband and was never seen again by her white relatives" (Heard, 139).[44]

The story of Lizzie Ross is a good example of a young captive who was able to move into white society without major readjustment. Her age was probably in her favor; she was taken from the Comanches in Oklahoma by the Ranger Sul Ross when she was only eight. Her white family was never located, so Ross adopted her, named her Lizzie, and paid for her education. Born white, she had been assimilated into Comanche life before Ross took her, but she was reassimilated into her culture of origin without strain. To cement her ties to this culture, she married a rich (white) merchant from California.[45]

The vast majority of the chronicles of women's transculturation concern white American women, but scattered examples exist to suggest the experiences of Mexicans who were captured and of American Indians who were transculturated into white culture. For example, Tomassa was born to a wealthy Mexican family about 1841, but was taken by Comanches and adopted into a Comanche family, where she stayed for several years until she was ransomed by the Mexican government.[46] Like Lizzie Ross, she had been taken so young that she could not remember enough information to locate her Mexican family, so she and a boy in a similar situation became servants to another Mexican family. Treated poorly, they determined to escape and find their adopted Comanche families, which they succeeded in doing after travelling hundreds of miles over rough terrain. There Tomassa stayed happily until she reached marriageable age, at which point she decided not to marry the Indian to whom she had been promised but a white ranch owner, Joseph Chandler. Although born into Mexican culture, Tomassa chose Comanche and subsequently Anglo culture and then used her skills to negotiate contact and communication among all three peoples: "She adopted many of the ways of white civilization and tried to help Indians follow her example. Frequently she warned white people of impending raids. Once she saved the lives of two Mexican captives by hiding them under the floor of her house" (Heard, 36).

While we have examined some stories of non-Indians—usually taken as children—being transculturated to Indian life, very little information exists in the captivity literature on the reverse process. White families were not likely to adopt American Indians, although "a considerable number of them were removed from their Indian families by missionaries or Government officials and sent to boarding schools" (Heard, 154). Therefore, the story of *The Little Osage Captive*, by Elias Cornelius, is rather unusual.[47] In his preface, Cornelius claims that the narrative's intent is to "make an impression upon the rising generation, in favor of the missionary cause" (8), and it is primarily propagandist children's literature. But it also includes information on an Indian child's transculturation into what seems to be a loving white family. Cornelius was travelling in 1817 to New Orleans when he came across a Cherokee war party with a captive Osage orphan girl, aged four or five. He tried to befriend her, but took no further action until he arrived in Natchez and told a wealthy Mississippi woman, Lydia Carter, about her. Carter offered a ransom of $150 for the child, who was named after her benefactress and adopted by a missionary and his wife, Reverend and Mrs. William Chamberlain: "To them, the immediate care of her education was committed. They received her into their family, and adopted her, as their own child. She was taught to call them father, and mother, and to feel towards them as such; while they addressed her as their daughter—and as the sister of another little daughter whom they had, whose name was Catharine" (*Osage 1*, 36–37). In due course, the Osage Indians demanded that she and another captive, John Ross, be returned, and accordingly, they embarked on the long journey back. Although it was finally decided that Lydia Carter could be returned once again to the Chamberlains, she died before she could be reunited with her foster family.

The images of women in the captivity literature cannot be reduced to one or two stereotypes, and even the five categories used in this chapter cannot do full justice to the complexity of their experiences. Yet the single strand that runs through the accounts both by and about women concerns the dissolution of the frontier family, whether the boundary was Massachusetts, Minnesota, Florida, or Utah, and the women's awareness of "the challenge of rearing a family and maintaining domestic order against the disordered life on the frontier" (Schlissel, 155).

Chapter Six

The Indian Captivity Narrative as Usable Past

"Ah, poor man, Rip Van Winkle was his name, but it's twenty years since he went away from home with his gun, and never has been heard of since—his dog came home without him; but whether he shot himself, or was carried away by Indians, nobody can tell."

—Washington Irving, "Rip Van Winkle" (1819)

> Our mother, while she turned her wheel
>   Or run the new-knit stocking-heel,
> Told how the Indian hordes came down
>   At midnight on Chocheco town,
> And how her own great-uncle bore
>   His cruel scalp-mark to fourscore.

—John Greenleaf Whittier, *Snow-Bound* (1866)

One merit the writer may at least claim: that of calling forth the passions and engaging the sympathy of the reader by means hitherto unemployed by preceding authors. Puerile superstition and exploded manners, Gothic castles and chimeras, are the materials usually employed for this end. The incidents of Indian hostility and the perils of the Western wilderness are far more suitable; and for a native of America to overlook these would admit of no apology.

—Charles Brockden Brown, *Edgar Huntly* (1799)

By the early nineteenth century, the reality of Indian captivity was already a generation or more removed from the consciousness of white Americans living in the East. While frontier warfare continued in the West until well into the latter part of the century, it long since had ceased in the East. Along with the end of warfare came a change in the way Easterners viewed the American Indian. Attempting to discover and define a national identity, white Americans turned to their past, hoping there to find a heritage worthy of what they considered their country's future promise. In the words of Peter Force, a nineteenth-century New

York mayor and government editor, "The tendency of the present age has been justly and philosophically designated as historick."[1] Indeed, during the nineteenth century, histories of all types were attracting an ever-widening audience. No longer a military threat, the Indian, together with the frontier, was perceived as part of a rapidly vanishing national heritage that needed immediate preservation. That Indians seemed to be disappearing from the American landscape, never more to return, made their appeal all the more alluring as a part of a rich historical legacy that could be safely romanticized. Consequently, white audiences began romanticizing the American Indian as part of what was perceived to be a glorious historical heritage, and along with this process the Indian captivity narrative entered yet another phase in its social and literary evolution. Shedding its overtly propagandistic character, it became instead part of a usable past that furnished cultural information for the imagination of historiographers, tellers of folklore, and novelists who together sought to forge an American national character from a past that was often less than noble.

The Captivity Narrative as History

The nineteenth century saw a tremendous interest at both local and national levels in collecting and preserving Indian captivity narratives as history. Often subsidized by municipal, state, and federal grants, nineteenth-century historians, under the influence of a general romantic interest in the past as well as a nationalistic impulse on the part of Americans to discover their historical roots, focused attention on aspects of the nation's pioneer heritage that, according to their thinking, illustrated the American character at its best.[2] Indian captivity was one such experience. Most American cities took pride in the exploits of a local captive—a Hannah Dustan, Mary Rowlandson, John Williams, or Mary Jemison—whose seeming grace under pressure exemplified the heroism and fortitude that, they claimed, characterized their pioneer heritage and foretold the future greatness of the nation. Including captivity narratives in historical works fulfilled an important cultural function. Insecure about its identity, nineteenth-century America needed self-definition. In the form of history, captivity narratives helped supply that definition. They were accordingly used by the white culture to engender regional and national patriotism and to preserve for posterity accounts of Indian/white relations that might otherwise have been lost.[3]

The most striking feature of captivity narratives written as local history is their wide geographic distribution. Accounts of Indian captivity appear with predictable frequency in the local histories of New England and Middle Atlantic states, where by the early part of the nineteenth century incessant warfare had reduced the Indian to little more than a memory. Stories of the captivity of local pioneers were printed in John Farmer and Jacob Moore's *Collections, Topographical, Historical, and Biographical, Relating Principally to New Hampshire* (1822– 24). Elihu Hoyt's *A Brief Sketch of the First Settlement of Deerfield* (1833) recounts the captivity of John Williams. Based on *The Redeemed Captive, Returning to Zion* (1707), Hoyt's history of Deerfield was written explicitly to "gratify the feelings of those who are descendants of the early settlers of the place" and to teach "those who are not immediate descendants from the sufferers" about the "exploits, the sufferings, [and] the hairbreadth escapes which were the lot of those who first ventured to take a stand on the borders between civilized man, and the savage state."[4] In his *History of the Counties of Dauphin and Lebanon* (1883), another local historian, William Egle, chronicles the captivities of two Pennsylvania youths, William Barnett and Thomas Mackey. Several narratives were published in the local histories of the South, where limited printing facilities had previously hindered the publication of narratives. Virgil Lewis's *History of West Virginia* (1889), for example, records the captivities of Margaret and Jennie Wiley, famous local figures. At least two local histories were written specifically to memorialize Indian captives. Robert Caverly's *Heroism of Hannah Duston* (1874) commemorates the unveiling of the Hannah Dustan Memorial Statue in Haverhill, Massachusetts. Samuel Green's *Historical Address Delivered at Groton, Massachusetts, February 20, 1880* praises the valor of several pioneers "captured from Groton at different times."

As the frontier moved westward, a number of narratives were also published in the local histories of Midwestern towns and states. Nehemiah Matson's *Pioneers of Illinois* (1882) contains accounts of the captivities of Mary Lee, captured in the 1812 Chicago massacre of Fort Dearborn, and of Amanda Wolsley, taken in 1813 near Cahokia. Eventually captivity narratives appear in the local histories of the West, but only after the danger of Indian/white military hostilities had ceased. The stories of several local captives, including that of Cynthia Ann Parker, mother of the famous chief Quanah Parker, were published, for example, in John Henry Brown's *Indian Wars and Pioneers of Texas* (1898).

If short, previously published narratives were sometimes reprinted verbatim as parts of local histories. More often, though, they were rewritten in the third person and condensed to form a chapter or episode in longer narrative sequences. Several narratives never before published appear for the first time in local histories. Joseph Doddridge's *Notes on the Settlement and Indian Wars of the Western Parts of Virginia and Pennsylvania* (1824) contains an abridged version of the captivities of the heroes of the American Revolution, Colonel Crawford, Dr. John Knight, and John Slover, whose stories were first published in *Narratives of the Late Expedition against the Indians* (1783), but it tells for the first time of several other captivities. In *A Chronological Register of Boscawen, in the County of Merrimack, in the State of New Hampshire* (1823), Ebenezer Price documents the story, originally publicized by Cotton Mather more than a century earlier and later retold by Timothy Dwight, John Greenleaf Whittier, Henry David Thoreau, and Nathaniel Hawthorne, among others, of Dustan's murderous rampage against her captors. Anxious to uphold the reputation of this local goodwife, Price, writing from the viewpoint of a regional historian, applauds Dustan's heroism, a position that her other biographers were far less willing to defend.

Reprinted, rewritten, and previously unrecorded narratives also appear regularly in nineteenth-century military histories, where they are included as examples of the hardships endured by white pioneers during times of border warfare. *A Particular History of the Five Years French and Indian War in New England* (1870), for instance, contains a reprinting of John Norton's *Redeemed Captive* (1748), the story of a captivity by the French and Indians during King George's War (1744–48). Henry White reprints the Williams and Rowlandson narratives and summarizes those of several other captives in his *Indian Battles* (1859). Thomas Dawson's *The Ute War* (1879) provides extended narratives of "the privations and hardships of captive white women" during the Ute uprisings of the 1870s. Similar tales of Indian captivity appear in Joseph Pritts's *Incidents of Border Life* (1859) and Charles McKnight's *Our Western Border* (1875).

Captivity narratives were also reshaped for inclusion in ethnic histories where, in accordance with the general romanticization given the Indian as the nineteenth century progressed, they were edited to emphasize favorable aspects of Indian life. *The Book of American Indians* (1854) contains a truncated version of John Dunn Hunter's *Manners and Customs* (1823). Parts of *A Narrative of the Captivity and Adventures of John Tanner* (1830) were reprinted with little alteration in *A Collection of Indian Anecdotes* (1837). The subtitle of Anna C. Miller's *The Iroquois; or, The Bright Side of Indian Character* (1855), a biography of Mary Jemison, reveals its favorable sentiments toward the American Indian. Even more significantly, an account of the death of Jane MacCrea, whose captivity and death during the American Revolution had long been used as propaganda against Indians, was reworked by William Stone for William Beach's *Indian Miscellany* (1877), a collection of Indian-related documents. Far from blaming Indians for MacCrea's murder, Stone argues that she was shot by American soldiers who intended to kill her captors and that her scalp was accidentally torn from her head by Indians who chivalrously tried to break her fall from a horse.

Still other historians and ethnologists simply reprinted verbatim as many captivity narratives as they could find. They believed that if these documents were accurately preserved posterity would differentiate fact from fiction. Dozens of captivity narratives are reprinted in Samuel Gardner Drake's *Indian Captivities* (1839) and Henry Rowe Schoolcraft's *The American Indians* (1851), works that were so assiduously collected that even today they remain valuable repositories of information about Indian/white relations. They stand in contrast to such collections as the *Affecting History of the Dreadful Distresses of Frederick Manheim's Family* (1793) and Archibald Loudon's *A Selection of Some of the Most Interesting Narratives of Outrages Committed by the Indians* (1808–11), where narratives were selected, edited, and structured to maximize their potential as anti-Indian propaganda.

While most of the historical writing about Indian captivity was hastily written and haphazardly researched, some notable literary exceptions do exist. Participating in the growing national interest in the past, skilled writers such as Washington Irving, George Bancroft, Francis Parkman, and Henry David Thoreau incorporated accounts of Indian captivity into their more sophisticated historical works. Espousing the general philosophy that "human progress had proceeded westward, from the Middle East to North America" (Levin, 27), where it culminated in the democratic institutions of the United States, these writers believed that history should be well-written. On a practical level, this theory meant that good historical writing should illustrate their philosophy of history in a way that was profound, dramatic, and inspiring. Incorporating stories of Indian captivity into their writings became one way for these historians to accomplish their goals.

Washington Irving was perhaps the least philosophical of the historians to write about Indian captivity. Familiar with Irving's *A Tour of the Prairies* (1835), an account of life among Indians and trappers on the frontier, John Jacob Astor commissioned the writer to compose a history

of Astor's fur-trading empire in the Northwest. The book that Irving
wrote was *Astoria* (1836), with its dramatic account of the captivity of the
explorer and mountain man John Colter by Blackfoot Indians at the
headwaters of the Missouri River in 1806. A member of the Lewis and
Clark expedition, Colter was given the chance to save his life by outrun-
ning a group of armed warriors. Managing to outmaneuver even the
fastest Indian runners, Colter was said to have escaped by hiding under a
beaver lodge until his pursuers believed him drowned. Although Irving
claims to have met Colter while researching *Astoria*, he extracted the
narrative almost verbatim from *Travels in the Interior of America* (1809) by
John Bradbury, who purportedly was told it by Colter. Highly interesting in itself, the Colter captivity develops added meaning within the
historical and philosophical framework that Irving gives it. According to
Irving, Colter was "another of those heroes" whose "story deserves
particular citation, as showing the hair-breadth adventures to which
these solitary rovers of the wilderness are exposed."[5] Like the sailors and
adventurers who preceded them, individuals like Colter make "vast
internal voyages" (*Astoria*, 147) across uncharted wilderness. Just as
explorers brought European civilization across the oceans to the Americas, people like Colter finish the process through their explorations and
adventures. As an inevitable part of this process, the "restless and
predatory tribe[s]" of "savages" who "infest" the frontier must be
subdued if white civilization is to triumph. Thus, Irving uses Colter's
captivity to illustrate the Indian's "vindictive cruelty" and "implacable
hostility to the white men," attitudes that, to Irving's thinking, required
the violent elimination of the Indian from the West (*Astoria*, 147).

The Indian captivity episodes in George Bancroft's 12-volume *History
of the United States* (1834–82) fulfill much the same rhetorical function as
the Colter episode in Irving's *Astoria*. An influential scholar and writer,
Bancroft sympathized with the plight of the Indians, but in keeping
with his philosophy of white Anglo-Saxon historical supremacy, he
believed that history necessitated their elimination. Thus, whenever
Bancroft recounts a war in which Indians were killed, he interjects a
captivity episode to reinforce his racist thesis that Indians were hopelessly attached to "savage" ways and therefore doomed to perish. Thus,
Captain John Smith was "a being of a higher order" whom the Virginia
"barbarians" would have murdered had not "the gentle feelings of
humanity" bloomed "unconsciously in the bosom of Pocahontas."[6] In
justifying the murder of Indians by the Puritans during King Philip's
War, Bancroft introduces Mary Rowlandson's captivity to emphasize

that "there was no security but to seek out the hiding-places of the natives, and destroy them by surprize" (*History*, II, 107). Because the Indians of New England refused to accept white civilization, "Destiny had marked" them for "extermination" (*History*, II, 109). The inclusion of the captivity and death of Jane MacCrea fulfills a double function. During the summer of 1777, Jane MacCrea had secretly left the safety of Fort Edward, New York, to marry David Jones, a Tory soldier in the army of General Burgoyne. MacCrea, however, never reached her destination. For reasons that historians still debate, she was killed and scalped, presumably by the Indian guides that the British had employed to protect her during her journey. The subject of numerous retellings, the MacCrea captivity was used during the American Revolution as a rallying point to foment public opinion against Great Britain for its use of Indian allies. According to Bancroft, although "the incident was not of unusual barbarity," it exemplifies "enormities too horrid to think of" which Indians might perpetrate if "left to themselves" (*History*, IX, 371). It also illustrates Bancroft's reasoning as to why the American colonists won the American Revolution. To Bancroft's thinking, the British were as barbaric as the Indians whom they hired to kill "innocent women and infants" (*History*, IX, 371).

Like Bancroft, Francis Parkman incorporated Indian captivity episodes into his historical writings. Educated at Harvard, Parkman devoted much of his life to researching and writing about the conflict between France and England for the control of North America. Essentially a literary man, Parkman immediately recognized the metaphoric function the captivity narrative could perform within the context of longer historical works. Like his portrayal of the wars between France and England, it was "dramatic, romantic, and tragic" (Levernier and Cohen, 143). In both *The Conspiracy of Pontiac* (1851) and *The Jesuits in North America* (1867), Parkman uses Indian captivity episodes for literary effect. Having essentially the same philosophy of history as Bancroft, Parkman felt it a foregone conclusion that Indians must make way for white civilization. In *The Conspiracy of Pontiac*, Parkman's massive investigation into the attempts of the Ottawa chief Pontiac to organize a rebellion against the English, he includes a section on the return of white captives according to the terms of a treaty between Colonel Henry Bouquet and the Indians (see Fig. 9). Sympathetic with the Indians, Parkman describes the affection that bonded captors and captives, but in keeping with his philosophy of white "progress," he uses the captivity episodes to reinforce why he felt the American Indian must be elimi-

Elaborate engraving captioned "The Indians delivering up the English Captives to Colonel Bouquet" from *An Historical Account of the Expedition against the Ohio Indians* (1766). This event took place in November 1764, at the end of the war known as Pontiac's Rebellion. The illustration shows the grief of the Delawares and Shawnees at having to surrender their adopted captives. *Courtesy of the Edward E. Ayer Collection, the Newberry Library.*

nated. Revealing his prejudices through his descriptions, Parkman calls the children of marriages between whites and Indians "hybrid offspring,"[7] and he notes that white captives, whom he describes as "wild young barbarians" (*Pontiac*, 419), are not adopted by the Indians until "the old, the sick, or the despairing had been tomahawked, as useless encumbrances" (*Pontiac*, 425) and "the vengeance of the conquerors is sated" through having "shot, stabbed, burned, or beaten to death, enough to satisfy the shades of their departed relatives" (*Pontiac*, 429).

In *The Jesuits in North America*, Parkman uses Indian captivity episodes to explain his theory about why England gained domination over both Indians and the French. Not only are the captivity episodes in this work designed to illustrate that Indians were opposed to progress and hence doomed to annihilation, but they also illustrate what Parkman perceived as the futile, misdirected, yet admirably heroic conduct of the French Jesuit missionaries whom Parkman simultaneously "admired" and "despised." According to Parkman, Indians were "bereft of the instincts of humanity" and therefore incapable of change: "Would the Iroquois, left undisturbed to work out their own destiny, have ever emerged from the savage state? Advanced as they were beyond most other American tribes, there is no indication whatever of a tendency to overpass the confines of a wild hunter and a warrior life. They were inveterately attached to it, impracticable conservatists of barbarism, and in ferocity and cruelty they matched the worst of their race."[8] At the same time, "The lives of these early Canadian Jesuits," states Parkman, "attest to the earnestness of their faith and the intensity of their zeal; but it was a zeal bridled, curbed and ruled by" the "equivocal morality" of a religion based on "superstition, bigotry, and corruption" (*Jesuits*, 98, 187). No amount of fortitude, however admirable, could eradicate the fact that in Parkman's opinion the "enthusiasm in which the Jesuit saw the direct inspiration of God" was actually "fostered by all the prestige of royalty and all the patronage of power." Jesuit colonization had failed because the Jesuits mistakenly considered "the vicious imbecile who sat on the throne of France" to be "the anointed champion of the Faith, and the cruel and ambitious priest who ruled king and nation alike" to be "the chosen instrument of Heaven" (*Jesuits*, 244–45). Within this context, accounts of the captivities of the Jesuit martyrs offer Parkman the opportunity to dramatize what he perceived as the cruelty of the Indians and the stupidity of the French, thereby valorizing his theory of British cultural superiority.

Like Irving, Bancroft, and Parkman, Henry David Thoreau used Indian captivity in his philosophical and historical writings. To dramatize the relationship between the past and the present, Thoreau incorporates a retelling of Hannah Dustan's captivity in his personal and social history, *A Week on the Concord and Merrimack Rivers* (1849). As Thoreau recognized, Dustan's brutal slaying of her Indian captors lent itself to philosophical and ethical considerations. The first to tell the tale, Cotton Mather saw the hand of God directing Dustan's actions. In Timothy Dwight's *Travels in New England and New York* (1821) and in John Greenleaf Whittier's *Legends of New England* (1831), Dustan is apologetically depicted as temporarily insane after having witnessed the violent death, a few days prior, of her infant. Totally unsympathetic toward Dustan, Nathaniel Hawthorne's sketch on "The Duston Family," which he published in 1836 while editor of *The American Magazine of Useful and Entertaining Knowledge*, roundly vilifies Dustan as a "bloody old hag" and "raging tigress."[9] To Thoreau, what Dustan represents is more important than what she did. As both a victim of brutality and an instrument of its perpetuation, Dustan symbolizes those violent impulses within the self illustrating destructive historical patterns that will, unless checked, inevitably repeat themselves in the present. Imbuing the tale with mythic overtones, Thoreau refers to an "apple-tree" three times in recounting his version of the Dustan captivity, and he artfully interpenetrates past with future when he states, "This seems a long time ago, yet it happened since Milton wrote his Paradise Lost."

The Captivity Narrative as Folklore

The same interest that led local antiquarians like Elihu Hoyt and epic historians like Bancroft and Parkman to write about Indian captivity also prompted the proliferation of tales, ballads, and legends about the subject among the folk of nineteenth-century America. In *Snow-Bound* (1866), for example, John Greenleaf Whittier, himself a collector of folk traditions, mentions his family's familiarity with the subject. According to Whittier, his mother

> Told how the Indians hordes came down
> At midnight on Chocheco town,
> And how her own great-uncle bore
> His cruel scalp-mark to fourscore.[10]

Like historical accounts of captivity, folk materials about the theme originate in the East after the threat of Indian/white warfare had passed and the folk could comfortably romanticize Indians as part of a vanishing heritage or vilify them to emphasize the fortitude and ingenuity of Yankee captives who survived and often escaped.

Several captivity ballads, for example, fit these criteria. "It Was Brilliant Autumn Time" recounts the captivity of Jane MacCrea. Another ballad, "Young Strongbow," tells about an Indian brave who attended Dartmouth, returned to his tribe, and later secured the release of his former roommate, a soldier captured during a war. As far as can be ascertained, both of these ballads originated in the East during the early nineteenth century and enjoyed widespread popularity among the folk.[11] Perhaps the most interesting example of balladry about captivity, however, is "The White Captive," about a young white woman heroically rescued from death at the stake by an Indian chief named Olbin. Its historical basis and origination remain obscure. It was first collected for the *Columbia Sentinel* of Boston in 1818, and variants have been found in states as geographically separated as Maine, Kentucky, Florida, Missouri, Texas, and Utah, under such different titles as "Amanda, the Captive," "Young Albin," "Bright Amanda," "Her White Bosom Bare," and even a garbled rendition called "The White-Bosomed Bear," in which the heroine, "Amandrew," was tied for a time to a "white-bosomed bear." According to tradition, the events in the ballad possibly took place near Lincoln, New Hampshire, on the Merrimack River. "Young Albin" has been identified as Metallak, a Coo-ash-auke Indian chief, who at the time of his death in 1847 in Stewartstown, New Hampshire, is thought to have been 120 years old. Metallak is said to have lost his tribal authority for having rescued a white woman from death by burning.[12]

Ultimately, however, how this ballad originated is of lesser consequence than what it reveals about the use of Indian captivity among the folk. Variants of the ballad illustrate how the theme was adapted to folk culture in different places at different times. In Western versions, for example, attention is drawn to Amanda's "charms," most notably "her white bosom bare."[13] In Eastern variants, these details are absent. Western variants are probably more sexually suggestive because they were sung by cowboys to a male audience around a campfire. Eastern versions were most likely recited to the family around a hearth. Perhaps the most striking differences, however, between Eastern and Western versions of the ballad center around the relationship between Indians and whites. In Eastern versions, a hint of romance, conspicuously absent from Western variants, is suggested between Amanda and the Indian chief: "Amanda returned to her village and home/Lamenting that Albion a savage was born."[14] Moreover, Eastern renditions conclude with a hope of reconciliation between Indians and whites that is absent in Western forms: "And long may the banner of peace o'er them save—/Amanda the captive, and Albin the brave!"[15] Free from the possibility of war with the Indians, the white popular culture of Vermont and New Hampshire could both accept and romanticize the American Indian. In the West, where Indian/white military confrontations continued to erupt until the 1880s, no such reconciliation was possible.

Like ballads, folktales about Indian captivity also received wide circulation during the nineteenth century. The vast majority of these tales emphasize the ingenuity of captives who outwit their captors and escape, thus reinforcing the premise, deep-seated in the white culture, that Indians deserved to lose their lands because they were too ignorant to develop them. One such tale is told about Daniel Abbott from Concord, New Hampshire, who was captured by Indians during the Seven Years' War and so successfully pretended to enjoy Indian culture that his captors adopted him into their tribe and promised to make him a chief. Among the booty taken from Concord were several pairs of skates, which the Indians unsuccessfully tried to use. A skilled skater, Abbott nonetheless acted as if he, too, were unable to skate. Later, after the Indians had given up, he put on the skates, disappeared around a corner, and fled down Lake Champlain to Albany.[16]

Similar tales of clever escapes held widespread currency throughout the East. The folk in New York, for example, recall how a local woman drugged her captors by slipping the leaves from a tree known to induce sleep into their tea. Not only did the woman escape, but she took with her the livestock and plunder her captors had stolen.[17] Another New York captive is said to have escaped from captivity by feigning illness to gain the opportunity to linger behind his captors and then hide in some brush. When his captors began searching for him, he raised his cap on a stick. The Indians shot at the cap, but when they came to scalp him he rose up and killed them instead (Neal, 204–6).

Indeed, folktales about escapes from Indian captivity were so popular throughout the nineteenth century that folk celebrities evolved whose legendary reputations sometimes rested on these accounts. Among these heroes was Tim Murphy, known in New York state as the "Savior of the Schoharie" because of his legendary exploits there as scout, soldier, and Indian fighter.[18] The actual details of Murphy's life are difficult to unravel. Legend holds that he was born in Minisink, New Jersey, in 1751, but that he grew up in Pennsylvania, where he married. According to tradition, Murphy's wife and children were murdered during an Indian attack while he was travelling. As a result, Murphy is said to have vowed revenge against all Indians, whom he is said to have spent the remainder of his life searching out and killing. Folktales about Murphy's escapes from captivity are legion. One tradition holds that Murphy outwitted his captors by leaping from a high cliff and hitting the ground so hard that he was buried to his knees. When confident that his captors had given him up for dead, he is said to have walked to the nearest town, borrowed a shovel, dug himself out, and then planted his crops.[19] In another tale Murphy is said to have enticed his Indian captors to the edge of a thin ice on a river and then turned so suddenly that they, unable to stop, fell in.[20]

In some instances, folktales about Indian captivity became so ingrained in the white popular culture that they became associated with several different folk personalities. One such tale is told about Indians who capture Murphy while he is splitting logs. Undaunted, Murphy requested their assistance in helping him to pull apart a log in which a wedge was stuck. When the Indians put their hands in the crack, Murphy removed the wedge and thus trapped them by their fingers so that he could kill them. As far as can be ascertained, this classic "trickster tale" originated with Murphy, but it has been told with little variation about the Pennsylvania scout Tom Quick, and versions have also been found in Maine, New Hampshire, Illinois, Kentucky, and Arkansas, among other places (Levernier and Cohen, 172). Perhaps the most interesting variant of this tale occurs in Missouri, where the motif was shaped into the type of tall-tale so common in Western lore. In it a pioneer tells his wife about killing four Indians by tricking them into placing their fingers into a crack in a log. His skeptical wife laughed at him, but "when he showed her the big brass pistol and the three tomahawks and some other things he took off the dead Indians, she didn't have no more to say."[21]

One striking difference between Eastern and Western variants of this tale centers on the fate of the entrapped Indians. In Eastern variants the Indians are occasionally released unharmed, and less attention is given to their execution than to the ingenuity of the captive who outmaneuvered them. In Western versions the Indians are mercilessly executed. The same cultural factors which shaped and reshaped variants of "The White Captive" apparently affected variant folktales about Indian captivity as they moved Westward with the frontier. In the West, white settlers considered Indians too great a threat to be treated leniently.

Eventually, oral folk traditions about Indian captivity were appropriated by a pseudofolkloristic literary culture, where they were used in a variety of literary and social contexts. Stories, for example, about the nearly miraculous escapes from captivity associated with folk celebrities such as Tim Murphy and Tom Quick were used by John Filson in his "Adventures of Col. Daniel Boon," published as part of his *The Discovery, Settlement, and Present State of Kentucke* (1784), and by Timothy Flint in his *Biographical Memoir of Daniel Boone* (1833) to embellish the burgeoning nineteenth-century reputation of Daniel Boone as pathfinder, scout, and frontier hero.[22] These same tales were also used by Southwestern humorists who created humorous, larger than life caricatures such as Sal Fink, the mythical daughter of Mike Fink, who burst loose from the bonds that held her and then roasted her Indian captors by dragging them into their own campfire. In the end, these same materials, by this time more overused and commercialized than even Cotton Mather's numerous retellings of the story of Hannah Dustan, became the substance of dime novels such as Edward Sylvester Ellis's *Seth Jones; or, the Captives of the Frontier* (1860) and Paul Bibbs's *Moccasin Bill; or, Cunning Serpent the Ojibwah* (1873), where they were read by tens of thousands of young readers in search of lively but cheap frontier fare.[23]

The Captivity Narrative as Children's Literature

The wave of cultural nationalism that brought narratives of Indian captivity to individuals as different as historians and the singers of folk ballads also brought the subject to the attention of writers generating literature for America's rising generation of young people.[24] Before the nineteenth century, American children's literature had been, as R. Gordon Kelly has noted, "simply a variant of English taste," but the spirit of cultural chauvinism that engulfed America, particularly during the decades preceding the Civil War, gave shape to a type of children's literature that, according to John C. Crandall, reflected "the nationalistic spirit which nurtured it."[25] Affirmations of the American Dream— stories of frontier life and adventure, biographies of American heroes, and tales of the rise from rags to riches—replaced Old World sagas about the exploits of kings, princesses, knights, and aristocrats as the literature that white nineteenth-century Americans, anxious to preserve and foster their country's democratic ideals, encouraged their youth to read. Even religious institutions, whose primary goal was to teach the Bible, not nationalism, insisted that Sunday school tracts be "thoroughly American in their coloring and environment."²⁶ Written or rewritten for children, narratives of Indian captivity were seen as a decidedly American medium to entertain and instruct the young in such subjects as reading, writing, history, and moral behavior—though not necessarily in that order—as well as to perpetuate conventional attitudes, among them, unfortunately, the conviction of white, Protestant, Anglo-Saxon superiority.

Because nineteenth-century educators considered fact more edifying than fiction, captivity stories written for children were usually based on an actual captivity, and because these captivities usually occurred on the frontier during times of border warfare, they were used to teach children about history and legend. *The Deerfield Captive* (1831), about the captivities of the Puritan minister John Williams and his family, is subtitled "A Narrative of Facts for the Instruction of the Young." Based on Williams's *The Redeemed Captive, Returning to Zion* (1707), the children's version clarifies obscure points of colonial history that serve as background to the narrative. Among the historical material it contains are discussions of the French and Indian Wars, the settlement of Plymouth by the Pilgrims, and the early histories of several towns in western Massachusetts, including Springfield, Northampton, and Deerfield. Reprinted from *The New Mirror for Travellers* (1828), James Kirke Paulding's satire on fashionable summer resorts in the Hudson River region, "Murderer's Creek," a selection in both *The Children's Picture Book of Indians* (1833) and McGuffey's *Newly Revised Eclectic Third Reader* (1846), uses folklore and legend to explain how the Otterkill, a stream that flows into the Hudson River at a juncture a few miles northwest of West Point, received its more romantic name of "Murderer's Creek." According to local legend, a pioneer family named Stacey was living near the banks of the Otterkill when the Indians of the area, long enraged by incessant white encroachments on their lands, planned a surprise attack. No one was to be spared. In order for the attack to succeed, secrecy was an absolute necessity, for if the settlers learned beforehand of the uprising, they would have time to warn their neighbors, and not only might the rebellion fail, but it might also very well result in the needless slaughter of many Indians. Fearful for the safety of his friends the Staceys, Naoman, an elderly Indian chief, warned the family of the uprising and urged them to leave the area at once. While fleeing down the Otterkill, the Staceys were captured by the hostile Indians and threatened with torture and death if they refused to tell who had warned them of the impending attack. Faithful to the Indian who had been faithful to them, the Staceys remained silent even when the Indians prepared to execute their children. Moved by this gesture of fidelity, Naoman confessed his complicity in the incident, and the Indians massacred both Naoman and the Staceys. Thus, the legend informs us, in memory of the place where the Stacey family lived and died, the Otterkill "is called 'Murderer's Creek.'"[27]

By emphasizing the fact that white pioneers willingly faced and even endured ordeals like Indian captivity so that their country might eventually become a place where Anglo-Saxon values might flourish, captivity narratives were also used to foster patriotism among the young. *The Deerfield Captive*, for instance, "shows, in a striking manner, what trials our ancestors were compelled to endure in laying out these fair settlements which it is our lot to inherit."[28] Its anonymous author hopes that "the sufferings of the first civilized inhabitants of New England" will fill "the tender mind[s]" of its readers with "the deepest gratitude for the privileges and the blessings" which the "labors and privations" of their ancestors have secured for them. "In order to possess the liberty of worshipping God, according to the dictates of their own consciences," explains the author, the Pilgrims and Puritans who first colonized America "sailed across the Atlantic ocean, a distance of three thousand miles, to a new and uncivilized country," forsaking a "land of comfort and plenty for an unknown wilderness" where, "surrounded by beasts of prey and savage barbarians," they "would have to encounter all manner of hardships"—captivities, of course, included (*Deerfield*, 8–10).

Reminiscent of earlier phases in the captivity tradition, captivity narratives written for children often used the captivity experience as a means for teaching religious and moral lessons. Explicit about what he wished to achieve, the Congregationalist missionary Elias Cornelius wrote *The Little Osage Captive* (1822) to persuade children and youth "to embrace the gospel themselves, and do what they can to send it to others."[29] In this work, Cornelius discourses on the value of missionary efforts to convert the world's pagan population, particularly those "heathen" (*Osage 2*, 59) who were fortunate or unfortunate enough to live in North America, within easy reach of zealots such as Cornelius. In *The Deerfield Captive*, Williams is described as "a good man" because "he was patient and submissive." Rather than "murmer or complain" about his fate, he "put his trust and confidence in God" and "was supported by his faith and his piety" (*Deerfield*, 34–36). According to Cornelius, the young captive girl in his narrative "was an excellent example to children who have had, from their infancy, a thousand comforts and privileges which she had not enjoyed." Unlike "many children who do not remember the kindnesses which they receive, nor feel thankful for them," this child "was *a very grateful little girl*" (*Osage 2*, 39).

Captivity narratives written for children were also used to perpetuate racial and religious prejudices, which, though painfully noticeable to the modern reader, apparently did not disturb the moral certitude of nineteenth-century pedagogues whose function it was to indoctrinate young Americans with a lifelong respect for the values, admirable or otherwise, of their elders. Because the Spanish, the French, and especially the American Indian threatened the spread of Anglo-Saxon culture westward, southward, and northward, they were depicted as retrogressive, anarchic, and, at least in the case of the Indian, degenerate and subhuman. In *The Stolen Boy* (1830), a story about the adventures of a Spanish youth captured by "Cumanches," Barbara Hofland takes every possible opportunity to articulate her theories about Anglo-Saxon racial superiority. While Hofland begrudgingly admits that Indians "have some good properties" (they can sometimes be "punctual" and even "hospitable"), she states that their vices "more than counter-balance their virtues."[30] These vices, which Hofland is quick to enumerate, include larceny, murder, revenge, bigotry, superstition, laziness, cruelty, cannibalism, and, of course, "that terrible propensity to drunkenness, which is such a remarkable trait in their characters," even among "their wisest and gravest chiefs" (*Boy*, 13). These supposed vices are also used to justify the seizure of Native American lands by the European:

. . . An Indian in general thinks that fighting is the great business of life; and so subject are the various nations of Indians to warfare, that they have always remained few in number, and with a beautiful and fruitful country, rich in all the means of life, and capable of giving abundance to myriads, have continued to be mere patches of population, scattered over the continent that may give birth to empires. Had they been united in mind, flourishing in numbers, and improving in the arts of life, no stranger could have entered their country and taken possession of their birthright: they could not have been so situated that other nations might say (as they have said, in fact,) and might do it with truth—"Give place to me, for I am worthier than thou." (*Boy*, 60)

In her haste to condemn Indians, Hofland accuses them of being "akin to the devil" (*Boy*, 24), the view once articulated by the Puritans and still expressed some 200 years later. When the Comanches who captured Manuel, the subject of the narrative, use their knowledge of woodcraft to escape from soldiers who are pursuing them, Hofland credits their success to supernatural powers obtained from the devil. Nevertheless, when Manuel escapes from captivity by means of wilderness skills that he acquired from the Indians, Hofland appreciatively comments that he exhibited a "firmness of endurance" that was "worthy of the highest praise" (*Boy*, 131). Not only are Indians thus considered incapable of doing good, but their vices become virtues when practiced by whites.

Hofland also criticizes the Spanish. Like the American Indians, the Spanish are "destined to be vanquished" because they are "much too indolent" (*Boy*, 14). Without industry, she explains, it is possible to "starve in the midst of plenty" and to "want" while "in possession of an immense expanse of fruitful country" (*Boy*, 51). No doubt Hofland, like many of her contemporaries, wished to secure that land for Anglo-, not Spanish-, American culture. As *The Stolen Boy* reveals, as early as 1830, white Americans had pointed the flag of Manifest Destiny toward Mexico, and many of the solders who later died while defending the claims of the United States to lands north of the Rio Grande may very well have been inspired to do so, at least in part, from youthful memories of such tales as *The Stolen Boy*.

The Casco Captive (1839) casts an equally covetous glance toward Canadian lands. Based on the episode in Mather's *Magnalia Christi Americana* (1702), *The Casco Captive* recounts the five-year captivity of the Puritan woman Hannah Swarton among the French and Indians of Canada at the end of the seventeenth century. Like Hofland's description of the Spanish who control Mexico, the French who inhabit Canada are depicted as "intolerant, cruel, and vicious."[31] Because they are under the influence of the "Church of Rome" (*Casco*, 10)—whose "artful priests" encourage "hypocrisy, bigotry, encroachment, fraud, violence, and bloodshed" (*Casco*, 16, 18)—the French have also failed to prosper, at least in contrast to their neighbors in the United States. "Such," proclaims the anonymous author of *The Casco Captive*, "is the offspring of a corrupt church! Such are the consequences of man's apostasy from God!" (*Casco*, 23). "While the Roman Catholic religion keeps the French of Canada from improvement and growth," continues the author, "we, with the Bible, the preacher and the schoolmaster, shall spread and spread over the wilderness, till, with a peaceful population, we crowd to the St. Lawrence, and scatter over the hills and valleys the cheerful school-house and the sacred place of public worship" (*Casco*, 48). Within this context, Catholic Indians were, of course, seen as the ultimate affront to Anglo-American social decorum. They combined, in the words of *The Casco Captive*, the "innate depravity" of their race with the "bigotry" and "superstition" of their French proselytizers and were, therefore, "immoral and wretched, as the heathen generally are" (*Casco*, 7).

The Civil War saw a decline in the cultural nationalism that had previously encouraged the writing and publication of children's stories about Indian captivity, and the captivity narrative was no longer considered appropriate reading for impressionable young minds. Among the factors that contributed to this shift in sensibilities were the gradual assimilation of the Indian into a consciously cultivated historical heritage, and, as Kelly has pointed out, a growing postwar spirit of sectionalism, industrialism, and urbanism that challenged the New England values that had dominated children's literature prior to the 1860s (Kelly, 101). So profound was this change in attitude that by the early decades of the twentieth century the United States Congress had established the Boy Scouts of America, whose goal was to encourage youth to practice crafts and values learned from the American Indian.

The Captivity Narrative as Novel

While the tendency to fictionalize the captivity experience had certainly been present in even the earliest captivity narratives, fiction was usually subordinate to the aims of propaganda. Not until the last decade of the eighteenth century did American writers shift their perspective about Indian captivity from fiction in the form of propaganda to fiction in the form of the novel. Just as changing cultural factors had prompted the production of the luridly sensationalized anti-Indian narratives, so too did cultural forces encourage the publication of novels about Indian captivity. When in 1818 Sydney Smith wrote in the *Edinburgh Review*, "In the four quarters of the globe, who reads an American book?",[32] aspiring American novelists were duly embarrassed. As Philip Freneau had earlier explained, "Dependence is a state of degradation, fraught with disgrace; and to be dependent on a foreign mind, for what we can ourselves produce, is to add to the crime of indolence, the weakness of stupidity."[33]

Acutely aware that while America had achieved political independence it still remained culturally indebted to Europe for the forms and themes of much of its literature, novelists turned to the American past in an attempt to provide an appropriately nationalistic backdrop for their writing. Indian captivity was a part of that past and one that for more than two centuries had clearly interested both Old World and New World audiences. In fact, fearful that Old World writers would usurp the subject before their American counterparts had mined its full imaginative potential, Rodman Drake rebuked his American literary colleagues for allowing the British poet Thomas Campbell to preempt the subject in Campbell's epic poem *Gertrude of Wyoming* (1809): "No native bard the patriot harp hath ta'en, / But left to minstrel of a foreign strand / To sing the beauteous scenes of nature's lovliest land."[34] As Charles Brockden Brown wrote in his preface to *Edgar Huntly* (1799), one of the first American novels based on the theme of Indian captivity, "Incidents of Indian hostility and the perils of the Western wilderness" are far more suitable themes for fiction than the "Puerile superstition and exploded manners, Gothic castles and chimeras" usually used by writers for the subject matter of their novels, "and for a native of America to overlook these would admit of no apology."[35]

As novelists like Brown earlier recognized, the Indian captivity narrative could, with only slight modification, be adapted to the prevailing literary forms of the late eighteenth- and early nineteenth-century English novel. Recognized as one of America's first novels, *The History of Maria Kittle* (1790) is, in the words of Roy Harvey Pearce, "simply a captivity narrative turned novel of sensibility" (Pearce, "Significances," 13). Its author, Ann Eliza Bleecker, was living in Tomahanick, New York, on the Albany frontier, at the time when she wrote the novel. Twice during the American Revolution, Bleecker and her family were forced to flee before an advancing army of marauding British soldiers and Indians. During one of these escapes, Bleecker's baby died of exhaustion and exposure. When her husband was captured by Tories in 1781, Bleecker became ill and never recovered, dying in 1783.

Although Bleecker herself narrowly escaped the Indian captivity she describes in *The History of Maria Kittle*, the novel is largely fictional and draws heavily upon the conventions of the sentimental novel so popular in England and America during the late eighteenth century. Set during the French and Indian Wars, its action centers around the captivity of a fictional heroine named Maria Kittle, who is abducted from her homestead in upstate New York. Taken to Montreal, Kittle is eventually ransomed by kindly French women, who welcome her into their community and commiserate with her losses and trials: "'Would to heaven!' said Madame De R., 'that the brutal nations were extinct, for never— never can the united humanity of France and Britain compensate for the horrid cruelties of their savage allies.'"[36] Assuming that his wife had been killed during the burning of their home, Mr. Kittle enlists in the army. The novel concludes with a tearful reunion between him and his wife, whom he accidentally encounters in Canada several years later.

Designed to evoke a maximum of sentimental response on the part of the reader, *The History of Maria Kittle* is filled with highly emotional scenes profusely described in the most sentimentalized diction. Commenting on his affection for his family, Mr. Kittle exclaims, "I feel my heart expand with love and gratitude to heaven every moment, nor can I ever be grateful enough" (*Maria*, 11). When her "tender husband" departed to seek help from neighbors, his "disconsolate" wife "burst into a flood of tears, which his endearments only augmented" (*Maria*, 15). When "the merciless hands of the savage" attack her family, Maria Kittle felt "unbearable anguish of her soul" and fell to "rending away her hair" and "roaring out her sorrows" (*Maria*, 21–22). When Mr. Kittle returns and finds his home in ruins and his family presumed dead, "his heart throbbed under the big emotion" and "uttering a deep groan, he fell insensible from his horse" (*Maria*, 28), only to recover and "in the furious extravagance of passion" tear "the hair from his head" and again fall "prostrate" to the ground (*Maria*, 30). When Mrs. Kittle is finally reunited with her husband, the emotions are so strong that she swoons with delight: "The tide of joy and surprise was too strong for the delicacy of her frame; she gave a faint of exclamation, and stretching out her arms to receive him, dropped senseless at his feet" (*Maria*, 65).

In the hands of Ann Eliza Bleecker, the trappings of the Indian captivity—the wilderness journeys, the miraculous escapes, the merciless enemy—are all transformed and converted into those of the sentimental novel. Kittle's captivity and forced march to Canada provide the occasion for a series of affecting scenes in which she "escapes one danger" only "to encounter others" (*Maria*, 15), from all of which, like the heroines in the novels of Henry Fielding and Samuel Richardson, she only narrowly escapes. Indians function as villains whose tyranny proves as traumatically terrifying as that in any sentimental novel. "'O hell!'", exclaims Mrs. Kittle in a particularly trying moment of pathos, "'are not thy flames impatient to cleave the center and engulf these wretches in thy ever burning waters? Are there no thunders in Heaven—no avenging Angel—no God to take notice of such Heaven defying cruelties?'" (*Maria*, 22). Even nature reinforces the sentiment evoked by the plot: "The shrill shrieks of owls, the loud cries of the wolf, and the mournful screams of panthers, which were redoubled by distant echoes as the terrible sounds seemed dying away, shook her frame with cold tremors" (*Maria*, 38).

In much the same way that Bleecker adapted the captivity narrative to the conventions of the sentimental novel, Charles Brockden Brown used it to provide structure and metaphor for the gothic novel. One of Brown's most important novels, *Edgar Huntly; or, Memoirs of a Sleepwalker* is basically a captivity narrative turned gothic thriller. Complicated and convoluted, *Edgar Huntly* is part murder mystery and part psychological thriller. Its plot centers around Indian captivity as it affects the efforts of Edgar Huntly to discover his fiancée's brother, Waldegrave. Huntly's efforts to determine the identify of Waldegrave's assassin led him to a local farmhand, Clithero Edny, whom he observed sleepwalking and subsequently suspects of Waldegrave's murder. Following Clithero into the wilderness, Huntly eventually rescues a young lady captured by Indians. On their return home, both Huntly and the woman are once again captured. Eventually Huntly finds his way out of the wilderness only to discover that Waldegrave was murdered by the same Indians who had just captured Huntly. Indian captivity episodes constitute most of the second half of the novel.

At its most elemental level, Indian captivity provides an American substitute for the structural conventions of the gothic novel so popular in England during the late eighteenth and early nineteenth centuries. Indians are depicted as gothic villains. "I never looked upon or called up the image of a savage without shuddering," exclaims Huntly, whose family had been massacred during a surprise Indian attack on their home (*Huntly*, 165). In like manner, the American wilderness provides a setting that Huntly himself likens to "an inextricable maze" (*Huntly*, 164), suggestive of the "Gothic castles and chimeras" (*Huntly*, 29) so familiar to readers of gothic romance. Finally, Brown's use of "the wilder American landscape as a gothic symbol of the unconscious psyche"[37] creates "a field of action conceived not so much as a place as a state of mind" that allows "the actual and the imaginary [to] intermingle."[38] In exploring the American wilderness, Brown also explores the subconscious, thus anticipating such works as Edgar Allan Poe's *Narrative of A. Gordon Pym* (1838), Nathaniel Hawthorne's *The House of the Seven Gables* (1851), Herman Melville's *Typee* (1846), *Mardi* (1849), *Pierre* (1852), *Benito Cereno* (1856), and *Billy-Budd* (1924), Robert Montgomery Bird's *Nick of the Woods* (1837), Mark Twain's *A Connecticut Yankee in King Arthur's Court* (1889), and even Henry James's *The Portrait of a Lady* (1881), all of which can be and have been read as captivity narratives in the tradition of Brown's *Edgar Huntly*.

The "incidents of Indian hostility and the perils of the wilderness" that drew the notice of Charles Brockden Brown also attracted the attention of nineteenth-century historical novelists in search of imbuing their materials with an American identity. During the nineteenth century, dozens of historical novels, among them Jesse Lynch Holman's *The Prisoners of Niagara* (1810), Catherine Sedgwick's *Hope Leslie* (1827), and William Gilmore Simms's *Yemassee* (1835), were written about Indian captivity. It was, however, with the historical romances of James Fenimore Cooper, particularly his Leatherstocking Tales, that "the Indian captivity narrative has made the most obvious impression on American, and indeed international, literary culture" (Levernier and Cohen, xxviii). Like Bleecker and Brown, Cooper was, as David T. Haberly explains, seeking "to use fiction to foster America's 'mental independence'"[39] from the writers and literary traditions of Europe. In researching fiction on American historical themes, Cooper read extensively in the frontier literature of early America, including the many captivity narratives popular in the East since the seventeenth century. As Haberly points out, Cooper's "passionate interest in the American past and the ready availability of such narratives—some dealing with his own area of upstate New York—would inevitably have led him to the captivities" (Haberly, 433).

Exactly which captivity narratives Cooper read is difficult to ascertain with certainty. Cooper's daughter, Susan Fenimore Cooper, wrote that he read such sources as John Heckewelder's *History, Manners, and Customs of the Indian Nations* (1818) and *Narrative of the Mission of the United Brethren among the Delaware and Mohegan Indians* (1820) and Cadwallader Colden's *The Five Indian Nations of Canada* (1747), all of which contain information about Indian captivity. Cooper is also known to have read such works about Indian captivity as Jonathan Carver's *Travels through the Interior Parts of North-America* (1778), David Humphrey's *An Essay on the Life of the Honourable Major-General Israel Putnam* (1788), and Alexander Henry's *Travels and Adventures in Canada and the Indian Territories* (1809).[40] In addition, many of the men and women in Cooper's narratives can be identified with legendary and folk personalities associated with Indian captivity, among them Daniel Boone, Tim Murphy, Tom Quick, and Jane MacCrea, as well as such obscure local celebrities as Ephraim Webster, the founder of Syracuse, said by some to be the basis for Cooper's Nathaniel Bumppo because, as Rosalyn Shapero explains, he "had as many narrow escapes and thrilling adventures as ever went into the story of pioneer days among the Indians."[41]

Clearly drawn to the tales of Indian captivity through his reading and research, Cooper first experimented with the subject in *The Last of the Mohicans* (1826) and returned to it throughout his career in such novels as *The Prairie* (1827), *The Wept of Wish-Ton Wish* (1829), *The Pathfinder* (1840), and *The Deerslayer* (1841), all of which are replete with captivity episodes. Indeed, through his captivity novels, Cooper became empowered to bring his readers into the world of the American frontier, permitting them to follow its emotional and ethical ramifications within a whirling narrative structure of pursuit, capture, escape, and pursuit.

Such is the case, for example, with *The Last of the Mohicans*. By structuring his novel around a series of captures and escapes, Cooper was able to give his novel the "mental independence" from the Old World that he urged American writers to seek. Not only do the captivity episodes provide a structural framework for an exciting wilderness adventure in the tradition of the captivity narratives of Mary Rowlandson and John Williams, but they also place it in a thoroughly American historical framework. Moreover, the relationship between the male Indians in the novel and their female captives allows Cooper to explore the emotional and ethical implications of the racial tensions present but often ignored in American culture. The result was a historical novel so brilliantly successful and influential that it was "for several generations one of the most popular of all American novels and a work which created an idea of America which put down deep and permanent roots in Europe, in Latin America, and in the recesses of our own minds" (Haberly, 432). Other novelists would emulate Cooper's use of the captivity materials, and Mark Twain would satirize it, but none would achieve the popular and critical success with the subject that Cooper did.

It has been said that, "It is not a nation's past that shapes its mythology but a nation's mythology that determines its past."[42] The Indian captivity narrative aptly illustrates this maxim. Through its long and complex history, it has acted like a litmus paper for writers to record and readers to interpret their historical and literary past. Like the United States, the captivity narrative evolved with the expanding frontier and reflected its preoccupations as well as its blind spots. On the surface, captivities contain accounts of courage and suffering; beneath the surface, they also chronicle cultural misunderstanding, bigotry, militarism, and racism. From the sixteenth- and seventeenth-century reports of Juan Ortiz, Captain John Smith, and Mary Rowlandson, through the sensationalized propaganda narratives of the eighteenth and nineteenth centuries, and eventually to the novels of Cooper and Twain, is a long and difficult journey for the literary historian to chronicle. Ultimately, the tradition is so complex that any attempts to generalize about it must be done with caution. But one thing remains certain: the subject continues to fascinate both writers, readers, and now television and movie viewers who absorb visual productions of captivity materials such as John Ford's *The Searchers* (1956), Thomas Berger's *Little Big Man* (1964), Larry McMurtry's *Lonesome Dove* (1985), Kevin Costner's Academy Award-winning *Dances with Wolves* (1991), and the much acclaimed remake of the *The Last of the Mohicans* (1992) with as much interest as did the seventeenth-century Puritans who read about Rowlandson and Dustan. As long as the American frontier exists as a real or imagined entity, permutations of the captivity narrative and the captivity psychology will no doubt continue to evolve.

Notes and References

Chapter One

1. Nathaniel Hawthorne, *The Scarlet Letter* (Columbus: Ohio State University Press, 1962 [orig. pub. 1850]), 61–62, 127.

2. Hector St. John de Crèvecoeur, *Letters from an American Farmer* (1782; Gloucester: P. Smith, 1968), 203, 219.

3. Colin G. Calloway, "An Uncertain Destiny: Indian Captivities on the Upper Connecticut River," *Journal of American Studies*, 17 (1983): 189; hereafter cited in text.

4. See Emma Coleman, *New England Captives Carried to Canada* (Portland, Maine: Southworth Press, 1925).

5. Alden T. Vaughan and Daniel K. Richter, "Crossing the Cultural Divide: Indians and New Englanders, 1605–1763," *Proceedings of the American Antiquarian Society*, 90 (1980): 91; hereafter cited in text.

6. Wilcomb E. Washburn, "Introduction," in *Narratives of North American Indian Captivity: A Selective Bibliography*, Alden T. Vaughan, ed. (New York: Garland, 1983), xviii; hereafter cited in text as "Introduction" for Washburn and *Bibliography* for Vaughan.

7. Washington Irving, *The Sketch-Book* (1818–19; New York and London: G. P. Putnam's Sons, 1910), 71.

8. Isaac Jogues, "Captivity of Father Isaac Jogues, of the Society of Jesus, Among the Mohawks" (1655), in *Held Captive by Indians: Selected Narratives, 1642–1836,* Richard VanDerBeets, ed. (Knoxville: University of Tennessee Press, 1973), 20, 35. Jogues's work hereafter cited in text as *Jogues*; VanDerBeets's work hereafter cited in text.

9. For a discussion that attempts to differentiate between myth and reality regarding the much publicized torture of captives, see Nathaniel Knowles, "The Torture of Captives by the Indians of Eastern North America," *Proceedings of the American Philosophical Society*, 82 (1940): 151–225.

10. Rachel Plummer, *Narrative of the Capture and Subsequent Sufferings of Mrs. Rachel Plummer* (1839), in *Held Captive by Indians*, VanDerBeets, ed., 360; hereafter cited in text as *RP*.

11. Mary Rowlandson, *A True History of the Captivity & Restoration of Mrs. Mary Rowlandson* (London: Joseph Poole, 1682), 32; hereafter cited in text as *MR*. All citations to Mary Rowlandson's narrative are from the above-cited London edition, the most authoritative of the extant editions. The 1682 editions published in Boston and Cambridge and titled *The Sovraignty & Goodness of God,*

together, with the Faithfulness of His Promises Displayed contain only minor variations from the London edition.

12. Elizabeth Hanson, *God's Mercy Surmounting Man's Cruelty* (Philadelphia: S. Keimer, 1728), 35–36; hereafter cited in text as *EH*.

13. Lonnie J. White, "White Women Captives of Southern Plains Indians, 1866–1875," *Journal of the West*, 8 (July 1969): 330; hereafter cited in text.

14. James T. DeShields, *Cynthia Ann Parker: The Story of Her Capture* (St. Louis: By the author, 1886), 22–23; hereafter cited in text as *Parker*.

15. Charles Johnston, *A Narrative of the Incidents Attending the Capture, Detention, and Ransom of Charles Johnston* (New York: J. and J. Harper, 1827), 53; hereafter cited in text as *CJ*.

16. Quoted by James Axtell in "The White Indians of Colonial America," *William and Mary Quarterly*, 32 (1975): 61; hereafter cited in text.

17. John Todd, *The Lost Sister of Wyoming. An Authentic Narrative* (Northampton: J. H. Butler, 1842), 140–41; hereafter cited in text as *Sister*.

18. Clifton Johnson, *An Unredeemed Captive* (Holyoke: Griffith, Axtel & Candy, 1897), 48.

19. Angie Debo, "Cynthia Ann Parker," *Notable American Women, 1607–1950*, vol. 3 (Cambridge, Mass.: Harvard University Press, 1971), 15–16.

20. James A. Levernier and Hennig Cohen, eds., *The Indians and Their Captives* (Wesport, Conn.: Greenwood Press, 1977), 98; hereafter cited in text.

21. Emeline L. Fuller, *Left by the Indians: Story of My Life* (Mt. Vernon, Iowa: Hawk-Eye, 1892), 29–30; hereafter cited in text as *Left*.

22. Robert Eastburn, *A Faithful Narrative of the Many Dangers and Sufferings as Well as Wonderful Deliverances of Robert Eastburn* (Philadelphia: William Dunlap, 1758), 39; hereafter cited in text as *RE*.

23. John Dunn Hunter, *Manners and Customs of Several Indian Tribes Located West of the Mississippi . . . to Which is Prefixed the History of the Author's Life during a Residence of Several Years among Them* (Philadelphia: J. Maxwell, 1823), 15; hereafter cited in text as *Manners*.

24. See R. W. G. Vail, *The Voice of the Old Frontier* (Philadelphia: University of Pennsylvania Press, 1949); hereafter cited in text.

25. See *Narratives of Captivity Among the Indians of North America* (Chicago: The Newberry Library, 1912) and Clara A. Smith, comp., *Supplement I* (Chicago: The Newberry Library, 1928).

26. See Alden T. Vaughan, ed., *Narratives of North American Indian Captivity: A Selected Bibliography* (New York: Garland, 1983); hereafter cited in text.

27. See Wilcomb E. Washburn, ed., *Narratives of North American Indian Captivities* (New York: Garland, 1977), vols. 1–111.

28. Roy Harvey Pearce, "The Significances of the Captivity Narrative," *American Literature*, 19 (1947): 16; hereafter cited in text.

29. James Russell, *Matilda: or, the Indian's Captive* (Toronto: William Briggs, 1833), i.

30. For a discussion of the historical debate surrounding the Hunter captivity, see Richard Drinnon, *White Savage: The Case of John Dunn Hunter* (New York: Schocken Books, 1972).

31. For a discussion of the Rusoe d'Eres narrative and the controversy surrounding its authorship, see Levernier and Cohen, 55–57.

32. Sarah L. Larimer, *The Capture and Escape; or, Life among the Sioux* (Philadelphia: Claxton, Remsen, and Hafelfinger, 1870); hereafter cited in text as *SL*.

33. Fanny Kelly, *Narrative of My Captivity among the Sioux Indians* (Hartford: Mutual Publishing Co., 1871), vi; hereafter cited in text as *FK*.

34. A comparison of the following pages in Larimer and Kelly indicates their textual closeness and strongly argues for Larimer's plagiarism: (1) *SL*, 54, and *FK*, 33; (2) *SL*, 59, and *FK*, 219; (3) *SL*, 59, and *FK*, 47; and (4) *SL*, 191, and *FK*, 92.

35. Caroline Harris, *History of the Captivity and Providential Release Therefrom of Mrs. Caroline Harris* (New York: Perry and Cooke, 1838); hereafter cited in text as *CH*.

36. Clarissa Plummer, *Narrative of the Captivity and Extreme Sufferings of Mrs. Clarissa Plummer* (New York: Perry and Cooke, 1838); hereafter cited in text as *CP*.

37. E. House, *A Narrative of the Captivity of Mrs. Horn with Mrs. Harris* (St. Louis: C. Keemle, 1839); hereafter cited in text as *Horn*.

38. Sarah Ann Horn, *An Authentic and Thrilling Narrative of the Captivity of Mrs. Horn . . . with Mrs. Harris* (Cincinnati: By the author, 1851); hereafter cited in text as *Horn and Harris*.

39. See Kathryn Zabelle Derounian, "The Publication, Promotion, and Distribution of Mary Rowlandson's Indian Captivity Narrative in the Seventeenth Century," *Early American Literature*, 23 (1988): 239–61.

40. For the publication history of the Johonnot and Hanson narratives, see Vail.

41. Cotton Mather, *Magnalia Christi Americana* (1702; Hartford, Conn.: Silas Andros, 1820), vol. 2, 666; hereafter cited in text as *Magnalia*.

42. James Everett Seaver, *Life of Mary Jemison*, 4th ed. (New York: Miller, Orton, and Mulligan, 1856), 12.

43. For previous discussions of the evolution of the captivity narratives through time, particularly regarding the various historic and cultural applications to which they were put, see Pearce, "Significances"; Richard VanDerBeets, "'A Thirst for Empire': The Indian Captivity Narrative as Propaganda," *Research Studies*, 40 (1972): 207–15; VanDerBeets, "A Surfeit of Style: The Indian Captivity Narrative as Penny Dreadful," *Research Studies*, 39 (1971): 297–306; VanDerBeets, *The Indian Captivity Narrative: An American Genre* (Lanham, Md.: University Press of America, 1984); and Levernier and Cohen, especially xv–xxx.

44. Massy Harbison, *A Narrative of the Sufferings of Massy Harbison* (Pittsburgh: S. Engles, 1825), 7; hereafter cited in text as *MH*.

45. Francis Joseph Bressani, "A Letter from a Jesuit in New France," in Levernier and Cohen, eds., *Indians*, 26.

46. John Williams, *The Redeemed Captive, Returning to Zion* (Boston: B. Green for Samuel Phillips, 1707), ii; hereafter cited in text as *Zion*.

47. Hannah Swarton, *A Narrative of Hannah Swarton*, in Cotton Mather, *Humiliations Follow'd with Deliverances* (Boston: B. Green and J. Allen, for Samuel Phillips, 1697), 55–56. Swarton's narrative hereafter cited in text as *HS*; Mather's work hereafter cited in text as *Humiliations*.

48. See Levernier and Cohen, xviii; and Increase Mather, *An Essay for the Recording of Illustrious Providences* (Boston: S. Green, 1682), 185.

49. Cotton Mather, *A Memorial of the Present Deplorable State of New-England* (Boston: S. Phillips, 1707), 31.

50. John Williams, *Reports of Divine Kindness* (Boston: S. Phillips, 1707), 1; hereafter referred to in text as *Reports*.

51. Cotton Mather, *Good Fetch'd Out of Evil* (Boston: B. Green, 1706), 7–8; hereafter cited in text as *Good*.

52. Jonathan Dickinson, *God's Protecting Providence* (Philadelphia: Reiner Jansen, 1699), i.

53. Alden T. Vaughan and Edward W. Clark, eds., *Puritans among the Indians: Accounts of Captivity and Redemption, 1676–1724* (Cambridge, Mass.: Harvard University Press, 1981), 21–22.

54. David Minter, "By Dens of Lions: Notes on Stylization in Early Puritan Captivity Narratives," *American Literature*, 45 (1973): 336, n. 7.

55. Cotton Mather, *Decennium Luctuosum* (Boston: B. Green and J. Allen, for Samuel Phillips, 1699), 138, 140; hereafter cited in text as *DL*.

56. Moses Coit Tyler, *History of American Literature, 1607–1765* (Ithaca, N. Y.: Cornell University Press, 1949), 363.

57. For the complete text of the Stewart narrative, together with a discussion of its significance and the role of almanacs in the development of the captivity narrative, see Levernier and Cohen, 60–63.

58. For the complete text of this broadside and a more extended analysis of both the Mason narrative and the Indian captivity as broadside, see Levernier and Cohen, 85–89.

59. Charles Saunders, *The Horrid Cruelty of the Indians Exemplified in the Life of Charles Saunders, Late of Charles-town, in South Carolina* (Birmingham: T. Warren, 1763), 4, 6, 7, 11, 12; hereafter cited in text as *CS*.

60. *A Narrative of the Extraordinary Life of John Conrad Shafford, the Dutch Hermit* (New York: C. L. Carpenter, 1840), 16.

61. William and Elizabeth Fleming, *A Narrative of the Sufferings and Surprizing Deliverance of William and Elizabeth Fleming* (Philadelphia: By the authors, 1756), 16; hereafter cited in text as *Fleming*.

62. Peter Williamson, *French and Indian Cruelty Exemplified in the Life and Various Vicissitudes of Fortune of Peter Williamson* (London: R. Griffiths, 1759); hereafter cited in text as *Williamson*.

63. John Thompson, *Travels and Surprizing Adventures* (New York: n. p., 1761), 8–9.

64. Jean Lowry, *A Journal of the Captivity of Jean Lowry and Her Children* (Philadelphia: William Bradford, 1760), 15; hereafter cited in text as *JL*.

65. *A Narrative of the Capture of Certain Americans at Westmorland by the Savages* (Hartford: n. p., c. 1780), 3; hereafter cited in text as *Westmorland*.

66. John Dodge, *A Narrative of the Capture and Treatment of John Dodge* (Philadelphia: T. Bradford, 1779), 5, 7; hereafter cited in text as *JD*. For a discussion of the Dodge narrative, its author, its background, and its significance as anti-British propaganda, see Levernier and Cohen, xxi, 50–51.

67. John Dodge, *An Entertaining Narrative of the Cruel and Barbarous Treatment and Extreme Sufferings of Mr. John Dodge* (2d ed., Danvers: R. Russell, 1780), 5.

68. For a discussion of the reprinting of captivity narratives for purposes of inciting anti-British sentiment, see Levernier and Cohen, 50–51; and Robert J. Denn, "Captivity Narratives of the American Revolution," *Journal of American Culture*, 2 (1980): 575–82.

69. Shepard Kollock, *A True Narrative of the Sufferings of Mary Kinnan* (Elizabethtown, N. J.: Shepard Kollock, 1795), 10–11; hereafter cited in text as *MK*.

70. Elias Darnall, *A Journal Containing an Accurate & Interesting Account of the Hardships, Sufferings, Battles, Defeat, & Captivity of Those Heroic Kentucky Volunteers* (Paris, Ken.: Joel R. Lyle, 1813), 3; hereafter cited in text as *Kentucky*.

71. Hugh Henry Brackenridge, ed., *Narratives of a Late Expedition against the Indians* (Philadelphia: Francis Bailey, 1782), 32; hereafter cited in text as *Expedition*.

72. For a discussion of the Fraser narrative and its relationship to the captivity tradition, see Levernier and Cohen, xxii, 266–67.

73. *Narrative of the Capture and Providential Escape of Misses Frances and Almira Hall* (New York: William Edwards, 1832), 17; hereafter cited in text as *Hall*.

74. *A Narrative of the Life and Sufferings of Mrs. Jane Johns* (Baltimore: Jas. Lucas and E. K. Deaver, 1837), 5; hereafter cited in text as *Johns*.

75. *Affecting History of the Dreadful Distresses of Frederick Manheim's Family* (Exeter, Mass.: Henry Ranlet, 1793), 4; hereafter cited in text as *Manheim*.

76. For discussions of the captivity narrative as history, see Levernier and Cohen, xxiv–xxvi, 131–59, and Levernier, "The Captivity Narrative as Regional, Military, and Ethnic History," *Research Studies* 45 (1977): 30–37.

77. For a discussion of the captivity narrative as children's literature, see

Levernier and Cohen, xxvi, 160–64; and Levernier, "The Captivity Narrative as Children's Literature," *Markham Review*, 8 (1979): 54–59.

78. See Philip Freneau, *A Poem on the Rising Glory of America* (Philadelphia: n. p., 1772).

79. For photographs of Cole's painting and Palmer's statue and for a discussion of their significance for the captivity tradition, see Levernier and Cohen, 252–56, 260–63.

Chapter Two

1. See, for example, Greg Sieminski, "The Puritan Captivity Narrative and the Politics of the American Revolution," *American Quarterly* 42 (1990): 35–56, for a discussion of the republication of Puritan texts in the eighteenth century.

2. Historian David D. Hall explains this phenomenon in terms of *extensive* (consumerist) and *intensive* (traditional) readerships and points out that early best-sellers of all kinds combined both practices to reach a wide audience from diverse economic, social, and educational backgrounds. See David D. Hall, "The World of Print and Collective Mentality in Seventeenth-Century New England," in John Higham and Paul K. Conkin, eds., *New Directions in American Intellectual History* (Baltimore, Md.: Johns Hopkins University Press, 1979), 168.

3. Richard VanDerBeets, "The Indian Captivity Narrative as Ritual," *American Literature* 43 (1972): 549; hereafter cited in text.

4. Richard Slotkin, *Regeneration through Violence: The Mythology of the American Frontier, 1600–1860* (Middletown, Conn.: Wesleyan University Press, 1973), 25; hereafter cited in text.

5. Phillips D. Carleton, "The Indian Captivity," *American Literature* 15 (1943): 171; hereafter cited in text.

6. Sir James George Frazer, *The Golden Bough*. 3d ed., 12 vols (1890; London: Macmillan, 1907–15). Part two of this monumental study, "Taboo and the Perils of the Soul," is particularly appropriate here. Readers new to this area may wish to consult the abridged edition, Theodor H. Gaster, rev. and ed., *The New Golden Bough* (1959; New York: Mentor, 1964). See also, John B. Vickery, *The Literary Impact of the Golden Bough* (Princeton, N.J.: Princeton University Press, 1973).

7. VanDerBeets, *Indian Captivity Narrative*.

8. Leslie A. Fiedler, *The Return of the Vanishing American*, rev. ed. (New York: Stein and Day, 1968); hereafter cited in text.

9. Annette Kolodny, *The Land before Her: Fantasy and Experience of the American Frontiers, 1630–1860* (Chapel Hill: University of North Carolina Press, 1984), xiii; hereafter cited in text.

10. Transculturation is discussed in more detail in chapter 3; transculturated women, specifically, receive extended analysis in chapter 5.

11. For an important assessment of Mary Jemison's account, see Susan Walsh, "'With Them Was My Home': Native American Autobiography and *A Narrative of the Life of Mrs. Mary Jemison*," *American Literature* 64 (1992): 49–70. See also, June Namias's "Introduction" to her edition of *A Narrative of the Life of Mrs. Mary Jemison*, by James E. Seaver (Norman: University of Oklahoma Press, 1992).

12. Dawn Lander Gherman, "From Parlour to Tepee: The White Squaw on the American Frontier," Ph.D. diss., University of Massachusetts, 1975; hereafter cited in text. While dissertations do not usually have a wide influence, Gherman's study is an exception and merits special attention here. Another important dissertation, which is forthcoming as a book, is June Namias, "White Captives: Gender and Ethnicity on Successive American Frontiers," Ph.D. diss., Brandeis University, 1989.

13. Abraham Panther [*pseud.*], *A Surprising Account of the Discovery of a Lady who was taken by the Indians in the year 1777, and after making her escape, she retired to a lonely Cave, where she lived nine years* in *Bickerstaff's Almanack, for . . . 1788* (Norwich, Conn.: J. Trumbull, 1787); hereafter cited in text as *Panther*. Although this is sometimes accepted as the first edition, Vail, 339, cites two other editions published in 1787 and says, "There is nothing to show which is the first edition."

14. For further discussion of the popularity and reprinting of the "Panther Captivity," see Slotkin, 256, and Vail, 339, 353–54, 396, 405–6, 417–18, 430, 437–38, 444, 454–55.

Chapter Three

1. See, for example, Francis Jennings, *The Invasion of America: Indians, Colonialism, and the Cant of Conquest* (Chapel Hill: University of North Carolina Press, 1975); and Alden T. Vaughan, *New England Frontier: Puritans and Indians, 1620–1675* (Boston: Little, Brown & Co., 1965).

2. For a listing and discussion of early American texts on this subject, see Vail.

3. Robert F. Berkhofer, Jr., *The White Man's Indian: Images of the American Indian from Columbus to the Present* (New York: Alfred A. Knopf, 1978), 28; hereafter cited in text.

4. Cecil Jane and L. A. Vigneras, trans., *The Journal of Christopher Columbus*, by Christopher Columbus (London: Hakluyt Society, 1960), 194, 200.

5. George Tyler Northup, trans., *Mundus Novus*, by Amerigo Vespucci, in *Vespucci Reprints, Texts and Studies*, vol. 2 (Princeton, N. J.: Princeton University Press, 1916), 4–6.

6. For an analysis of European attitudes toward the American Indian during the fifteenth, sixteenth, and seventeenth centuries, see Lee Eldridge Huddleston, *Origins of the American Indians: European Concepts, 1492–1729*

(Austin: University of Texas Press, 1967); Howard Peckham and Charles Gibson, eds., *Attitudes of Colonial Powers Toward the American Indian* (Salt Lake City: University of Utah Press, 1969); Edward Dudley and Maximillian E. Novak, eds., *The Wild Man Within: An Image in Western Thought from the Renaissance to Romanticism* (Pittsburgh: University of Pittsburgh Press, 1973); James Axtell's two studies, "The Scholastic Philosophy of the Wilderness," *William and Mary Quarterly*, 29 (1972): 335–66, and "Through a Glass Darkly: Colonial Attitudes toward the Native Americans," *American Indian Culture and Research Journal*, 1 (1974): 17–28; and Berkhofer. For an analysis of early Puritan attitudes toward the American Indian during this time, see Roy Harvey Pearce, "'The Ruines of Mankind': The Indian and the Puritan Mind," *Journal of the History of Ideas*, 13 (1952): 200–17; Slotkin; G. E. Thomas, "Puritans, Indians, and the Concept of Race," *New England Quarterly*, 48 (1975): 3–27; and William S. Simmons, "Cultural Bias in the New England Puritans' Perception of Indians," *William and Mary Quarterly*, 38 (1981): 56–72. For a previous discussion of early Colonial captivity narratives and European concepts of the Indians, together with examples of narratives illustrating these views, see Levernier and Cohen, especially xv–xix, 3–42.

7. Quoted by Stanley L. Robe from Paul III's *Sublimus Deus* in "Wild Men and Spain's Brave New World," in Dudley and Novak, 47.

8. Robe, 50–51.

9. For a reprinting of the Ortiz narrative and an earlier discussion of its significance in terms of sixteenth- and seventeenth-century Spanish views of the Indian, see Levernier and Cohen, 3-11.

10. See also, Dudley and Novak, eds., *Wild Man Within*, 57.

11. Michael Drayton, *The Works of Michael Drayton*, ed. J. William Hebel (Oxford: Shakespeare Head Press, 1941), vol. 2, 364.

12. Quoted by Richard Ashcraft in "Leviathan Triumphant: Thomas Hobbes and the Politics of Wild Men," in Dudley and Novak, eds., *Wild Man Within*, 152.

13. Quoted by Gary B. Nash in "The Image of the Indian in the Southern Colonial Mind," *William and Mary Quarterly*, 29 (1972): 208.

14. E. G. R. Taylor, ed., *The Original Writings and Correspondence of the Two Richard Hakluyts*, ser. 2, vol. 1 (London: Hakluyt Society, 1935), 164–65.

15. Captain John Smith, *The Generall Historie of Virginia, New-England, and the Summer Isles* (London: Michael Sparkes, 1624), 48–49.

16. For a discussion of the facts surrounding the historicity of Smith's alleged rescue by Pocahontas, see Levernier and Cohen, 12–14.

17. "The Charter of the Colony of Massachusetts Bay in New England 1628–29," in *Records of the Governor and Company of Massachusettes Bay in New England: 1628–1641*, vol. 1. ed. Nathaniel B. Shurtleff (Boston: W. White, 1853), 17.

18. William Hubbard, *A General History of New England from the Discovery to MDCLXXX* (Cambridge, Mass.: Hilliard and Metcalf, 1815), 34–35.

19. Increase Mather, *The History of King Philip's War*, ed. Samuel G. Drake (Boston: Printed for the author, 1862), 208–9.

20. For discussions of the evolution of the captivity narrative from documents based on personal experiences to fictional thrillers, see Pearce, "Significances," 1–20; and Richard VanDerBeets, "Thirst for Empire," 207–15; "Surfeit of Style," 297–306; and *Indian Captivity Narrative*; and Levernier and Cohen, especially xix–xxiii.

21. William Scudder, *The Journal of William Scudder* (New York: By the author, 1794), 41–42; hereafter cited in text as *WS*.

22. Hannah Lewis, *Narrative of the Captivity and Sufferings of Mrs. Hannah Lewis and Her Three Children* (Boston: Henry Trumbull, 1817), 22; hereafter cited in text as *HL*.

23. Theresa Gowanlock, *Two Months in the Camp of Big Bear: The Life and Adventures of Theresa Gowanlock and Theresa Delaney* (Parkdale, Canada: Times Office, 1885), 20; hereafter cited in text as *Bear*.

24. Henry Grace, *The History of the Life and Sufferings of Henry Grace* (Reading, England: Printed for the author, 1764), 20–21; hereafter cited in text as *HG*.

25. Mary Smith, *An Affecting Narrative of the Captivity and Sufferings of Mrs. Mary Smith* (Providence: L. Scott, 1815), 41; hereafter cited in text as *MS*.

26. Eunice Barber, *Narrative of the Tragical Death of Mr. Darius Barber, and His Seven Children, Who Were Inhumanly Butchered by the Indians* (Boston: David Hazen, 1818), 21; hereafter cited in text as *Barber*.

27. John Maylem, *Gallic Perfidy: A Poem* (Boston: Benjamin Mecom, 1758), 15.

28. For a discussion of the subject of ritualistic cannibalism among Indian tribes, see Frederick Webb Hodge, ed., *Handbook of American Indians North of Mexico* (Grosse Pointe, Mich.: Scholarly Press, 1968), vol. 1, 200–1.

29. Eliza Swan, *An Affecting Account of the Tragical Death of Major Swan* (Boston: Henry Trumbull, 1815), 19–20; hereafter cited in text as *Swan*.

30. Archibald Loudon, *A Selection of Some of the Most Interesting Narratives of Outrages Committed by the Indians in Their Wars with the White People* (Carlisle, Penn.: A. Loudon, 1808).

31. Jane Wilson, *A Thrilling Narrative of the Sufferings of Mrs. Jane Adeline Wilson during Her Captivity among the Comanche Indians* (1854; Fairfield, Wash.: Ye Galleon Press, 1971), 98.

32. *Old Record of the Captivity of Margaret Erskine* (Baltimore: The Lord Baltimore Press, 1912), 10.

33. Jane Lewis, *Narrative of the Captivity and Providential Escape of Mrs. Jane Lewis* (New York: n. p., 1833), 24.

34. *General Sheridan's Squaw Spy and Mrs. Blynn's Captivity* (Philadelphia: Co-operative Publishing House, 1869), 19.

35. For other studies about the experiences of transculturized captives, see

Erwin H. Ackernecht, "'White Indians': Psychological and Physiological Pe-
culiarities of White Children Abducted and Reared by North American Indi-
ans," *Bulletin of the History of Medicine*, 15 (1944): 15–36; William S. Ewing,
"Indian Captives Released by Colonel Bouquet," *Western Pennsylvania Historical
Magazine*, 39 (1956): 187–203; A. Irving Hallowell, "American Indians,
White and Black: The Phenomenon of Transculturation," *Current Anthropology*,
4 (1963): 519–31; and J. Norman Heard, *White into Red: A Study of the
Assimilation of White Persons Captured by Indians* (Metuchen, N. J.: Scarecrow
Press, 1973); and Levernier and Cohen, xxiii, 97–128.

36. James Everett Seaver, *A Narrative of the Life of Mrs. Mary Jemison*
(Canandaigua: J. D. Bemis, 1824), xiii; hereafter cited in text as *MJ*.

37. James Smith, *An Account of the Remarkable Occurrences in the Life and
Travels of Col. James Smith* (Lexington, Ky.: John Bradford, 1799), 3; hereafter
cited in text as *JS*.

38. Edwin James, *A Narrative of the Captivity and Adventures of John Tanner
during Thirty Years Residence among the Indians in the Interior of America* (New York:
G. & C. H. Carvell, 1830), 5; hereafter cited in text as *JT*.

39. John Franklin Meginness, *Biography of Frances Slocum* (Williamsport,
Penn.: Heller Bros., 1891), 57; hereafter cited in text as *Frances*.

40. Seaver, *Mary Jemison*, 4th ed., 7.

41. J. Z. Ballard, ed., *The Life and Adventures of William Filley* (Chicago:
Filley & Ballard, 1867), 101; hereafter cited in text as *WF*.

42. Charles Dennis Rusoe d'Eres, *Memoirs of Charles Dennis Rusoe d'Eres*
(Exeter, N. H.: Henry Ranlet, 1800), 143; hereafter cited in text as *d'Eres*.

43. Alexander Henry, *Travels and Adventures in Canada and the Indian
Territories* (New York: I. Riley, 1809), 73; hereafter cited in text as *Travels*.

44. John Davenport, "Mr. John Davenport's *Narrative*," in Elias Darnall,
Kentucky, 1–2.

45. Josiah Mooso, *The Life and Travels of Josiah Mooso* (Winfield, Kans.:
Telegram Print, 1888), 101.

Chapter Four

1. For more information on these editions see Robert K. Diebold, "A
Critical Edition of Mrs. Mary Rowlandson's Captivity Narrative" (Ph.D. diss.,
Yale University, 1972), ix, clii–clix; hereafter cited in text.

2. Following is a selective list of books and articles concerning Rowland-
son not cited elsewhere in this chapter: Mitchell R. Breitwieser, *American
Puritanism and the Defense of Mourning: Religion, Grief, and Ethnology in Mary
White Rowlandson's Captivity Narrative* (Madison: University of Wisconsin Press,
1990); Margaret H. Davis, "Mary White Rowlandson's Self-Fashioning as
Puritan Goodwife," *Early American Literature* 27 (1992): 49–60; Annette
Kolodny, "Captives in Paradise: Women on the Early American Frontier," in
Lenore Hoffman and Margo Culley, eds., *Women's Personal Narratives: Essays in*

Criticism and Pedagogy (New York: Modern Language Association, 1985), 93–111; Amy Schrager Lang, ed., introduction to and text of Rowlandson's *A True History* in William L. Andrews, ed., *Journeys in New Worlds: Early American Women's Narratives* (Madison: University of Wisconsin Press, 1990); Frank Luther Mott, *Golden Multitudes: The Story of Best Sellers in the United States* (New York: Bowker, 1947); John Seelye, *Prophetic Waters: The River in American Life and Literature* (New York: Oxford University Press, 1977); Slotkin; Richard Slotkin and James K. Folsom, eds., *So Dreadfull a Judgment: Puritan Responses to King Philip's War, 1676–1677* (Middletown, Conn.: Wesleyan University Press, 1978); Ann Stanford, "Mary Rowlandson's Journey to Redemption," *Ariel* 7 (1976): 27–37; Vail.

3. For more genealogical information, see Kathryn Zabelle Derounian, "A Note on Mary (White) Rowlandson's English Origins," *Early American Literature* 24 (1989): 70–72 and Kathryn Zabelle Derounian-Stodola and David L. Greene, "Additions and Corrections to 'A Note on Mary (White) Rowlandson's English Origins,'" *Early American Literature* 25 (1990): 305–6.

4. Diebold, viii, n. 3, lists the contemporary histories that refer to Rowlandson's capture.

5. David L. Greene, "New Light on Mary Rowlandson," *Early American Literature* 20 (1985): 24–38.

6. Rowlandson is typical of many other women captives who remarried—though they generally did so because their husbands died before or during capture—and subsequently disappeared from records under their previous surnames. With greater efforts to recover genealogical information and trace new surnames, these women might become more visible and vocal.

7. For more information on this case, see Greene, 31–35.

8. Douglas Edward Leach, "The 'When's' of Mary Rowlandson's Captivity," *New England Quarterly* 34 (1961): 352–55.

9. For more detailed information on composition and publication, see Derounian, "Publication, Promotion," 240–42.

10. Hall, "World of Print," in Higham and Conkin, 167–68.

11. See David Downing, "'Streams of Scripture Comfort': Mary Rowlandson's Typological Use of the Bible," *Early American Literature* 15 (1981): 252–59.

12. See Minter, "By Dens of Lions," 341.

13. See Kathryn Zabelle Derounian, "Puritan Orthodoxy and the 'Survivor Syndrome' in Mary Rowlandson's Indian Captivity Narrative," *Early American Literature* 22 (1987): 82–93.

14. Daniel B. Shea's *Spiritual Autobiography in Early America* (1968; Madison: University of Wisconsin Press, 1988) is still the most comprehensive analysis of the genre.

15. Quoted from "The Message: Trinity Episcopal Cathedral," Little Rock, Ark., 10 February 1991, n. p.

16. William G. Niederland, "Clinical Observations of the 'Survivor Syndrome,'" *International Journal of Psycho-Analysis* 49 (1968): 313; hereafter cited in text.

17. Mary Schwandt-Schmidt, *The Story of Mary Schwandt*, in *Collections of the Minnesota Historical Society* 6 (1894): 461–74; Urania (Mrs. N. D.) White, *Captivity among the Sioux, August 18 to September 26, 1862*, in *Collections of the Minnesota Historical Society* 9 (1901): 395–426; and Minnie Buce Carrigan, *Captured by the Indians: Reminiscences of Pioneer Life in Minnesota* (Forest City, S. Dak.: Forest City Press, 1907). Schwandt-Schmidt's work hereafter cited in text as *Schwandt*; White's work hereafter cited in text as *Sioux Captivity*; and Carrigan's work hereafter cited in text as *Captured*. See also the section "Traumatized Women," in chapter 5 herein, "Images of Women."

18. Mary Barber, *The True Narrative of the Five Years' Suffering & Perilous Adventures* (Philadelphia: Barclay, 1872).

Chapter Five

1. For further information on statistics, see chapter 1.

2. Carol F. Karlsen, *The Devil in the Shape of a Woman: Witchcraft in Colonial New England* (New York: Norton, 1987), 163.

3. Lillian Schlissel, ed., *Women's Diaries of the Westward Journey* (New York: Schocken, 1982), 158; hereafter cited in text.

4. Complete bibliographical information on all first editions of captivity narratives before 1800 can be found in Vail.

5. Owing to availability, we have used the third edition, Reuben Weiser, *Regina, the German Captive; or, True Piety among the Lowly* (1856; Baltimore: T. Newton Kurtz, 1860); hereafter cited in text as *Regina*.

6. *Die Erzehlungen von Maria le Roy and Barbara Leininger, Welche Vierthalb Jahr unter den Indianem Gefangen Gewesen* (Philadelphia: Deutsche Buchdruckerei, 1759) and *The Narrative of Marie Le Roy and Barbara Leininger* (Philadelphia, 1759); hereafter cited in text as *Le Roy and Leininger*. For information on these editions, see Vail, 267–69.

7. Vail, 268, says that Regina was known as Hartman until definitely proved to be the lost Regina Leininger in 1765. However, by 1856, when Weiser published *Regina, the German Captive; or, True Piety among the Lowly*, her real name had been known for almost a century, so it obviously suited him to maintain, or rather to impose, the fictional framework on his retelling.

8. Jannette De Camp Sweet, *Mrs. J. E. De Camp Sweet's Narrative of Her Captivity in the Sioux Outbreak of 1862*, in *Collections of the Minnesota Historical Society* 6 (1894): 354–80; Nancy Huggan McClure, *The Story of Nancy McClure*, 438–60; *Schwandt*, 461–74; hereafter cited in text as *Sweet* and *McClure*, respectively.

9. A sampling of recent scholarship in this area includes Gherman; David D. Hall, *Worlds of Wonder, Days of Judgment: Popular Religious Belief in*

Early New England (New York: Alfred A. Knopf, 1989); Lyle Koehler, *A Search for Power: The "Weaker Sex" in Seventeenth-Century New England* (Urbana: University of Illinois Press, 1980); Kolodny, *Land*; Namias, "White Captives"; Glenda Riley, *Women and Indians on the Frontier 1825–1915* (Albuquerque: University of New Mexico Press, 1984); Slotkin; Laurel Thatcher Ulrich, *Good Wives: Image and Reality in the Lives of Women in Northern New England, 1650–1750* (New York: Random House, 1982); all hereafter cited in text.

10. Heard, *White into Red*, 2; hereafter cited in text.

11. Originally published in serial form in the *Buffalo Lake News* (1903).

12. *An Authentic Narrative of the Seminole War; and of the Miraculous Escape of Mrs. Mary Godfrey, and Her Four Female Children* (New York: D. F. Blanchard, 1836), 10; hereafter cited in text as *MG*.

13. Royal B. Stratton, *Life among the Indians: Being an Interesting Narrative of the Captivity of the Oatman Girls*, 1st ed. (San Francisco: Whitton, Towne & Co., 1857), 94; hereafter cited in text as *Oatman 1*.

14. Royal B. Stratton, *Captivity of the Oatman Girls* (New York: Carlton & Porter, 1858); hereafter cited in text as *Oatman 3* .

15. Royal B. Stratton, *Captivity of the Oatman Girls: Being an Interesting Narrative of Life among the Apache and Mohave Indians*, 2d ed. changed (San Francisco: Whitton, Towne & Co., 1857); hereafter cited in text as *Oatman 2*.

16. John Frost, *Heroic Women of the West* (Philadelphia: A. Hart, 1854), 258 and 260; hereafter cited in text.

17. Gherman includes an appendix titled "Sexual Abuse or Rape," in which she suggests that even proof of rape by Plains Indians had been overgeneralized "to represent the entire history of white-Indian relations in the United States" (230). She goes on to show that the evidence of Plains tribes ritually gang-raping captive women ("passing them over the prairie," in the frontier slang) has probably been exaggerated and needs further investigation (235). See also Susan Brownmiller, *Against Our Will: Men, Women and Rape* (New York: Simon and Schuster, 1975), 140–73.

18. Grace E. Meredith, *Girl Captives of the Cheyennes* (Los Angeles, Calif.: Gem, 1927); hereafter cited in text as *Girl Captives*.

19. For analyses of the reworkings of Hannah Dustan's story, see Robert D. Arner, "The Story of Hannah Dustan: Cotton Mather to Thoreau," *American Transcendental Quarterly* 18 (1973): 19–23, and Kathryn Whitford, "Hannah Dustin: The Judgement of History," *Essex Institute Historical Collections* 108 (1972): 304–25.

20. Samuel Sewall, *The Diary of Samuel Sewall 1674–1729*, ed. M. Halsey Thomas, 2 vols. (New York: Farrar, Straus and Giroux, 1973), vol. 1, 372–73.

21. The full petition is quoted in Robert B. Caverly, *Heroism of Hannah Dustan Together with the Indian Wars of New England* (Boston: Russell, 1874), 39.

22. [H. D. Kilgore], *The Story of Hannah Dustan*, rev. ed. (Haverhill, Mass.: Duston-Dustin Family Association, 1984), 9–11; hereafter cited in text.

23. "Sal Fink, the Mississippi Screamer: How She Cooked Injuns," in the *Crockett Almanac for 1854. Containing Life, Manners and Adventures in the Backwoods, and Rows, Sprees, and Scrapes on the Western Waters* (Philadelphia: Fisher, 1854). Reprinted in Levernier and Cohen, 186–88.

24. Hannah Willis, *A Surprizing Account of the Captivity of Miss Hannah Willis* (Stonington-Port, Conn.: S. Trumbull, 1799); hereafter cited in text as *HW*.

25. Helen M. Tarble, *The Story of My Capture and Escape during the Minnesota Indian Massacre of 1862* (St. Paul, Minn.: Abbott, 1904), 19; hereafter cited in text as *Capture and Escape*.

26. Gertrude Morgan, *Gertrude Morgan: or, Life and Adventures among the Indians of the Far West* (Philadelphia: Barclay, 1866); hereafter cited in text as *GM*.

27. Geneva Bible, 2 Corinthians 4:16–18.

28. John Norton, *The Redeemed Captive* (Boston: S. Kneeland, 1748), 14.

29. Susannah Willard Johnson (Hastings), *A Narrative of the Captivity of Mrs. Johnson* (Walpole. N. H.: D. Carlisle, 1796), 89; hereafter cited in text as *SJ*.

30. Susannah Willard Johnson (Hastings), *A Narrative of the Captivity of Mrs. Johnson* (Windsor, Vt., 1814), 89.

31. William Elsey Connelley, *Eastern Kentucky Papers: The Founding of Harman's Station with an Account of the Indian Captivity of Mrs. Jennie Wiley* (New York: Torch Press, 1910); hereafter cited in text as *Founding*.

32. Jemima Howe, *A Genuine and Correct Account of the Captivity, Sufferings & Deliverance of Mrs. Jemima Howe* (Boston: Belknap and Young, 1792); hereafter cited in text as *JH*.

33. Anne Jamison, *An Interesting Narrative* (Pittsburgh: J. Patterson, 1824); hereafter cited in text as *Interesting Narrative*.

34. Susan Thompson Lewis Parrish, "Following the Pot of Gold at the Rainbow's End, 1850," Manuscript Diary. Quoted in Schlissel, 69. Olive Oatman in fact stayed with the Thompson family only four months, not four years.

35. See Heard for analyses and case studies of men and women who became assimilated to Indian culture, either temporarily or permanently.

36. Axtell, "White Indians," 55–88, and Heard have suggested that one reason for transculturation was the freedom and adventure of an Indian lifestyle compared to the drudgery of white frontier life. Heard, for example, says this of transculturated people: "Taken at an impressionable age, cherished by Indian adopted parents, introduced to a life of freedom and adventure, it is understandable that many of them lost the desire to return to the grinding toll of a white family on the frontier" (14). We suspect that the reasons were generally more complicated.

37. These women receive fuller attention in Charlotte Alice Baker, *True Stories of New England Captives Carried to Canada during the Old French and Indian*

Wars (Cambridge, Mass.: By the author, 1897), and in Ulrich. They are also the subjects of two recent essays: Barbara E. Austin, "Captured . . . Never Came Back: Social Networks among New England Female Captives in Canada, 1689–1763," and Alice N. Nash, "Two Stories of New England Captives: Grizel and Christine Otis of Dover, New Hampshire," both in *New England/New France, 1600–1850*, 28–38 and 39–48 respectively. (Boston: Boston University Scholarly Publications, 1992. Annual Proceedings of the Dublin Seminar for New England Folklife, 14 [1989]).

38. It is interesting to note that the title of Williams's text is ironic in light of Eunice's story, for while he had indeed been redeemed, Eunice and others remained unredeemed by choice.

39. The full text of this letter is included in the chapter on Eunice Williams in Baker, 144–46.

40. The full text of this letter is quoted in Gherman, 86.

41. For an important perspective on Jemison's narrative, see Walsh, 49–70.

42. See A. L. Kroeber and Clifton B. Kroeber, "Olive Oatman's First Account of Her Captivity among the Mohave," *California Historical Society Quarterly* 41 (1962), 314–15, n.10, for a very convincing argument that the Oatman party was not attacked by Apaches—a term whites at the time used to include Yavapais too—but by Yavapais alone.

43. Debate still continues about the significance of Oatman's tattoos because her exact status among the Mohaves at the time she was tattooed (slave? wife? adopted daughter?) has not been confirmed. Alford E. Turner, in "The Oatman Massacre," *Real West* (Spring 1983), 17, points out that "tattooing on a Mojave woman's chin, which Olive had, usually indicated marriage," and he also mentions that "a wealthy Mojave Indian named John Oatman" claimed to be Olive Oatman's son. However, Paul Taylor, in "Oatman Massacre Causes National Furor," *Indian Trader* (October 1985), 16–17, refers readers to evidence that the Mohaves used (and still use) tattoos for religious purposes to ensure their entrance to the "land of the dead." For information on the process of tattooing among the Mohaves—including references to Oatman—see "Mojave Tattooing and Face Painting," *Frontier Chronicles* 3 (April 1992): 4–9.

44. These stories appear in C. Hale Sipe, *The Indian Wars of Pennsylvania* (Harrisburg, Penn.: Telegraph Press, 1931). Heard, 138–39, summarizes them.

45. This case appears in Hugh D. Corwin, *Comanche and Kiowa Captivities in Oklahoma and Texas* (Lawton, Okla.: Corwin, 1959), 117–21. It is summarized by Heard, 140.

46. Josiah Butler, "Pioneer School Teaching at the Comanche-Kiowa Agency School, 1870–03," *Chronicles of Oklahoma* 6 (1928): 499–500. Also retold by Heard, 35–36. Other transculturated women of Mexican origin receive attention in Carl Coke Rister, *Border Captives: The Traffic in Prisoners by*

Southern Plains Indians, 1835–1875 (Norman: University of Oklahoma Press, 1940), 181–87.

47. Elias Cornelius, *The Little Osage Captive* (Boston: Samuel T. Armstrong and Crocker & Brewster, 1822); hereafter cited in text as *Osage 1*. See Heard, 149–59, for some other case studies of Indian children's transculturation or acculturation to white society.

Chapter Six

1. Quoted by Eric F. Goldman, "The Historians," in Robert Spiller, ed., *Literary History of the United States* (3d rev. ed., New York: Macmillan, 1963), 526–27.

2. For a discussion of nineteenth-century historiography and the encouragement that government grants gave to the collecting and editing of historical documents such as Indian captivity narratives, see Goldman, 526–27; and David Levin, *History as Romantic Art* (1959; New York: Harcourt, Brace, and World, 1963), particularly 6; hereafter cited in text.

3. For a more extended discussion of the Indian captivity narrative as popular history, see Levernier, "Captivity Narrative," 30–37.

4. For the text and an analysis of the Hoyt account of the Deerfield captivities, see Levernier and Cohen, 131–34.

5. Washington Irving, *Astoria, or Anecdotes of an Enterprise beyond the Rocky Mountains* (1836; Norman: University of Oklahoma Press, 1964), 146–47; hereafter cited in text as *Astoria*. For texts and a more extended analysis of captivity selections from the writings of Irving, Bancroft, and Parkman, see Levernier and Cohen, 135-55.

6. George Bancroft, *A History of the United States from the Discovery of the American Continent* (Boston: Little, Brown & Co., 1873), vol. I, 130–31; hereafter cited in text as *History*.

7. Francis Parkman, *The Conspiracy of Pontiac* (1850; New York: Collier Books, 1966), 426; hereafter cited in text as *Pontiac*.

8. Francis Parkman, *The Jesuits in North America* (1867; Boston: Little, Brown & Co., 1963), 59; hereafter cited in text as *Jesuits*.

9. The various versions and interpretations of the Dustan legend are analyzed at length by Whitford, 304–25; and by Arner, 19–23. For texts of the Thoreau and Hawthorne versions of the Dustan captivity, along with a more extended analysis of their significance, see Levernier and Cohen, 156–59, 224–30.

10. John Greenleaf Whittier, *Snow-Bound*, rpt. in Robert Penn Warren, *John Greenleaf Whittier: An Appraisal and Selections* (Minneapolis: University of Minnesota Press, 1971), 175.

11. For commentary on the MacCrea ballad, see Harold W. Thompson, *New York State Folktales, Legends, and Ballads* (1939; New York: Dover, 1967),

328; and for a discussion of "Young Strongbow," see Phillips Barry, *The Maine Woods Songster* (Cambridge, Mass.: Harvard University Press), 210–12.

12. For discussion of the origin and proliferation of this ballad, see Vance Randolph and Floyd C. Shoemaker, *Ozark Folksongs* (Columbia, Mo.: State Historical Society, 1946–50), 118; Robert E. Pike, "Amanda the Captive," *Journal of American Folk-Lore*, 56 (1945): 137; and Charles Peabody, "A Texas Version of 'The White Captive,'" *Journal of American Folk-Lore*, 25 (1912): 169; and Levernier and Cohen, 165-70.

13. John A. Loman, *Cowboy Songs* (New York: Macmillan, 1910), 271.

14. Pike, 139.

15. Helen Harkness Flanders and Elizabeth Flanders Ballard, eds., *New Green Mountain Songster: Traditional Folksongs of Vermont* (New Haven, Conn.: Yale University Press, 1939), 257.

16. Mrs. Moody P. Gore and Mrs. Guy E. Speare, eds., *New Hampshire Folk Tales* (Plymouth: New Hampshire Federation of Women's Clubs, 1932), 31–32.

17. Janice C. Neal, "Heroic Settlers of the Upper Susquehanna," *New York Folklore Quarterly*, 4 (1948): 198–99; hereafter cited in text.

18. For a more extended discussion of Murphy and the folktales about Indian captivity associated with him, see Levernier and Cohen, 171-73.

19. Emelyn Gardner, "Folk-lore from Schoharie County, New York," *Journal of American Folk-Lore*, 26 (1914), 305.

20. Emelyn Gardner, *Folklore from the Schoharie Hills, New York* (Ann Arbor: University of Michigan Press, 1937), 27.

21. Vance Randolph, *Who Blow'd up the Church House? and Other Ozark Folk Tales* (New York: Columbia University Press, 1952), 203.

22. For texts of the Boone materials relating to Indian captivity and a more extended analysis of their significance for the captivity tradition, see Levernier and Cohen, 174–177.

23. For examples and an analysis of the use of the captivity tradition by Southwestern humorists and dime novelists, see Levernier and Cohen, 186–99.

24. For a discussion of this subject, see Levernier, "Children's Literature," 54–59.

25. R. Gordon Kelly, "American Children's Literature: An Historiographical Review," *American Literary Realism*, 6 (1973): 95; John C. Crandall, "Patriotism and Humanitarian Reform in Children's Literature, 1825– 1860," *American Quarterly*, 21 (1969): 3–4.

26. Quoted by Crandall (4) from Edwin W. Rice, *The Sunday School Movement, 1780–1917, and the American Sunday School Union, 1817–1917* (Philadelphia: American Sunday-School Union, 1917).

27. For a reprinting of the text of "Murderer's Creek" and a discussion of its background and significance for the captivity tradition, see Levernier and Cohen, 160–64.

28. *The Deerfield Captive: An Interesting Indian Story, Being a Narrative of Facts for the Instruction of the Young* (Greenfield, Mass.: A. Phelps, 1830), 5; hereafter cited in text as *Deerfield*.

29. Elias Cornelius, *The Little Osage Captive* (2d ed., Boston: Massachusetts Sabbath School Society, 1832), 59–60; hereafter cited in text as *Osage 2*.

30. Barbara Hofland, *The Stolen Boy* (New York: G. L. Austin and Co., 1830), 9–10; hereafter cited in text as *Boy*.

31. *Hannah Swarton, the Casco Captive; or the Catholic Religion in Canada, and Its Influence on the Indians of Maine* (Boston: Massachusetts Sabbath School Society, 1839), 9–10; hereafter cited in text as *Casco*.

32. Quoted by Robert E. Spiller in "The Verdict of Sydney Smith," *American Literature*, 1 (1929), 5–6.

33. Quoted by Lewis Leary in "Poets and Essayists," *Literary History of the United States* (3d rev. ed., New York: Macmillan, 1963), 176.

34. Quoted by Leary, 176.

35. Charles Brockden Brown, *Edgar Huntly; or Memoirs of a Sleepwalker* (1799; New Haven, Conn.: College and University Press, 1973), 29; hereafter cited in text as *Huntly*.

36. Ann Eliza Bleecker, *The History of Maria Kittle* (Hartford: Elisha Babcock, 1797); hereafter cited in text as *Maria*.

37. Paul Levine, "The American Novel Begins," *American Scholar*, 35 (1966): 146.

38. Quoted from Richard Chase, *The American Novel and Its Tradition* (Garden City, N. J.: Doubleday, 1957) by David Stineback in the "Introduction" to his edition of *Edgar Huntly* (New Haven, Conn.: College and University Press, 1973), 7.

39. David T. Haberly, "Women and Indians: *The Last of the Mohicans* and the Captivity Tradition," *American Quarterly*, 28 (1976): 423; hereafter cited in text.

40. For a discussion of identifiable captivity sources for Cooper's fiction, see John T. Frederick, "Cooper's Eloquent Indians," *Publications of the Modern Language Association*, 71 (1956): 1004–17; Gregory Lansing Paine, "The Indians of the Leather-Stocking Tales," *Sewanee Review*, 23 (1926): 16–39; Thomas Philbrick, "The Sources of Cooper's Knowledge of Fort William Henry," *American Literature*, 36 (1964): 209–14; and Richard VanDerBeets, "Cooper and the 'Semblance of Reality': A Source for *The Deerslayer*," *American Literature*, 45 (1971): 335–47.

41. See Levernier and Cohen, 231–32; and Rosalyn Shapero, "Indians and Pioneers of the Syracuse Region," *New York Folklore Quarterly*, 7 (1951): 226–28.

42. Richard Stengel, "American Myth 101," *Time*, 23 December 1991, 78.

Selected Bibliography

BIBLIOGRAPHIES

Narratives of Captivity among the Indians of North America. Chicago: The Newberry Library, 1912.

Smith, Clara A., comp. *Narratives of Captivity among the Indians of North America: Supplement 1.* Chicago: The Newberry Library, 1928.

Vail, R. W. G. *The Voice of the Old Frontier.* 1949; New York: Octagon, 1970.

Vaughan, Alden T. *Narratives of North American Indian Captivity: A Selected Bibliography.* New York: Garland, 1983.

PRIMARY SOURCES

Calloway, Colin G., ed. *North Country Captives: Narratives of Indian Captivity from Vermont and New Hampshire.* Hanover, N.H.: University Press of New England, 1992.

Diebold, Robert K. "A Critical Edition of Mrs. Mary Rowlandson's Captivity Narrative." Ph.D. diss., Yale University, 1972.

Levernier, James A., and Hennig Cohen, eds. *The Indians and Their Captives.* Westport, Conn.: Greenwood Press, 1977.

Slotkin, Richard, and James K. Folsom, eds. *So Dreadfull a Judgment: Puritan Responses to King Philip's War, 1676–1677.* Middletown, Conn.: Wesleyan University Press, 1978.

VanDerBeets, Richard, ed. *Held Captive by Indians: Selected Narratives, 1642–1836.* Knoxville: University of Tennessee Press, 1973.

Vaughan, Alden T., and Edward W. Clark, eds. *Puritans among the Indians: Accounts of Captivity and Redemption, 1676–1724.* Cambridge, Mass.: Harvard University Press, 1981.

Washburn, Wilcomb E., ed. *Narratives of North American Indian Captivities.* Vols. 1–111. New York: Garland, 1977.

SECONDARY SOURCES

Ackernecht, Erwin H. "'White Indians': Psychological and Physiological Peculiarities of White Children Abducted and Reared by North American Indians." *Bulletin of the History of Medicine* 15 (1944): 15–36.

Allen, Phoebe S. "The Double Exposure of Texas Captives." *Western Folklore* 32 (1973): 249–61.

Arner, Robert D. "The Story of Hannah Dustan: Cotton Mather to Thoreau." *American Transcendental Quarterly* 18 (1973): 19–23.

Austen, Barbara E. "Captured . . . Never Came Back: Social Networks among New England Female Captives in Canada, 1689–1763." In *New England/New France, 1600–1850,* 28–38. Boston: Boston University Scholarly Publications, 1992 (Annual Proceedings of the Dublin Seminar for New England Folklife, 14 [1989]).

Axtell, James. *After Columbus: Essays in the Ethnohistory of Colonial North America.* New York: Oxford University Press, 1988.

————. *The Invasion Within: The Contest of Cultures in Colonial New England.* New York: Oxford University Press, 1985.

————. "The Scholastic Philosophy of the Wilderness." *William and Mary Quarterly* 29 (1972): 335–66.

————. "The White Indians of Colonial America." *William and Mary Quarterly* 32 (1975): 55–88.

Baker, Charlotte Alice. *True Stories of New England Captives Carried to Canada during the Old French and Indian Wars.* Cambridge, Mass.: By the author, 1897.

Barbeau, Marius. "Indian Captivities." *Proceedings of the American Philosophical Society* 94 (1950): 522–48.

Barnett, Louise K. *The Ignoble Savage: American Literary Racism, 1790–1890.* Westport, Conn.: Greenwood Press, 1975.

Berkhofer, Robert F., Jr. *The White Man's Indian: Images of the American Indian from Columbus to the Present.* New York: Alfred A. Knopf, 1978.

Breitwieser, Mitchell R. *American Puritanism and the Defense of Mourning: Religion, Grief, and Ethnology in Mary White Rowlandson's Captivity Narrative.* Madison: University of Wisconsin Press, 1990.

Brown, Parker B. "The Historical Accuracy of the Captivity Narrative of Doctor John Knight." *Western Pennsylvania Historical Magazine* 70 (1987): 53–67.

Brownmiller, Susan. *Against Our Will: Men, Women and Rape.* New York: Simon and Schuster, 1975.

Calloway, Colin G. "An Uncertain Destiny: Indian Captivities on the Upper Connecticut River." *Journal of American Studies* 17 (1983): 189–210.

Carleton, Phillips D. "The Indian Captivity." *American Literature* 15 (1943): 169–80.

Coleman, Emma L. *New England Captives Carried to Canada.* Portland, Maine: Southworth Press, 1925.

Corwin, Hugh D. *Comanche and Kiowa Captives in Oklahoma and Texas.* Lawton, Okla.: By the Author, 1959.

Davis, Margaret H. "Mary White Rowlandson's Self-Fashioning as Puritan Goodwife," *Early American Literature* 27 (1992): 49–60.

Denn, Robert J. "Captivity Narratives of the American Revolution." *Journal of American Culture* 2 (1980): 575–82.

Derounian, Kathryn Zabelle. "The Publication, Promotion, and Distribution of Mary Rowlandson's Indian Captivity Narrative in the Seventeenth Century." *Early American Literature* 23 (1988): 239–61.

———. "Puritan Orthodoxy and the 'Survivor Syndrome' in Mary Rowlandson's Indian Captivity Narrative." *Early American Literature* 22 (1987): 82–93.

Dondore, Dorothy A. "White Captives among the Indians." *New York History* 13 (1932): 292–300.

Downing, David. "'Streams of Scripture Comfort': Mary Rowlandson's Typological Use of the Bible." *Early American Literature* 15 (1981): 252–59.

Drinnon, Richard. *Facing West: The Metaphysics of Indian-Hating and Empire-Building.* Minneapolis: University of Minnesota Press, 1980.

Ewing, Williams S. "Indian Captives Released by Colonel Bouquet." *Western Pennsylvania Historical Magazine* 39 (1956): 187–203.

Fiedler, Leslie A. *The Return of the Vanishing American.* Rev. ed. New York: Stein and Day, 1968.

Fitzpatrick, Tara. "The Figure of Captivity: The Cultural Work of the Puritan Captivity Narrative." *American Literary History* 3 (1991): 1–26.

Gherman, Dawn Lander. "From Parlour to Tepee: The White Squaw on the American Frontier." Ph.D. diss., University of Massachusetts, 1975.

Green, Rayna P. "Traits of Indian Character: The 'Indian' Anecdote in American Vernacular Tradition." *Southern Folklore Quarterly* 39 (1975): 233–62.

Greene, David L. "New Light on Mary Rowlandson." *Early American Literature* 20 (1985): 24–38.

Griffin, Edward M. "Patricia Hearst and Her Foremothers: The Captivity Fable in America." *The Centennial Review* 36 (1992): 311–26.

Haberly, David T. "Women and Indians: *The Last of the Mohicans* and the Captivity Tradition." *American Quarterly* 28 (1976): 431–41.

Hallowell, A. Irving. "American Indians, White and Black: The Phenomenon of Transculturation." *Current Anthropology* 4 (1963): 519–31.

Heard, J. Norman. *White into Red: A Study of the Assimilation of White Persons Captured by Indians.* Metuchen, N. J.: Scarecrow Press, 1973.

Holte, James Craig. *The Conversion Experience in America: A Sourcebook on Religious Conversion Autobiography.* Westport, Conn.: Greenwood Press, 1992.

Huddleston, Lee Eldridge. *Origins of the American Indians: European Concepts, 1492–1729.* Austin: University of Texas Press, 1967.

Jennings, Francis. *The Invasion of America: Indians, Colonialism, and the Cant of Conquest.* Chapel Hill: University of North Carolina Press, 1975.

Knowles, Nathaniel. "The Torture of Captives by the Indians of Eastern North America." *Proceedings of the American Philosophical Society* 82 (1940): 151–225.

Koehler, Lyle. *A Search for Power: The "Weaker Sex" in Seventeenth-Century New England*. Urbana: University of Illinois Press, 1980.

Kolodny, Annette. *The Land before Her: Fantasy and Experience of the American Frontiers, 1630–1860*. Chapel Hill: University of North Carolina Press, 1984.

———. "Review Essay." *Early American Literature* 14 (1979): 228–35.

Leach, Douglas Edward. "The 'When's' of Mary Rowlandson's Captivity." *New England Quarterly* 34 (1961): 353–63.

Levernier, James A. "The Captivity Narrative as Children's Literature." *Markham Review* 8 (1979): 54–59.

———. "The Captivity Narrative as Regional, Military, and Ethnic History." *Research Studies* 45 (1977): 30–37.

Minter, David. "By Dens of Lions: Notes on Stylization in Early Puritan Captivity Narratives." *American Literature* 45 (1973): 335–47.

Monical, David C. "Changes in American Attitudes toward the Indian as Evidenced in Captive Literature." *Plains Anthropologist* 14 (1969): 130–36.

Mott, Frank Luther. *Golden Multitudes: The Story of Best Sellers in the United States*. New York: Bowker, 1947.

Namias, June, ed. *A Narrative of the Life of Mrs. Mary Jemison*, by James E. Seaver. Norman: University of Oklahoma Press, 1992.

———. "White Captives: Gender and Ethnicity on Successive American Frontiers." Ph.D. diss., Brandeis University, 1989.

Nash, Alice N. "Two Stories of New England Captives: Grizel and Christine Otis of Dover, New Hampshire." In *New England/New France, 1600–1850*, 39–48. Boston: Boston University Scholarly Publications, 1992 (Annual Proceedings of the Dublin Seminar for New England Folklife, 14 [1989]).

Nash, Gary B. "The Image of the Indian in the Southern Colonial Mind." *William and Mary Quarterly* 29 (1972): 197–230.

Pearce, Roy Harvey. "'The Ruines of Mankind': The Indian and the Puritan Mind." *Journal of the History of Ideas* 13 (1952): 200–17.

———. "The Significances of the Captivity Narrative." *American Literature* 19 (1947): 1–20.

Riley, Glenda. *Women and Indians on the Frontier 1825–1915*. Albuquerque: University of New Mexico Press, 1984.

Rister, Carl Coke. *Border Captives: The Traffic in Prisoners by Southern Plains Indians, 1835–1875*. Norman: University of Oklahoma Press, 1940.

Robe, Stanley L. "Wild Men and Spain's Brave New World." In *The Wild Man Within: An Image in Western Thought from the Renaissance to Romanticism*, edited by Edward Dudley and Maximillian E. Novak, 39–54. Pittsburgh: University of Pittsburgh Press, 1973.

Russell, Jason Almus. "The Narratives of the Indian Captives." *Education* 51 (1930): 84–88.

Seelye, John. *Prophetic Waters: The River in American Life and Literature.* New York: Oxford University Press, 1977.

Sieminski, Greg. "The Puritan Captivity Narrative and the Politics of the American Revolution." *American Quarterly* 42 (1990): 35–56.

Simmons, William S. "Cultural Bias in the New England Puritans' Perception of Indians." *William and Mary Quarterly* 38 (1981): 56–72.

Slotkin, Richard. *Regeneration through Violence: The Mythology of the American Frontier, 1600–1860.* Middletown, Conn.: Wesleyan University Press, 1973.

Smith, Dwight L. "Shawnee Captivity Ethnology." *Ethnohistory* 2 (1955): 29–41.

Stanford, Ann. "Mary Rowlandson's Journey to Redemption." *Ariel* 7 (1976): 27–37.

Swanton, John R. "Notes on the Mental Assimilation of Races." *Journal of the Washington Academy of Sciences* 16 (1926): 493–502.

Thomas, G. E. "Puritans, Indians, and the Concept of Race." *New England Quarterly* 48 (1975): 3–27.

Ulrich, Laurel Thatcher. *Good Wives: Image and Reality in the Lives of Women in Northern New England, 1650–1750.* New York: Random House, 1982.

VanDerBeets, Richard. *The Indian Captivity Narrative: An American Genre.* Lanham, Md.: University Press of America, 1984.

———. "The Indian Captivity Narrative as Ritual." *American Literature* 43 (1972): 548–62.

———. "A Surfeit of Style: The Indian Captivity Narrative as Penny Dreadful." *Research Studies* 39 (1971): 297–306.

———. "'A Thirst for Empire': The Indian Captivity Narrative as Propaganda." *Research Studies* 40 (1972): 207–15.

Vaughan, Alden T. *New England Frontier: Puritans and Indians 1620–1675.* Boston: Little, Brown & Co., 1965.

———, and Daniel K. Richter. "Crossing the Cultural Divide: Indians and New Englanders, 1605–1763." *Proceedings of the American Antiquarian Society* 90 (1980): 23–99.

Walsh, Susan. "'With Them Was My Home': Native American Autobiography and *A Narrative of the Life of Mrs. Mary Jemison*." *American Literature* 64 (1992): 49–70.

Washburn, Wilcomb E. "Introduction." In *Narratives of North American Indian Captivity: A Selective Bibliography*, edited by Alden T. Vaughan, xi–liii. New York: Garland, 1983.

White, Lonnie J. "White Women Captives of Southern Plains Indians, 1866–1875." *Journal of the West* 8 (1969): 327–54.

Whitford, Kathryn. "Hannah Dustin: The Judgement of History." *Essex Institute Historical Collections* 108 (1972): 304–25.

Zanger, Jules. "Living on the Edge: Indian Captivity Narrative and Fairy Tale." *CLIO* 13 (1984): 123–31.

Alphabetical Checklist of Title Abbreviations

Astoria

Washington Irving, *Astoria, or Anecdotes of an Enterprise beyond the Rocky Mountains*. 1836; Norman: University of Oklahoma Press, 1964.

Barber

Eunice Barber, *Narrative of the Tragical Death of Mr. Darius Barber, and His Seven Children, Who Were Inhumanly Butchered by the Indians*. Boston: David Hazen, 1818.

Bear

Theresa Gowanlock, *Two Months in the Camp of Big Bear: The Life and Adventures of Theresa Gowanlock and Theresa Delaney*. Parkdale, Canada: Times Office, 1885.

Boy

Barbara Hofland, *The Stolen Boy*. New York: G. L. Austin and Co., 1830.

Capture and Escape

Helen M. Tarble, *The Story of My Capture and Escape During the Minnesota Indian Massacre of 1862*. St. Paul, Minn.: Abbott, 1904.

Captured

Minnie Buce Carrigan. *Captured by the Indians: Reminiscences of Pioneer Life in Minnesota*. Forest City, S.Dak.: Forest City Press, 1907.

Casco

Hannah Swarton, the Casco Captive; or the Catholic Religion in Canada, and Its Influence on the Indians in Maine. Boston: Massachusetts Sabbath School Society, 1839.

CH

Caroline Harris, *History of the Captivity and Providential Release Therefrom of Mrs. Caroline Harris*. New York: Perry and Cooke, 1838.

CJ

Charles Johnston, *A Narrative of the Incidents Attending the Capture, Detention, and Ransom of Charles Johnston*. New York: J. and J. Harper, 1827.

CP

Clarissa Plummer, *Narrative of the Captivity and Extreme Sufferings of Mrs. Clarissa Plummer*. New York: Perry and Cooke, 1838.

CS

Charles Saunders, *The Horrid Cruelty of the Indians, Exemplified in the Life of Charles Saunders*. Birmingham: T. Warren, 1763.

Deerfield

The Deerfield Captive: An Interesting Indian Story, Being a Narrative of Facts for the Instruction of the Young. Greenfield, Mass.: A. Phelps, 1830.

d'Eres

Charles Dennis Rusoe d'Eres, *Memoirs of Charles Dennis Rusoe d'Eres*. Exeter, N.H.: Henry Ranlet, 1800.

DL

Cotton Mather, *Decennium Luctuosum*. Boston: B. Green and J. Allen, for Samuel Phillips, 1699.

EH

Elizabeth Hanson, *God's Mercy Surmounting Man's Cruelty, Exemplified in the Captivity and Redemption of Elizabeth Hanson*. Philadelphia: S. Keimer, 1728.

Expedition

Hugh Henry Brackenridge, ed., *Narratives of a Late Expedition against the Indians*. Philadelphia: Francis Bailey, 1782.

FK

Fanny Kelly, *Narrative of My Captivity among the Sioux Indians*. Hartford, Conn.: Mutual Pub. Co., 1871.

Fleming

William and Elizabeth Fleming, *A Narrative of the Sufferings and Surprizing Deliverance of William and Elizabeth Fleming.* Philadelphia: By the authors, 1756.

Founding

William Elsey Connelley, *Eastern Kentucky Papers: The Founding of Harman's Station with an Account of the Indian Captivity of Mrs. Jennie Wiley.* New York: Torch Press, 1910.

Frances

John Franklin Meginness, *Biography of Frances Slocum.* Williamsport, Penn.: Heller Bros., 1891.

Girl Captives

Grace E. Meredith, *Girl Captives of the Cheyennes.* Los Angeles: Gem, 1927.

GM

Gertrude Morgan, *Gertrude Morgan: or, Life and Adventures among the Indians of the Far West.* Philadelphia: Barclay, 1866.

Good

Cotton Mather, *Good Fetch'd Out of Evil.* Boston: B. Green, 1706.

Hall

Narrative of the Capture and Providential Escape of Misses Frances and Almira Hall. New York: William Edwards, 1832.

HG

Henry Grace, *The History of the Life and Sufferings of Henry Grace.* Reading, England: By the author, 1764.

History

George Bancroft, *A History of the United States from the Discovery of the American Continent.* Boston: Little, Brown, & Co., 1873.

HL

Hannah Lewis, *Narrative of the Captivity and Sufferings of Mrs. Hannah Lewis and Her Three Children.* Boston: Henry Trumbull, 1817.

Horn

E. House, *A Narrative of the Captivity of Mrs. Horn with Mrs. Harris.* St. Louis: C. Keemle, 1839.

Horn and Harris

An Authentic and Thrilling Narrative of the Captivity of Mrs. Horn . . . with Mrs. Harris. Cincinnati: By the author, 1851.

HS

Hannah Swarton, *Narrative*, in Cotton Mather, *Humiliations Follow'd with Deliverances.* Boston: B. Green and J. Allen, for Samuel Phillips, 1697.

Humiliations

Cotton Mather, *Humiliations Follow'd with Deliverances.* Boston: B. Green and J. Allen, for Samuel Phillips, 1697.

Huntly

Charles Brockden Brown, *Edgar Huntly; or Memoirs of a Sleepwalker.* 1799; New Haven, Conn.: College and University Press, 1973.

HW

Hannah Willis, *A Surprizing Account of the Captivity of Miss Hannah Willis.* Stonington-Port, Conn.: S. Trumbull, 1799.

Interesting Narrative

Anne Jamison, *An Interesting Narrative.* Pittsburgh: J. Patterson, 1824.

JD

John Dodge, *A Narrative of the Capture and Treatment of John Dodge.* Philadelphia: T. Bradford, 1779.

Jesuits

Francis Parkman, *The Jesuits in North America.* 1867; Boston: Little, Brown, & Co., 1963.

JH

Jemima Howe, *A Genuine and Correct Account of the Captivity, Sufferings & Deliverance of Mrs. Jemima Howe.* Boston: Belknap and Young, 1792.

JL

Jean Lowry, *A Journal of the Captivity of Jean Lowry and Her Children.* Philadelphia: William Bradford, 1760.

Jogues

"Captivity of Father Isaac Jogues, of the Society of Jesus, Among the Mohawks" (1655), in Richard VanDerBeets, ed., *Held Captive by Indians: Selected Narratives, 1642–1836.* Knoxville: University of Tennessee Press, 1973.

Johns

A Narrative of the Life and Sufferings of Mrs. Jane Johns. Baltimore: Jas. Lucas and E. K. Deaver, 1837.

JS

James Smith, *An Account of the Remarkable Occurrences in the Life and Travels of Col. James Smith.* Lexington, Ky.: John Bradford, 1799.

JT

Edwin James, *A Narrative of the Captivity and Adventures of John Tanner during Thirty Years Residence among the Indians in the Interior of America.* New York: G. and C. H. Carvell, 1830.

Kentucky

Elias Darnall, *A Journal Containing an Accurate & Interesting Account of The Hardships, Sufferings, Battles, Defeat, & Captivity of Those Heroic Kentucky Volunteers.* Paris, Ky.: Joel R. Lyle, 1813.

Le Roy and Leininger

The Narrative of Marie Le Roy and Barbara Leininger. Philadelphia: Deutsche Buchdruckerei, 1759.

Left

Emeline L. Fuller, *Left by the Indians: Story of My Life.* Mt. Vernon, Iowa: Hawk-Eye, 1892.

Magnalia

Cotton Mather, *Magnalia Christi Americana.* 1702; Hartford, Conn.: Silas Andros, 1820.

Manheim

Affecting History of the Dreadful Distresses of Frederick Manheim's Family. Exeter, Mass.: Henry Ranlet, 1793.

Manners

John Dunn Hunter, *Manners and Customs of Several Indian Tribes Located West of the Mississippi . . . to Which Is Prefixed the History of the Author's Life during a Residence of Several Years among Them.* Philadelphia: J. Maxwell, 1823.

Maria

Ann Eliza Bleecker, *The History of Maria Kittle.* Hartford: Elisha Babcock, 1797.

McClure

Nancy Huggan McClure, *The Story of Nancy McClure*, in *Collections of the Minnesota Historical Society* 6 (1894): 438–60.

MG

An Authentic Narrative of the Seminole War; and of the Miraculous Escape of Mrs. Mary Godfrey, and Her Four Female Children. New York: D. F. Blanchard, 1836.

MH

Massy Harbison, *A Narrative of the Sufferings of Massy Harbison.* Pittsburgh: S. Engles, 1825.

MJ

James Everett Seaver, *A Narrative of the Life of Mrs. Mary Jemison.* Canandaigua, N.Y.: J. D. Bemis, 1824.

MK

Shepard Kollock, *A True Narrative of the Sufferings of Mary Kinnan.* Elizabeth-town, N.J.: S. Kollock, 1795.

MR

Mary Rowlandson, *A True History of the Captivity & Restoration of Mrs. Mary Rowlandson.* London: Joseph Poole, 1682.

MS

Mary Smith, *An Affecting Narrative of the Captivity and Sufferings of Mrs. Mary Smith*. Providence: L. Scott, 1815.

Oatman 1

Royal B. Stratton, *Life among the Indians: Being an Interesting Narrative of the Captivity of the Oatman Girls*. San Francisco: Whitton, Towne & Co., 1857.

Oatman 2

Royal B. Stratton, *Captivity of the Oatman Girls: Being an Interesting Narrative of Life among the Apache and Mohave Indians*. San Francisco: Whitton, Towne & Co., 1857.

Oatman 3

Royal B. Stratton, *Captivity of the Oatman Girls*. New York: Carlton & Porter, 1858.

Osage 1

Elias Cornelius, *The Little Osage Captive*. Boston: Samuel T. Armstrong and Crocker & Brewster, 1822.

Osage 2

Elias Cornelius, *The Little Osage Captive*. 2d ed. Boston: Massachusetts Sabbath School Society, 1832.

Panther

Abraham Panther, *pseud.*, *A Surprising account of the Discovery of a Lady who was taken by the Indians in the year 1777, and after making her escape, she retired to a lonely Cave, where she lived nine years*, in *Bickerstaff's Almanack, for . . . 1788*. Norwich, Conn.: J. Trumbull, 1787.

Parker

James T. DeShields, *Cynthia Ann Parker: The Story of Her Capture*. St. Louis: James T. DeShields, 1886.

Pontiac

Francis Parkman, *The Conspiracy of Pontiac*. 1850; New York: Collier Books, 1966.

RE

Robert Eastburn, *A Faithful Narrative of the Many Dangers and Sufferings as Well as Wonderful Deliverances of Robert Eastburn*. Philadelphia: William Dunlap, 1758.

Regina

Reuben Weiser, *Regina, the German Captive; or, True Piety among the Lowly*. Baltimore: T. Newton Kurtz, 1860.

Reports

John Williams, *Reports of Divine Kindess*. Boston: S. Phillips, 1707.

RP

Rachel Plummer, *Narrative of the Capture and Subsequent Sufferings of Mrs. Rachel Plummer* (1839), in Richard VanDerBeets, ed., *Held Captive by Indians: Selected Narratives 1642–1836*. Knoxville: University of Tennessee Press, 1973.

Schwandt

Mary Schwandt-Schmidt, *The Story of Mary Schwandt*, in *Collections of the Minnesota Historical Society* 6 (1894): 461–74.

Sioux Captivity

Urania (Mrs. N. D.) White, *Captivity among the Sioux, August 18 to September 26, 1862*, in *Collectinos of the Minnesota Historical Society* 9 (1901): 395–426.

Sister

John Todd, *The Lost Sister of Wyoming: An Authentic Narrative*. Northampton: J. H. Butler, 1842.

SJ

Susannah Willard Johnson (Hastings), *A Narrative of the Captivity of Mrs. Johnson*. Walpole, N.H.: David Carlisle, 1796.

SL

Sarah L. Larimer, *The Capture and Escape; or, Life among the Sioux*. Philadelphia: Claxton, Remsen, and Hafelfinger, 1870.

Swan

Eliza Swan, *An Affecting Account of the Tragical Death of Major Swan*. Boston: Henry Trumbull, 1815.

Sweet

Jannette De Camp Sweet, *Mrs. J. E. De Camp Sweet's Narrative of Her Captivity in the Sioux Outbreak of 1862*, in *Collections of the Minnesota Historical Society* 6 (1894): 354–80.

Travels

Alexander Henry, *Travels and Adventures in Canada and the Indian Territories*. New York: I. Riley, 1809.

Westmorland

A Narrative of the Capture of Certain Americans at Westmorland by the Savages. Hartford: n.p., c. 1780.

Williamson

Peter Williamson, *French and Indian Cruelty Exemplified in the Life and Various Vicissitudes of Fortune of Peter Williamson*. London: R. Griffiths, 1759.

WF

J. Z. Ballard, ed., *The Life and Adventures of William Filley*. Chicago: Filley & Ballard, 1867.

WS

William Scudder, *The Journal of William Scudder*. New York: By the author, 1794.

Zion

John Williams, *The Redeemed Captive, Returning to Zion*. Boston: B. Green, for Samuel Phillips, 1707.

Index

The Authors

Kathryn Zabelle Derounian-Stodola is professor of English at the University of Arkansas at Little Rock. She has edited *The Journal and Occasional Writings of Sarah Wister* (Fairleigh Dickinson University Press, 1987) and has both edited and contributed to *Early American Literature and Culture: Essays Honoring Harrison T. Meserole* (University of Delaware Press, 1992). Her special fields are early American women writers and the Indian captivity narrative form, and she has published on these topics in such journals as *Early American Literature*, *American Transcendental Quarterly*, *Studies in Puritan American Spirituality*, and *The Pennsylvania Magazine of History and Biography*.

James A. Levernier teaches American literature at the University of Arkansas at Little Rock, where he is professor of English and coordinator of the American studies program. With Hennig Cohen, he coedited *The Indians and Their Captives* (Greenwood Press, 1977), and with Douglas R. Wilmes, he coedited *American Writers before 1800: A Biographical and Critical Dictionary* (3 vols., Greenwood Press, 1983). He has also edited or coedited two volumes of Puritan sermons for Scholars' Facsimiles and Reprints, and he is coauthor of *Structuring Paragraphs: A Guide to Effective Writing* (3d ed., St. Martin's Press, 1991). In addition, he has published articles on American literature and American studies in such journals as *ESQ: A Journal of the American Renaissance, Early American Literature, The Markham Review, The Explicator, Resources for American Literary Studies*, and *Research Studies*.

The Editor

Pattie Cowell received her Ph.D. from the University of Massachusetts, Amherst in 1977. Since that time her research has been directed by combined interests in early American literature and women's studies. She has published *Women Poets in Pre-Revolutionary America* (1981) and several related articles and notes on individual colonial women writers. Additionally she has co-edited (with Ann Stanford) *Critical Essays on Anne Bradstreet* (1983) and prepared a facsimile edition of Cotton Mather's *Ornaments for the Daughters of Zion* (1978). She is currently at work on a second edition of *Women Poets in Pre-Revolutionary America* and on a cultural study of early New England women poets. She chairs the English Department at Colorado State University.

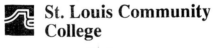

St. Louis Community College

Forest Park
Florissant Valley
Meramec

Instructional Resources
St. Louis, Missouri